Mexican and Central American Population and U.S. Immigration Policy

FRANK D. BEAN is Ashbel Smith Professor of Sociology and Director of the Population Research Center, at the University of Texas at Austin. He received his M.A. and Ph.D. from Duke University. He is the co-author of *Mexican American Fertility Patterns* (1985) and of *The Hispanic Population of the United States* (1987).

JURGEN SCHMANDT is Professor of Public Affairs at the LBJ School of Public Affairs at the University of Texas at Austin, and Director of the Center for Growth Studies at the Houston Area Research Center. He received his Ph.D. from Bonn University. He is the co-author of *Acid Rain and Friendly Neighbors: The Policy Dispute between the United States and Canada* (Revised, 1988) and of *Telecommunications Policy and Economic Development: The New State Role* (forthcoming).

SIDNEY WEINTRAUB is the Dean Rusk Professor of International Affairs at the LBJ School of Public Affairs, University of Texas at Austin. He holds an M.A. from Yale University and a Ph.D. from American University. He is the author of *Free Trade between Mexico and the United States?* (1984) and of *Mexican Trade Policy and the North American Community* (1988).

Mexican and Central American Population and U.S. Immigration Policy

edited by
Frank D. Bean
Jurgen Schmandt
Sidney Weintraub

THE CENTER FOR MEXICAN AMERICAN STUDIES
THE UNIVERSITY OF TEXAS AT AUSTIN

Copyright © 1989 by the Center for Mexican American Studies,
University of Texas at Austin. All rights reserved.

A CENTER FOR MEXICAN AMERICAN STUDIES BOOK

General Editor: Ricardo Romo
Managing Editor: Víctor J. Guerra
Editorial Assistants: Martha Vogel, Robert Carranza
Cover Design: David S. Cavazos

For information, or permission to reproduce material from
this work, address
CMAS Publications
Student Services Bldg.
University of Texas
Austin, TX 78712-1195

Distributed by arrangement with
University of Texas Press
Box 7819
Austin, TX 78713

Library of Congress Cataloging-in-Publication Data

Mexican and Central American population and U.S. immigration policy /
  edited by Frank D. Bean, Jurgen Schmandt, and Sidney Weintraub. —
  1st ed.
    p. cm.
  Bibliography: p.
  ISBN 0-292-75115-X. — ISBN 0-292-75116-8 (pbk.)
  1. United States—Emigration and immigration—Government policy.
2. Mexico—Emigration and immigration. 3. Central America—
Emigration and immigration. 4. Mexico—Population. 5. Central
America—Population.   I. Bean, Frank D. II. Schmandt, Jurgen.
III. Weintraub, Sidney, 1922– .
JV6483.M47   1989   89-32166
                                                                CIP

Manufactured in the United States of America

First Edition, 1989

CONTENTS

Introduction   *1*
Frank D. Bean, Jurgen Schmandt, and Sidney Weintraub

1. The Mexican Demographic Situation   *5*
   Francisco Alba

2. The Central American Demographic Situation: Trends and Implications   *33*
   Sergio Díaz-Briquets

3. The Spanish-Origin Population in the American Southwest   *65*
   Frank D. Bean, W. Parker Frisbie, B. Lindsay Lowell, and Edward E. Telles

4. Growing Imbalances between Labor Supply and Labor Demand in the Caribbean Basin   *113*
   Thomas J. Espenshade

5. Population and Immigration Policy: State and Federal Roles   *161*
   Charles B. Keely

6. Implications of Mexican Demographic Developments for the United States   *179*
   Sidney Weintraub

7. Final Report of the Regional Assembly for the Southwestern Region   *201*

APPENDIX. Participants, Regional Assembly for the Southwestern Region   *208*

Mexican and Central American Population and U.S. Immigration Policy

Introduction

Frank D. Bean, Jurgen Schmandt, and Sidney Weintraub

Since the early 1960s the volume and composition of immigration to the United States have changed considerably. The 1965 amendments to the Immigration and Nationality Act abolished the restrictive provisions of the National Origins Quota System, raised the annual ceiling on the number of immigrants from 158,000 to 270,000, and increased the number of categories of persons who could enter the country exempt from numerical limitations. Subsequent legislation made it much easier for political refugees to enter the country, particularly those from Cuba and Indochina. Following the termination of the bracero program in 1964, an increase in undocumented immigration to the United States also occurred, a phenomenon that was part of the worldwide emergence during the 1960s of labor migration from less- to more-developed countries.

One effect of these changes was to double, approximately, the number of legal immigrants coming to the United States. Another was to alter the ethnic composition of legal immigrants from a preponderance of Europeans to a preponderance of Asians and Latin Americans. During the 1950s Europeans made up over half of all legal immigrants, whereas in the years since 1970 they have composed only about 15 percent. Persons of Latin American origin increased their share over this same period from about 25 to nearly 40 percent. Asians have also shown a sizable increase in their fraction of legal immigration.

These shifts in immigration patterns have drawn increasing attention to U.S. immigration policy in recent years. They also emphasize that immigration policy is an important aspect of U.S. population policy, both domestically and internationally. This point is illustrated by two events that occurred in 1986: the Seventy-first American Assembly of Columbia University, held in April, and the passage of the Immigration Reform and Control Act in November.

The Seventy-first American Assembly, "World Population and U.S. Policy," undertook a reexamination of the world's population situation and the policy options available to the United States in helping other nations deal with their population problems. Particular attention was paid to the relationships between population growth rates and other variables, including economic development, maternal and child health, and the socioeconomic well-being of women and children. The policy of the United States over the previous twenty years to support and provide assistance to family-planning programs was also reassessed, especially in light of the change in U.S. policy announced in 1984 at the United Nations Conference on Population in Mexico City. This change recommended less reliance on family planning per se and more on economic reforms that would emphasize a market economy, to "put a society back on the road toward growth and, as an aftereffect, toward slower population increase as well." The conclusion of the Assembly was that international family-planning programs should continue to be an important part of a U.S. population policy aimed at achieving population growth rates that would maximize the economic and social well-being and health of residents of the nations being assisted.

With its focus on the world population situation and on international family-planning programs, the Seventy-first American Assembly was unable to devote much attention to immigration. As noted, however, U.S. immigration policy is an important component of U.S. population policy. Moreover, it has particularly critical implications for Mexico, Central America, and the American Southwest. In recognition of this, it was suggested after the Seventy-first Assembly that a regional assembly convene for the purpose of exploring the relationships of the population situations of Mexico, other Central American countries, and the Southwest with U.S. immigration policy. Modeled after the American Assembly, this meeting was held in October of 1987.

Also giving impetus to the need for an examination of U.S. immigration policy in relation to the population situations of Mexico, Central American countries, and the American Southwest was the passage of the Immigration Reform and Control Act (IRCA) in November 1986. This legislation marked the first major change in U.S. immigration policy since 1965. The momentum for its passage began with the passage of the previously mentioned 1965 amendments to the Immigration and Nationality Act. As the size and visibility of the foreign-born population grew, questions were increasingly voiced about whether legal immigrants were beneficial for the country and about whether the flow of illegal immigrants might be "out of control." A policy that not only was ineffectual in curtailing illegal immigration but that also kept tens of thousands of legal petitioners from obtaining entry visas was viewed by many policymakers as inequitable and unacceptable. Such concerns led to a strong movement to change immigration law.

Appropriate data, however, especially on illegal immigration, were often not readily available, so important research questions relevant to proposed reforms were difficult or impossible to address. Even when data could be examined, the completion of relevant research often lagged substantially behind the changes in immigration patterns that were giving rise to the calls for reform. A sense of urgency developed as many policymakers perceived a need for action even though insufficient time had elapsed for a national consensus on immigration policy to emerge. All of these factors contributed to a growing controversy over the issue of immigration reform. After several narrow defeats, the reform movement resulted in IRCA's passage in November 1986.

Although IRCA was passed despite an apparent lack of consensus concerning the volume and impact of immigration on the United States, it is clear that the Act may have implications for the population situations of Mexico and Central American countries, as well as for the American Southwest. The Regional Assembly that took place in October 1987 in Houston—named the Southwest Symposium on Mexican and Central American Population Issues—was thus devoted to examining U.S. immigration policy and the population situations of the aforementioned areas. Six background papers were prepared and read by the participants before they attended the Assembly. One by Francisco Alba of the Colegio de México focused on the demographic situation in Mexico. A paper by Sergio Díaz-Briquets of the Commission on International Migration and Cooperative Economic Development examined the demographic situation of Central America. Another by Frank D. Bean, Parker Frisbie, Edward Telles, and B. Lindsay Lowell of the University of Texas focused on the population situation in the American Southwest, especially the population of Spanish and Mexican origin in that region. Thomas J. Espenshade of Princeton University examined the important question of the relationship between labor supply and labor demand in the Caribbean Basin and its implications for immigration patterns. At the policy level, Charles B. Keely of Georgetown University examined the role of state and federal governments in shaping population and immigration policy. Finally, Sidney Weintraub, the Dean Rusk Professor of International Affairs at the LBJ School of Public Affairs at the University of Texas at Austin, discussed the implications of recent Mexican demographic developments for the United States.

The meeting included a group of distinguished persons from various parts of the United States, Mexico, and Central America. Discussions were organized around an agenda prepared by Dr. Jurgen Schmandt, director of the Center for Growth Studies at the Houston Area Research Center; Dr. Frank D. Bean, Ashbel Smith Professor of Sociology and director, Population Research Center, the University of Texas at Austin; and Dr. Sidney Weintraub. At the end of the Regional Assembly, the participants jointly compiled a report and formulated a set of policy recommendations. This report and the recommendations are included as Chapter 7 of this book. We hope that this volume will better inform views on immigration policy and help to make the facts relevant to debates about the role of immigration policy as an instrument of U.S. population policy more widely known.

We would like to express our appreciation for the funding for the Regional Assembly and this book that was provided by the Hewlett Foundation, the American Assembly, the University of Texas at Austin through the C. B. Smith Chair in U.S.–Mexico relations, and the Houston Area Research Center. The opinions expressed in this volume are those of the individual authors and not necessarily those of the sponsors, the American Assembly, or the Houston Area Research Center, which organized and hosted the meeting.

1.

The Mexican Demographic Situation

Francisco Alba

Some of the until recently accepted tenets pertaining to demographic conditions in Mexico are being challenged by even more recent developments. Fertility, traditionally high, has been slow to respond to rapid economic and social development; however, since the early 1970s fertility has declined sharply. The total fertility rate was estimated at 6.7 births in the early 1970s, whereas estimates put it near 4.0 births in 1986. This evolution has come about in association with the new population policy of 1973 and the implementation thereafter of public family-planning programs. However, the dramatic decline in the standard of living after 1981 has led many to wonder about the future of this variable.

In the 1940–1980 period, the social and economic advancement of Mexico was generally perceived as requiring a development style able to cope with the very high rate of population growth and even greater urbanization. This perception was based on the ascending trajectory of important national economic and social indicators. Regarding the labor force specifically, it appeared that labor absorption was proceeding according to expected norms. The share of the labor force engaged in agriculture was steadily declining, whereas labor's share in manufacturing and services was rapidly expanding. This sectorial shift reflects a movement from less productive, traditional (rural-agricultural) jobs and occupations toward more productive ones (urban-industrial). Although shortcomings in the development process were already apparent by the late 1960s and early 1970s, the severe economic crisis initiated in 1982 forced a revision of the mechanisms that accommodated population and suspended previous assumptions about economic and social transformation.

Regarding U.S.–Mexico relations, almost without interruption since 1942, Mexican labor has found a place in specific sectors of the U.S. economy. This has become a deep-rooted binational characteristic. Migration has mainly been of a temporary and rotating nature. More often than not, movement has not resulted in the relocation of the individuals and their families; response to the Immigration Reform and Control Act of November 6, 1986, however, might alter both the size of the flow and its traditional pattern. Although no one knows what the results of the Simpson-Rodino legislation will be, a significant curtailment in the size of the flow is likely. The implications for population distribution and urbanization trends of declining fertility patterns, new trends in labor absorption, and changing Mexico–U.S. migration are a matter of conjecture. Although there are signs of slackening of past tendencies, it does not seem that the secular features of the Mexican regional and urban landscape—high concentration coupled with high dispersion and disequilibrium—will be greatly modified in the near future, that is, before the year 2000.

This chapter is an attempt to document and assess the nature of Mexican demographic change and to review briefly the main features of the recent economic and social evolution of Mexico. It is against this background (domestic and international) that the demographic situation is being discussed.

Development and Population Trends

After Mexico institutionalized a new political system in the 1930s, its economic and social conditions were transformed by the development strategy that took hold in the following years. This development style has been characterized by deep and diversified import-substitution industrialization and by the creation of a modern agricultural sector.

The structural transformation of the economy is best summarized by the sectorial shifts of the domestic product. The primary sector, which accounted for 20 percent of the GDP in 1940, only contributed 12 percent in 1970 and less than 10 percent in 1985. On the other hand the industrial sectors have gained importance in product generation, from 25.1 percent in 1940, to 32.7 percent in 1970, and 34.9 percent in 1985. During this period, services accounted for more than 50 percent of domestic product (table 1).

Economic growth became the main objective of the emergent sociopolitical coalition and stands out as a distinctive feature of Mexico's development. Average annual GDP growth was between 6 and 7 percent until 1970. In the late 1950s and during the 1960s, in particular, the economy combined sustained growth with internal (price) and external (balance-of-payments) stability. Inflation averaged between 3 and 4 percent annually, and in any given year, the external deficit never exceeded one billion dollars, or 3 percent of GDP.

The Echeverría Alvarez (1970–1976) and López Portillo (1976–1982) administrations devised expansionary economic strategies to confront the employment and income distribution problems that they considered neglected by a development strategy that was characterized as "stabilizing development" (*desarrollo estabilizador*). Yet, during these sexenios GDP

Table 1.1 **Gross Domestic Product, Mexico, 1940–1985**

Year	Total (billions pesos)	Primary Sector (%)	Industries (%)	Services[a] (%)
1940	46.7[b]	19.4	25.1	55.5
1950	83.3[b]	19.2	26.5	54.3
1960	150.5[b]	15.9	29.2	54.9
1970	444.3[c]	12.2	32.7	55.2
1980	841.9[c]	9.0	35.2	55.8
1985	912.3[c]	9.6	34.9	55.6

SOURCES: 1940–1960: Banco de México, Annual Reports. 1979–1985: Secretaría de Programación y Presupuesto, Mexico, National Accounting System.
[a]Adjustment for banking services is excluded.
[b]1960 pesos.
[c]1970 pesos.

average annual growth was slightly slower than in the past, only 5.0 percent and 5.4 percent, respectively. Moreover, the expansionary strategies were accompanied by temporary economic instability, higher inflation, important trade deficits, capital flight, and devaluations. Inflation averaged 13.9 percent in the 1971–1976 period and 30.6 percent in the 1977–1982 period, and current account deficits reached $3.7 billion in the first period and soared to $12.5 billion in the second.

After 1982, beginning in the De la Madrid administration (1982–1988), the economy for the first time in Mexico's recent history experienced negative growth rates, -5.2 percent in 1983 and -3.8 percent in 1986. Negative economic growth has been accompanied by very high inflation rates, 80.8 percent in 1983, and 105.7 percent in 1986, huge outflows of capital to meet payments on a sizable foreign debt, and austerity measures that have sharply reduced income earnings. Obviously, GDP per capita has suffered a serious setback: in 1983 and 1986 the GDP per capita was negative; in 1985 the advance was almost nil; and in 1984 it was a mere 1 percent.

However, notwithstanding recent shortcomings, the process of economic growth has been accompanied by important social modernization. Today Mexico is no longer a predominantly rural and agrarian society, although profound rural characteristics persist. The expansion of a "middle class," together with the growth of the upper ranks of the industrial proletariat, is an achievement as well as legacy of the "Mexican miracle."

Poverty was receding until the 1970s, although it continued to be particularly concentrated in rural areas. Table 2 records major changes in some of the conventional indicators of socioeconomic development. The trend is upward and shows, in a broad and indirect way, a notable improvement in living standard. For example, the literate population increased from 43.2

Table 1.2 **Indicators of Social and Economic Development, Mexico, 1940–1980**

Indicator	1940	1950	1960	1970	1980
Labor force in agriculture (%)	65.4	50.2	49.4[a]	39.2	25.8
Literate population[b] (%)	43.2	55.9	65.5	74.1	82.7
Urban population[c] (%)	20.0	28.0	36.5	44.9	51.8
Rural population[d] (%)	70.0	56.7	48.3	40.4	33.7
Houses with running water (%)	—	17.0	23.4	61.4	70.2
Houses with sewer (%)	—	—	29.7	41.0	51.2
One-room houses (%)	—	60.4	57.8	39.8	29.8
Occupants per house (no.)	—	4.9	5.5	5.8	5.5
Population under age 15 (%)	41.2	43.1[e]	45.6[e]	46.7[e]	44.7[e]
Life expectancy at birth (yrs.)[f]	39.7	48.4	57.9	61.0	66.2

Source: National censuses.
[a] Estimate (Altimir 1974).
[b] Among population aged 15 and over.
[c] Localities with more than 15,000 inhabitants.
[d] Localities with fewer than 2,500 inhabitants.
[e] Instituto Nacional de Estadística, Geografía e Informática et al. 1983.
[f] Estimates (Camposortega 1987).

percent in 1940, to 74.1 percent in 1970; and to 82.7 percent in 1980; houses with running water increased from 17 percent in 1950 to 61.4 percent in 1970 and to 70.2 percent in 1980. Not shown in table 2 are the advances in social security coverage. Social security was initiated in 1943 with the creation of the Mexican Social Security Institute (IMSS). Later, other institutions were created. By 1983 nearly half of the population (47.2 percent) was covered by one of the social security institutions, and the IMSS accounted for 80 percent of the total population covered. Internationally, Mexico is ranked in the upper middle-income category (World Bank classification) of the new industrializing countries.

The social and economic changes experienced in Mexico since 1940 have been achieved within the context of a rapidly increasing population. The sustained drop in mortality levels that began in the 1930s set the stage for an acceleration of the population growth rate, which had shown a moderate and relatively stable increase of 1 to 1.5 percent since the latter part of the nineteenth century. Mortality rates dropped dramatically, from 23.3 deaths per thousand in the 1935–1939 period to 8.6 in 1970–1974. Life expectancy at birth increased by almost 20 years for men—from 40.4 years in 1940 to 60.1 in 1970—and by more than 20 years for women—from 42.5 in 1940 to 64.0 in 1970 (Benítez and Cabrera 1967; Cabrera et al. 1973). This decline was more pronounced between 1940 and 1960, and slowed down in the 1960s. Because during this long period the total fertility rate remained in the vicinity of 7 births per woman, Mexico's population growth rate doubled, from an average rate of 1.7 percent in the 1930s to above 3 percent per year since the 1950s. Consequently, population increased from 20 million in 1940, to 51 million in 1970, and 69 million in 1980 (table 3).

Lower mortality levels were considered more an indicator of the positive results associated with economic and social development than anything else. And they continue to be seen that way. Moreover, in this period, population growth was welcomed rather than feared; it was considered a sign of national vitality. The memories of the territories lost to the Colossus of the North and of the lives lost during the 1910 Revolution were still too vivid. The country was perceived as being rich and underpopulated.

Mortality decline also had other important demographic consequences. The age structure of the Mexican population, which was already young in 1940 (41.2 percent under fifteen years), further rejuvenated. In 1970, 46.7 percent of the total population was under fifteen years of age. After 1970, mortality levels declined. In the decade of the 1970s, life expectancy at birth gained more than 5 years, from 61 to 66.2. The gain for men was 4 years, to 63.2 years; women's gain was over 6 years, to 69.4 years. This increment in life expectancy is comparable to the increase that occurred during the 1940s (Camposortega 1987). In 1980 the crude death rate was 6.6 per thousand.

Table 1.3 **Census Enumerations and Corrected Population, Mexico, 1895–1980**

Year	Population Census[a]	Average Annual Growth (%)	Corrected Population (thousands)	Average Annual Growth (%)
1895	12,632,427	—	—	—
1900	13,607,259	1.50	—	—
1910	15,160,369	1.09	—	—
1921	14,334,780	-0.50	—	—
1930	16,552,722	1.72	17,063[b]	—
1940	19,653,552	1.73	20,244[b]	1.72
1950	25,791,017	2.73	27,376[c]	3.06
1960	34,923,129	3.07	37,073[c]	3.08
1970	48,225,238	3.41	51,176[c]	3.28
1980	66,846,833	3.26	69,393[c]	3.09

SOURCES:
[a]*Censos generales de población,* various years.
[b]For corrected population, 1930 and 1940: Centro de Estudios Económicos y Demográficos, *Dinámica de la población de México* (Mexico City: Colegio de México, 1970).
[c]Instituto Nacional de Estadística, Geografía e Informática et al. 1983.

Despite the low mortality level and the declining trend, there is still ample room for improvement; infant mortality amounts to 53 deaths per thousand births,[1] a rate that is two and a half times higher than rates recorded in other countries in the region.

The recent transition toward low fertility is revolutionizing the development of the Mexican population. The starting point of the decline is the early 1970s. It began in the context of an explicit policy of fertility regulation and had as background a socioeconomic situation characterized by a very dynamic and fluid social milieu in association with potent economic growth and prosperity. In the absence of a better explanation, it seems that the combination of these two sets of factors created the conditions for a sustained decline in fertility levels.

These socioeconomic and policy conditions will, in due time, change other demographic conditions in Mexico. Fertility change is already having major consequences for the size, growth rate, and age composition of the population. In turn, this changing demographic landscape will have broader economic and social implications.

The Transition toward Lower Fertility

Until the 1970s, Mexico's demographic history was associated with an unusually high fertility rate. Yet, in slightly over one decade, fertility patterns were significantly altered. A decline in fertility now appears to be a well-established fact. The estimated crude birth rate went down from 43.9 in the 1970–1972 period to 30.4 in 1983 (Consejo Nacional de Población 1985a). Data from the National Demographic Survey conducted in 1982 indicate that the total fertility rate for 1981 was 4.3, largely due to a reduction by 2 births per woman compared to the early 1970s. Table 4 documents the change that actually took place in the population's reproductive behavior. As seen, between 1970 and 1981 the total fertility rate fell by nearly 40 percent. Fertility dropped fastest after 1976. It is estimated that fertility stood at 4.0 births per woman in 1986.

Available information covering the 1970–1981 period shows that fertility rates are moving downward in all age groups. Fertility rates in 1981 were more than 50 percent lower than in 1970 among the 35 to 39 year old group; a third lower among the 20 to 34 year olds; and 15 percent lower among the 15 to 19 year olds (table 5).

From the intermediate variables standpoint, fertility decline has been attributed mainly to increased use of contraceptives. Table 6 shows the proportion of women in conjugal union who practice contraception and the distribution of these women by method of contraception. The proportion of users increased from 29 percent in 1976 to 48 percent in 1982, a 66 percent

Table 1.4 Fertility Estimates, Mexico, 1970–1981

Year	Total Fertility Rate	Crude Birth Rate (per 1,000)
1970	6.7	46
1975–76	5.7	41
1979	4.7	36
1981	4.3	33

SOURCE: Alba and Potter (1986).

Table 1.5 Fertility Rates by Age, Mexico, 1970–1981 (3-year moving averages)

Age Group	1970	1975	1981[a]
15–19	.124	.116	.106
20–24	.304	.263	.203
25–29	.335	.283	.211
30–34	.260	.245	.172
35–39	.215	.148	.122
40–44	(.101)[b]	.092	.043
45–49	(.019)[c]	(.019)[c]	.018
Total Fertility Rate	6.790	5.830	4.375

SOURCE: Consejo Nacional de Población (n.d.*a*).
[a] 1980 and 1981 average.
[b] 1973 rate.
[c] 1979 rate.

Table 1.6 Women in Conjugal Union Practicing Contraception, and the Distribution of Practice by Method, 1976–1982 (%)

	1976	1979	1982
Practicing contraception	29	38	48
Pills	37	33	30
IUD or injectables	25	22	24
Sterilization	7	24	29
Other	31	21	17
Total	100	100	100

SOURCE: Alba and Potter (1986).

change. The pill was and continues to be the most important method, one used by around a third of the women. IUD's and injectables account for another quarter. In the same period, female sterilization gained ground, from 7 percent to 29 percent, at the expense of other less effective or more traditional methods.

The process of fertility decline has, understandably, not wiped out previous regional and social differentials. Some differentials might even have been unmasked. Between 1940 and 1970 crude birth rates were above forty births per thousand in all regions of the country. Although different age structures may have some influence, in 1980 the crude birth rate in the region with the lowest level was below thirty; other regions exhibited intermediate levels in the middle thirties; and in the region with the highest level, the rate was still well above forty births per thousand (Consejo Nacional de Población 1985b). Recent results (Consejo Nacional de Población n.d.*a*) support, in general, the expected relationships between fertility levels and regional socioeconomic development (inverse), size of place of residence (inverse), educational levels (inverse), and women's participation in the labor force (inverse).

There are also indications that fertility decline in Mexico has been greater among the groups that exhibited the highest levels at the start of the present phase of fertility decline, namely, the less-educated and rural women. As a result, there was some reduction in fertility differentials between 1977 and 1981, when fertility was falling fastest. Among women aged 20 to 44, fertility (TFR) declined 24 percent, from 5.38 in 1977, to 4.08 in 1981. However the less-educated women (with less than four years of schooling) experienced a 31 percent decline, from 6.74 to 4.6. Among rural women, TFR declined 27 percent, from 6.68 to 4.86, and among urban women it dropped 20 percent, from 4.20 to 3.36 (Pullman, Casterline, and Juárez 1985).

These indicators suggest that fertility transition has a good chance to continue its present course. CONAPO (the national population council) estimates that the expected population growth rates are being reached as programmed; currently, population growth stands at 2 percent. However, the demographic (fertility) trajectory of the last five years must still be adequately documented. (The DHS Mexico project will soon provide results on this matter.)

A big question regarding future reproductive behavior arises from the prolonged economic and social crisis that has seriously reduced living standards in Mexico. Will this situation halt the declining fertility trend? In my opinion, it will not. In the post-1982 socioeconomic environment, development has become problematic. There is increasing tension between aspirations and realizations. The generally optimistic Weltanshauung of the past is substituted by a more uncertain and cost-oriented outlook. The positive developments of the past have given ground to the fertility transition of the future. However, one has to take into consideration the determination of the Mexican government to pursue the demographic objective of further reducing population growth by lowering fertility levels.

Whereas earlier population laws sought to encourage population growth by reducing mortality and encouraging births and immigration, the General Population Law of 1974 called for the introduction of programs to stabilize and regulate population growth.[2] A generalized shift in attitude toward favoring a lower fertility rate followed the announcement of the new policy. Based on the premise that it was in the nation's interest to limit population growth, successive administrations have laid down important guidelines and instituted specific programs to attain that goal.

When the moment came to implement the new policy, attention was directed at organizing various government-sponsored family-planning programs. Beginning in 1973, the Ministry of Health (Secretaría de Salubridad y Asistencia, SSA) and the Mexican Social Security Institute (IMSS) rapidly extended the delivery of family-planning services through their respective networks of health centers and hospitals.[3]

By the end of 1976 considerable headway had been made in advertising the availability of these services. The López Portillo administration set quantitative goals that transcended its period in office. Targets were set for the rate of population growth: 2.5 percent in 1982; 1.8 percent by 1988; and around 1 percent by 2000. The administration gave evidence of the government's commitment to attaining the 1982 demographic target of 2.5 percent population growth by providing the needed resources and motivation to those charged with delivering services and carrying out related activities, such as mass media campaigns and reforms in the school curricula.

The government's actions were guided by the position, adopted since the initial legislation, that family-planning programs were to be strictly voluntary and that the approach to altering the population's behavior was to be multisectorial and multifaceted. The government's strategy in promoting transformations in reproductive behavior has been to emphasize not only the benefits of family planning and smaller families, but also the benefits of sex education and the enhancement of women's position in the family and the labor market. Mass media materials and texts used in the educational system were revised to reflect this message. The government has always considered health and family planning as mutually reinforcing elements of population change. Maternal and child health care programs have been components of family-planning programs since their inception.

This strategy has been continued under the National Population Program 1984–1988, to the point that one could state that there is a stable and hereto-stay consensus on population policy objectives and implementation. This consensus involves the view that growth (fertility) policy cannot be divorced from migration policy. Indeed, the Mexican government has made it clear, since the change of the official stance regarding population in 1973, that on this matter it has two overriding concerns: harmonizing population growth with the country's resources, and matching territorial distribution of the population with the potential of regional economic and social development. This policy position has remained unchanged during three successive administrations.[4]

Consequences of Demographic Change

It is known that population trends carry with them long-term inertia. Thus, fertility transition is just beginning to influence secular population trends. There is every reason to expect that the current change will continue and serve as a harbinger of what the new secular, post-transition trends will be. However, the medium-term demographic prospects in Mexico will be a combination of current events and past tendencies.

Tables 7 and 8 sum up population projections to the year 2010. The projections are called programmatic, because it is assumed that the behavior of fertility trends will actually follow a programmed path. Fertility is expected to decline steadily into the twenty-first century. TFR drops from the 4.4 of 1980 to half this value by the year 2010 (Núñez and Moreno 1986). A first consequence of this decline has to do with the slowdown of the rate of population growth, from 2.5 percent in early 1980 to 1.6 percent in the 1990–1995 period. After the early 1990s, the tendency moves at a slower pace: 1.4 percent by the year 2000, and 1.2 percent in the 2005–2010 period. During the projection period international migration is assumed to be negative, in the range of 0.15 to 0.1 percent annually.

How does this change affect the absolute numbers of Mexico's population? At first glance, the effect is not impressive. Population projections that were elaborated in the early 1970s, on the eve of the fertility change, estimated that population in 1985 would stand between 81.3 million, in the low-fertility hypothesis, and 84.8 million, in the high- or constant-fertility hypothesis (Centro de Estudios Económicos y Demográficos et al. 1974). In 1985 population was calculated at 78.0 million, a reduction of 3 to 6 million. However, by the year 2000 the difference would be quite sizable. A national programmatic population of 100 to 104 million is significantly lower than the 123.1 to 147.8 million population projected little more than a dozen years ago.[5]

These deductions notwithstanding, from now to the year 2000 population will increase by 20 million to 25 million. Although still quite a sizable addition, the country's demographic future will be more manageable. For example, the number of births will in effect stabilize in the rage of 2.2 to

Table 1.7 **Population Projections, Mexico, 1980–2000**

	Programmatic Projection		Alternative Projection	
Year	Population (thousands)	Average Annual Growth (%)	Population (thousands)	Average Annual Growth (%)
1980	69,393	—	69,393	—
1985	78,524	2.47	78,996	2.59
1990	86,215	1.87	89,012	2.39
1995	92,996	1.51	99,165	2.16
2000	99,604	1.37	109,180	1.92

SOURCE: Instituto Nacional de Estadística, Geografía e Informática et al. (1983).

Table 1.8 **Population Projections, Mexico, 1985–2010**

	Programmatic Projection		Alternative Projection	
Year	Population (thousands)	Average Annual Growth (%)	Population (thousands)	Average Annual Growth (%)
1985	77,938	—	77,938	—
1990	85,784	1.92	86,154	2.00
1995	92,939	1.60	94,781	1.91
2000	100,039	1.47	103,996	1.85
2005	107,059	1.36	113,570	1.76
2010	113,787	1.22	123,158	1.62

SOURCE: Instituto Nacional de Estadística, Geografía e Informática and Consejo Nacional de Población (1985).

2.1 million per year, after having experienced a long period of annual increments that culminated in the period 1975–1980 with 2.4 million births per annum (table 9).

A similar statement can be made regarding the age structure of the population. In the near future, before the dependency ratio begins to increase again sometime in the twenty-first century, the working-age population (aged fifteen to sixty-four) will dramatically increase its share, from 52.5 percent in 1980 to 68.5 percent in 2010, reversing the traditionally very young age structure, which climaxed in 1970, when the group under age fifteen represented 46.7 percent of the total population. By the year 2000 this group should represent only 28.7 percent. The population aged sixty-five and older will certainly increase in absolute as well as relative numbers, from 2.3 million (3.3 percent) in 1980 to 4.8 million (4.8 percent) in the year 2000. This trend will continue into the next century, when a different set of issues will probably dominate demoeconomic considerations.

Table 1.9 **Demographic Indicators, Mexico, 1980–2010 (annual averages)**

Indicator	1980–84	1985–89	1990–94	1995–99	2000–04	2005–09
Crude death rate (%)	30.1	26.1	22.4	20.9	19.7	18.5
Crude birth rate (%)	6.3	5.6	5.2	5.1	5.1	5.3
Growth rate (%)	2.2	1.9	1.6	1.5	1.4	1.2
Births (thousands)	2,225	2,133	2,001	2,016	2,041	2,038

Population Distribution (%)	1980	1985	1990	1995	2000	2005	2010
0–14 years	44.2	40.3	35.6	31.7	28.7	26.6	25.3
15–64 years	52.4	56.2	60.6	64.0	66.5	68.0	68.5
65 and up	3.3	3.5	3.8	4.3	4.8	5.4	6.2

Source: Instituto Nacional de Estadística, Geografía e Informática and Consejo Nacional de Población (1985).

The implications of current demographic change on economic and social spheres could follow well-known sequences. For example, a steady number of births and a "more balanced" age structure would have an impact on public expenditures by changing the combination of needs in health, education, social security, and so on. The labor market situation is more complex, because of the demographic lag involved and mainly because the labor force absorption process is the result of both labor supply and demand.

Labor Force Absorption

The social and economic advancement of Mexico in the 1940–1980 period was accompanied by very high rates of population growth and rapid urbanization. Yet, Mexico was widely perceived until the late 1960s as a country whose economy was able to provide employment for a rapidly expanding labor force. That is no longer true. Some authors have viewed the economic events of the 1970s, in part, as forceful government efforts to provide employment to the large cohorts of labor force entrants.

The exceptional rapidity in the growth of the labor force is illustrated by the rate at which the working-age population expanded. Table 10 contains estimates of absolute numbers and rates of growth for this group for successive five-year periods between 1950 and 2000. It shows a growth rate surpassing the 2.5 percent mark since the 1950s, rising to a peak of 3.6 percent in the period 1980–1985, remaining close to the peak, which extends into the 1990s, and declining to 2.7 percent by the year 2000. Of course, labor force trends do not reproduce exactly the experience of this age group, but

Table 1.10 **Working-Age Population (15–64 Years), Mexico, 1950–2000**

Year	Total (thousands)	Average Annual Increment (thousands)	Average Annual Change (%)
1950	14,649	—	—
1955	16,587	388	2.5
1960	18,906	463	2.7
1965	21,749	568	2.8
1970	25,508	752	3.2
1975	30,206	940	3.4
1980	35,914	1,142	3.5
1985	42,868	1,391	3.6
1990	50,877	1,602	3.5
1995	59,067	1,638	3.0
2000	67,330	1,653	2.7

SOURCE: Instituto Nacional de Estadística, Geografía e Informática et al. (1983).

Table 1.11 **Economically Active Population, Mexico, 1940–1980**

Year	Agriculture (thousands)	(%)	Nonagriculture (thousands)	(%)	Total (thousands)
1940	3,831	63.3	2,224	36.7	6,055
1950	4,824	58.3	3,448	41.7	8,272
1960	6,145	54.2	5,187	45.8	11,332
1960[a]	(5,045)	(49.4)	(5,086)	(49.8)	(10,213)
1970	5,293	40.9	7,662	59.1	12,944
1980	5,700	25.8	9,690	43.9	22,066[b]

SOURCE: Population censuses. (1940–1970: Unspecified assigned to diverse activity sectors [Gómez Oliver 1978].)

[a]Estimates (Altimir 1974).
[b]1980: Unspecified = 29.7 percent.

they do tend to follow it. Likewise, population censuses show near doubling of the labor force every twenty years, twice between 1940 and 1980, from six to eleven million, and then to twenty-two million (table 11).[6]

Most of the increases in labor supply have certainly been due to net additions of young nationals to the labor force. Immigration does not appear to have been a significant factor in this period. Emigration, on the contrary, has played a special role, as we shall see later, in labor force absorption patterns.

How has Mexico coped with its growing labor force? First, a few observations on the developments that seemed to take care of labor force growth. In 1940, Mexico was a predominantly rural and agrarian nation. Almost two-thirds, 3.8 million, of the 6 million economically active people were engaged in agricultural activities. When the country entered the 1940s, two sets of agricultural policies combined to elicit a rather stable pattern of labor force accommodation in rural areas: on the one hand, agrarian reform (redistribution) provided land for settlement of campesino labor, which was rapidly reproducing and growing; on the other hand, modern agriculture and frontier expansion also made room for part of the same steady growth of the rural labor force.

Total land (old and new) under cultivation expanded by as much as 5.5 percent annually during most of the 1945–1964 period (Gómez Oliver 1978). Land expansion became a mechanism by which both the economy and society partially coped with labor increases. In this way, the polity was able to respond to a constant and sustained demand for land while maintaining political stability. Additionally, entrepreneurial farmers, especially in the newly irrigated areas, provided permanent and temporary employment to many agricultural workers and campesinos. Both modern and campesino agriculture shared responsibility for accommodating rural labor. One must point out, however, that this pattern also meant the perpetuation of highly uneven rural development, characterized by a relatively small number of "farmers" and a mass of "campesinos."

In my opinion, these institutions could be credited with the labor force increases in agriculture that showed up between 1940 and 1960. The net additions to the labor force in agriculture amounted to one million in the 1940s and at least a quarter of a million more in the 1950s (table 11). Although these developments were important, the most dynamic elements of the economy were outside the rural areas. The cities were the focal points of the country's transformation.

Rapid growth did not deter major structural changes in the composition of the labor force. Table 12 shows a significant shift of the labor force in the twenty-year interval from 1950 to 1970, from less productive, rural-agricultural jobs toward more productive occupations in the urban-industrial and services sectors. Industry increased its labor share in the period to 26.5 percent, and services increased to 32.6 percent. Together, nonagricultural sectors absorbed 4.2 million people, or 90 percent of total labor force growth in the period. Industry alone absorbed 1.5 million people. The expansion of the urban middle classes was certainly a manifestation of that pattern of labor force absorption. Moreover, it is generally accepted that the price of labor increased, at least slightly.

But the absorptive capacity of the strategy had its limitations. In retrospect, one can see some of the costs associated with this process, and

Table 1.12 Economically Active Population by Sector, Mexico, 1950 and 1970

	1950		1970	
Sector[a]	(thousands)	(%)	(thousands)	(%)
Agriculture	4,864.9	58.3	5,292.7[b]	40.9
Mining, energy, & manufacturing	1,237.5	14.8	2,829.1[c]	21.8
Construction	263.8	3.2	609.9	4.7
Commerce & finance	732.6	8.8	1,397.0	10.8
Other services	1,246.4	14.9	2,826.5	21.8
Total	8,345.2	100.0	12,955.2	100.0

SOURCE: Population censuses.
[a]Sectorial aggregation (Altimir 1974).
[b]Excludes agricultural services supplied to groups of farm units.
[c]Excludes that part of gas distribution included under commerce and finance. Also excludes water supply and sewage facilities, which are included under other services in the government sector.

some of its longer-term implications. Land availability—through distribution and frontier expansion—reached a limit. Between 1966 and 1975 the rate at which land was put into cultivation came to a standstill (Gómez Oliver 1978). Other inauspicious trends, which had probably been in place since the early stages of the process, did not become apparent until about 1970. The number of working days for *jornaleros* (agricultural workers) declined, and the number of campesinos without land was on the rise. By 1970 the number of landless people reached one million. Migration to the United States did not subside. The skills of the labor force improved, but only modestly. Consequently, the labor market equation in the country was not transformed, and the price of labor continued to be low.

Table 13 offers an additional indication of the consequences of the development pattern Mexico followed. The absorption of the labor force by the formal sectors of the economy slowed during the 1960s while the informal sectors continued gaining strength. Table 13 directs attention to the continued great importance of labor segmentation in the market and to the increases of "informal" employment, particularly after 1960. The figures suggest that in the 1960s there was an inflection point in the dynamics of employment generation. The rapid structural transformation of the 1950s does not show up in the 1960s; the gains of formal urban employment are modest and less than the gains of informal urban employment (1.7 versus 4.5 percentage points). This path fits with information stemming from different sources. It has been estimated that the annual rate of labor absorption by the industrial sector was 5 percent between 1950 and 1968, and 3

Table 1.13 **Segmentation of the Economically Active Population, Mexico, 1950, 1960, 1970, 1980 (%)**

	1950	1960	1970	1980[a]
Total	100.0	100.0	100.0	100.0
Subtotal urban	34.5	45.7	52.1	61.5
Formal	21.6	32.2	33.9	39.5
Informal	9.7	10.0	14.5	18.3
Domestic service	3.2	3.5	3.7	3.7
Subtotal rural	64.4	53.0	46.8	37.6
Modern	20.4	25.4	21.9	19.2
Traditional	44.0	27.6	24.9	18.4
Mining	1.1	1.3	1.1	0.9

SOURCE: Programa Regional del Empleo para América Latina y el Caribe (1982).
[a]Estimated.

percent in the period 1968–1978 (Casar and Ros 1981). Unfortunately, the downturn of formal labor demand appeared precisely when the system had to face prolonged increments in labor supply.

Estimates for 1980 confirm the continuous presence of informal employment in the urban scene *pari passu* with advances in the formal sectors of the economy (table 13). Formal urban employment gained 5.6 percentage points—an increase of 16.5 percent— and informal urban employment, 3.8 percentage points—an increase of 26.2 percent. It is apparent that formal and informal activities are a function of the (urban) economy in Mexico, but the situation is marked by both strong labor market segmentation and very heterogeneous employment conditions.

The emergence in the 1960s and 1970s of (open) unemployment could be considered an additional sign of fatigue. However, unemployment came with the increased formalization of the economy and the labor market and reflected (cyclical) fluctuation in economic activity during the 1970s and early 1980s rather than labor supply changes. More recent unemployment figures present a puzzle. Unemployment seems insensitive to current economic conjuncture. A very tempting explanation would be to view current circumstances as part of a process of adjustment of major proportions in which long-term labor supply tendencies are significant.

In spite of the positive changes in the structure of the labor force between 1940 and 1980, a tentative conclusion regarding past labor absorption experience is that the development strategy did not prove able to transform fully the economic and social conditions of the country in a setting of a very rapidly growing labor force and intense urban displacement. One of the overriding aims during the frantic years of the oil boom (1979–1981) seems to have been the acceleration of the pace of labor absorption. Employment grew at rates higher than the rate of increase of the labor supply, estimated at 4 percent. However, general wages did not keep step with labor demand. But the new trends abruptly ceased in 1982. Since then, labor demand by the formal economy has been almost nil. This economic situation is untenable in the long run.

The size of the working-age population will still be growing at 2.7 percent per annum between 1995 and 2000. Assuming an overall activity rate in the range of 50 percent, nearly 800,000 new jobs will be required annually to keep pace with the supply. Most of these jobs will have to be created in the cities, where rural-urban migration pressures do not seem likely to subside soon. The rural working-age population is expected to grow beyond the year 2000, but only slightly, with an increase of almost a quarter of a million people annually in the 1980s, and nearly one hundred thousand in the 1990s (Núñez and Moreno 1986). Therefore, most of the growth of the working-age population will take place in urban areas. The outlook for accommodating this population in the promising patterns of the past seems cloudy.

An increase in informal activities and a dramatic change in relative prices—to the detriment of the price of labor—will shape future absorption patterns. Indeed, to forestall the dismissal of workers and a complete stoppage of new hiring, wage levels have declined dramatically since 1982, some 35 to 40 percent in terms of the real value of the minimum wage. New export-oriented enterprises will demand labor when low wages prevail. The surge of subcontracting activities along the Mexico–U.S. border is a response to the new conditions. But other domestic and international economic and social adjustments might be required to match labor demand with labor supply.

International Migration

International migration has had a peculiar character in Mexico. Temporal emigration is predominant, and recent demographic change does not seem to affect it. Domestic and foreign (mainly U.S.) factors of an economic and historical nature shape and help to explain these patterns, but new U.S. legislation attempts to change the rules that have governed this phenomenon for almost a century. The panorama, already complex, is becoming even more so, and immigration to Mexico from Central America has been on the rise, adding new dimensions to the issue.

Until 1980 immigration does not appear to have been significant in the growth of population, or in the supply of labor. Except for the Spanish immigrants of the late 1930s and a few other migrants during World War II,

Mexico has been considered more a country of emigration than of immigration. The number of foreign nationals recorded in the censuses represented only 0.5 percent of the total population in 1960 and 1970, and 0.4 percent in 1980. Mexican nationals residing outside the country probably amount to 2 to 3 percent of the total population, and another one percent annually move out and in. But this appreciation has to be qualified by the peculiarities of temporary migrant labor, which is the main flow.

Since the early 1940s, Mexican workers have crossed the border into the United States and returned seasonally, with only some emigrating permanently. This movement of temporary workers was the object of legal agreements by both countries between 1942 and 1964. The number of work (agricultural) contracts during this twenty-two year period has been estimated at more than four million. However, the number of Mexican workers in this figure is much less, as many of them were yearly repeaters. After the end of the Bracero Program in 1964, the movement continued, this time undocumented. The number of migratory workers in 1984 whose habitual place of residence was Mexico has been estimated at three quarters of a million (García y Griego and Giner de los Ríos 1985).

Mexicans admitted legally to the United States have averaged about sixty thousand annually in the period since 1970. Available evidence from the 1980 U.S. census suggests that each year approximately one hundred thousand undocumented Mexican migrants make the United States their place of residence (Passel and Woodrow 1984). Yet, the volume of returned migrants, whether migration was legal or undocumented, is unknown. However, it seems that for projection purposes legal migration has been equated to permanent emigration. Probably taking these figures and other results from surveys on the subject into consideration, Mexico's population for the period 1960–1980 has been calculated assuming an annual emigration of seventy thousand nationals. This assumption is maintained in the projections of population until the year 2000 (Instituto Nacional de Estadística, Geografía e Informática 1983). A more recent projection for the period 1980–2010 assumes the annual number of emigrants to rise slightly above the one hundred thousand mark (Instituto Nacional de Estadística, Geografía e Informática, and Consejo Nacional de Población 1985).

Estimates of the number of undocumented Mexican immigrants in the United States vary widely. Still, no matter how sizable this number is, the migratory flow continues to be characteristically temporary. The majority of those who leave Mexico return after relatively short periods of time, usually less than a year.[7] The literature on Mexican migration to the United States generally supports the view that the migratory phenomenon is of a rotating nature. One or more members of a family unit might go to work abroad, but the move does not result in the relocation of the whole unit.

This arrangement may be considered a feedback process that consolidates the temporary migratory pattern.

Thus, migrants are not cut off completely from their domestic labor market, notwithstanding the significant stock of Mexican workers in the United States at any point in time. Likewise, temporary migration to the United States does not mean a direct removal of labor from the Mexican market, nor a transformation of the labor equation within the Mexican economy; but it has proved to be a resilient mechanism of labor absorption by a larger labor market, one that in many respects incorporates the Mexican and American economies. After decades of continued migration, this phenomenon has turned out to be a sui generis institutional arrangement of labor absorption both between and within the two countries.

Is the Immigration Reform and Control Act of 1986 going to change the "secular pattern" of temporary labor migration from Mexico to the United States? Probably. To what extent? Nobody knows. What will be the consequences of the Act? All depends on what nobody knows. However, a few highly speculative observations can be made.

It is certainly too early to chart the direction of future changes. Scattered, unsystematic information points toward a decrease in the number of migrants who might choose to establish permanent claim on transborder work and U.S. residence. The return of some migrants may just be fearful initial reactions to these legal changes. However, employers' sanctions will certainly close some job opportunities. In other words, the price of entry into this stream will be higher.

On the other hand, the legalization of a de facto situation might turn into a definitive migration, what in previous circumstances would have been only a prolonged journey away from home. It is difficult to gauge how this possibility, along with employers' sanctions, could affect the size and characteristics of the future flow. Could the Simpson–Rodino law disrupt migrant-related labor markets? For the time being the door is open for agricultural workers. Later, will it be business as usual? Will the migration pattern of Mexican temporary workers be replaced, or joined by a more conventional, permanent movement? Will this change affect the selectivity of the flow? These questions are extremely difficult to answer.

For specific regions and communities the curtailment of this secular source of income might trigger population movements toward the traditional areas of attraction, namely, the big cities and the cities along the Mexico–U.S. border. Will this eventually translate into social and political pressures? Certainly so. How serious could these pressures be? Even if serious, they can probably be absorbed by the system. But, in the near future the northern border will surely be in a state of flux. Indeed, changes in migration and the expansion of subcontracting industries might bring about quick, although highly volatile, regional development.

A similar state of affairs seems to characterize Mexico's southern border, where the country has experienced an influx of immigrants in recent years. During the 1970s Mexico had an open-door policy toward persons from various South American countries displaced by political changes and violence. Many of the migrants who came were skilled people. More recently, a more complex and heterogeneous stream is arriving from several Central American nations. The old, regionally localized, temporary flow of Guatemalan workers that used to enter to pick seasonal crops in Chiapas has been superseded by new, important, and sizable "political" flows that began around 1980.

By 1985 there were around forty thousand Guatemalan refugees, accepted as such by Mexican authorities. Estimates indicate that since the late 1970s, as many as one million additional people may have entered the country, displaced by political violence, insecurity, and economic hardship in the region. Of this number, it is difficult to assess how many remain in Mexico and how many simply crossed the country on their way to the United States. These transient international migrants link northern and southern borders to foreign events and problems, making the international migration outlook even fuzzier.

Population Distribution

The rapid development of medium-sized cities and their rising importance—in demographic, economic, and political terms—is perhaps the best indicator of trends that might shape the future population distribution in Mexico. The nation's capital will continue to grow, but its prominence will have to be increasingly parceled out with what seems to be the emergence and consolidation of a varied and diverse urban mosaic by intense domestic migration and very rapid urbanization. Since 1940, Mexico has been transformed from a country that was rural, with 80 percent of its population living outside urban localities.[8] Sustained rural-urban migration changed that landscape. In 1970, 45 percent of the population was urban. If the more conventional definition of urban population is used (localities with twenty-five hundred or more inhabitants), 60 percent of the population fell in this category by 1970. Although the population in localities with less than twenty-five hundred inhabitants did not quite double in the 1940–1970 period (from 13.7 to 19.4 million), urban population grew nearly fivefold (from 4.9 to 21.6 million).

This transformation was associated with population concentration in a few urban centers, most prominently in the Mexico City metropolitan area. In the 1940–1970 period, population concentration was mainly due to expansion of cities with more than one hundred thousand inhabitants. The number of these cities went up from 6 in 1940 to 35 in 1970, and their population share increased from 11.9 percent in 1940 to 35.2 percent in 1970. Metropolitan Mexico City alone, which contained 8 percent of the country's population in 1940, boasted 22 percent by 1970. However, the number of small- and medium-sized urban centers (between fifteen thousand and one hundred thousand inhabitants) also rose, from 49 to 143, although their population share changed relatively little (from 8 percent in 1940, to 9.5 percent in 1970) (Unikel et al. 1976). Indeed, migration flows turned to a few urban areas. For example, in the 1960–1970 period, 65 percent of net population shifts went to only five cities: Mexico City, Guadalajara, Monterrey, Puebla, and Acapulco.[9]

Notwithstanding this process of urban concentration, population dispersion in small localities did not fade away. In 1970 Mexico still had 94,200 widely dispersed localities with fewer than twenty-five hundred inhabitants, of which 90,200 were under one thousand inhabitants, compared with 104,800 and 102,900 localities, respectively, in 1940. These increases in rural communities, despite massive migration from the countryside to cities, can, of course, only be understood in the context of Mexico's overall accelerated population growth.

As part of the population concentration in a few urban centers, regional disparities in economic, social, and political resources consolidated a demographic redistribution that favored the Valley of Mexico (Region VII, table 14) and the Northern Plains (Regions I, II, and III). Table 14 shows that the entire country has been involved in these processes, although the Central regions (IV, V, and VI) have been the main suppliers of population. Their share of population diminished from 39.8 percent in 1940 to only 32.9 percent in 1970. The South-Southwest Region (VIII), which maintained its share of population between 1900 and 1940, became part of the unbalancing process after 1940. In 1970 it had only 14.6 percent of the total population, compared with 17.6 percent in 1940.

These tendencies followed a course well documented since 1900, but accelerated after 1940 (Unikel et al. 1976). Although these regional population shifts correspond roughly with the concentration of population in urban centers, they also reflect the movement of nonurban population toward regions—the Northeast (I) and the Gulf (III)—suited to the production of commercial crops following development of large-scale agricultural infrastructure.

Population policy also attempts to change the territorial distribution of the population. It has already been noted that Mexican population policy has two overriding concerns: to reduce population growth, and to balance regional distribution of the population. Indeed, the Law on Human Settlements (May 20, 1976) seeks to modify the territorial distribution patterns of the population, reorganizing economic and social activities among the

Table 1.14 **Percentage Distribution of Population by Region, Mexico, 1940–1980**

Regions[a]	1940	1950	1960	1970	1980
I	6.2	6.7	7.4	8.1	8.2
II	11.2	11.4	11.4	11.1	10.8
III	10.5	10.7	10.7	10.9	10.9
IV	7.2	6.6	6.0	5.3	5.0
V	18.9	17.9	17.8	16.8	15.9
VI	13.7	12.9	11.7	10.8	10.7
VII	14.7	17.2	19.3	22.4	24.5
VIII	17.6	16.6	15.7	14.6	14.0
Total	100.0	100.0	100.0	100.0	100.0
	(19,649,162)	(25,779,254)	(34,923,129)	(48,381,547)	(66,846,833)

SOURCES: 1940–1970: Unikel et al. (1976). 1980: X Censo General de Población y Vivienda, 1980. Instituto Nacional de Estadística, Geografía e Informática (1984).

[a]Regional division from Unikel et al. (1976). (See map, figure 1.)

metropolitan areas and other regions of the country. In this respect, population-related objectives have been added to distribution objectives, specifically to achieve regionally balanced socioeconomic development.

The attempt to correct what is considered highly centralized economic and social development is nothing new. Objectives include slowing the growth of the primary city and other metropolitan areas, promotion of medium-sized and intermediate cities, development of selected regions (the northern border region and others that are either of great potential or that are lagging) and of some rural districts (rain-fed areas), among others. The policy instruments used are also of a wide variety: public infrastructure subsidies, tax incentives to new industries or for the relocation of already established industry, restrictions and controls on industrial location, direct state investment, industrial corridors and parks, and various rural development programs. Programs already under way to decentralize the federal administrative machinery were strengthened after the 1985 earthquakes. Thus, the demographic distribution goals are linked to the objectives of other plans: the National Plan of Urban Development, the National Agrarian Plan, the National Industrialization Plan, the National Plan of Administrative Reform, among others.

However, results in this area have been inconclusive. The 1970s saw a continuation of the pattern observed in previous decades: the coexistence of high concentration and considerable dispersion. The population in localities with 15,000 and more inhabitants represented 51.8 percent of the total population in 1980, an absolute increase during the decade of 13 million of a total increment of 19 million. The Mexico City metropolitan area

Figure 1.1 **Mexico**

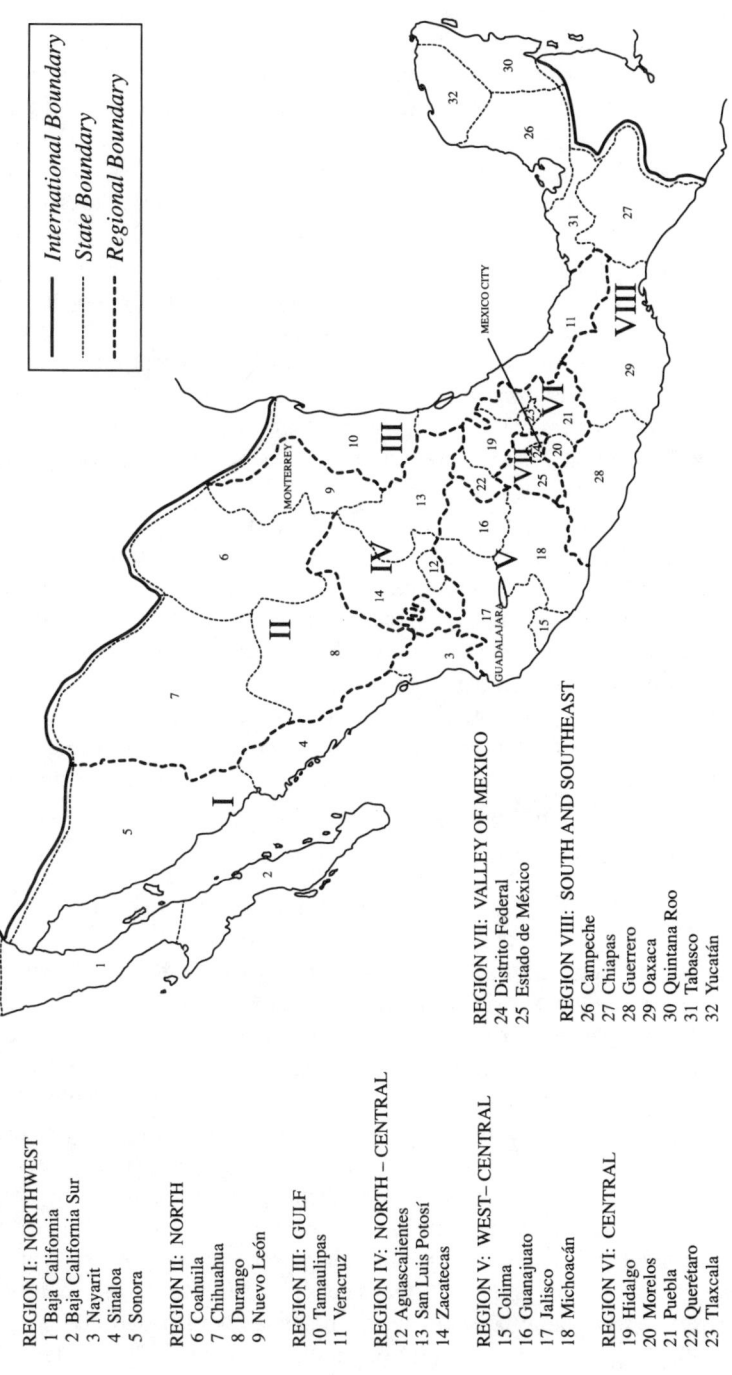

REGION I: NORTHWEST
1 Baja California
2 Baja California Sur
3 Nayarit
4 Sinaloa
5 Sonora

REGION II: NORTH
6 Coahuila
7 Chihuahua
8 Durango
9 Nuevo León

REGION III: GULF
10 Tamaulipas
11 Veracruz

REGION IV: NORTH–CENTRAL
12 Aguascalientes
13 San Luis Potosí
14 Zacatecas

REGION V: WEST–CENTRAL
15 Colima
16 Guanajuato
17 Jalisco
18 Michoacán

REGION VI: CENTRAL
19 Hidalgo
20 Morelos
21 Puebla
22 Querétaro
23 Tlaxcala

REGION VII: VALLEY OF MEXICO
24 Distrito Federal
25 Estado de México

REGION VIII: SOUTH AND SOUTHEAST
26 Campeche
27 Chiapas
28 Guerrero
29 Oaxaca
30 Quintana Roo
31 Tabasco
32 Yucatán

SOURCE: Unikel et al. (1076).

alone increased from 8.6 to 13.3 million inhabitants, and the estimated population of this area in 1986 was 18 million. The Valley of Mexico (Region VII) continued to increase its population share, and the northern regions (I and II) maintained theirs (table 14). The three major urban areas—Mexico City, Guadalajara, and Monterrey—also increased their share of total population, from 23.4 percent in 1970 (11.3 million) to 26.3 percent in 1980 (17.5 million). On the other extreme, the number of localities with fewer than 1,000 inhabitants increased from 90,000 in 1970 to 118,000 in 1980, and their population grew by 1.8 million.

Thus the basic features of the territorial distribution of the population apparently remained undisturbed in the decade of the 1970s. Nevertheless, many medium-sized cities are currently growing more rapidly than, or as rapidly as, the three largest metropolitan areas. Average annual growth of the eighteen most dynamic medium-sized cities is estimated at 6.9 percent versus 6.0 percent for Mexico City, Guadalajara, and Monterrey (Consejo Nacional de Población n.d.*b*).

On the other hand, rural population is not expected to diminish, although growth will be almost minimal. It is expected that during the 1980s, there will be a gain in rural population (in localities of less than 2,500 inhabitants) of one million people. Thereafter, until 2010, there will be an almost fixed rural population of 24.3 million. Nevertheless, the proportion of rural population will diminish from one-third in 1980, to one-fourth in 2000, and to just little more than one-fifth in 2010 (Núñez and Moreno 1986). The plans to motivate future population to move from the central highlands—the traditional centers—to the coastal areas—in the Gulf and on the Pacific—seem to be awaiting a decisive thrust.

Conclusions

A notable population change has occurred over the last fifteen years, since demographic considerations gained salience in public policy. This development has been accompanied by the recognition that population policy cannot be an independent policy. At the macro level, a major assumption is the existence of strong linkages between population, development, resources, and environment. Analysis of demographic variables has shown that significant progress has been made in reducing population growth and monitoring population tendencies. Success in fertility regulation is not credited to any single population program but to the fact that secular levels of income, nutrition, education, employment, and housing have improved over time, and that access to and use of information and appropriate technology are now more adequate and diffused.[10]

Mexico's policy to curb rapid population growth has promoted family planning and awareness. The impetus for this strategy originated at the highest level of the administration, and its effectiveness derived from the power of the Executive branch to make policy felt throughout the many tiers of the state bureaucracy. The institutions called on to produce results were, by virtue of their financial resources and organizational coherence, well equipped to take on the additional responsibilities of informing and delivering services. This experience does serve as an example of the speed and efficacy with which public opinion and governmental infrastructure can be mobilized and extended, given the political will to do so.

The initial, centralized decision to institute population programs is being complemented by attempts to decentralize the nation's vast system of public administration. The strategy seeks to advance population policy—growth and distribution—by motivating and monitoring the activities that will become the responsibility of authorities in the respective states.

Population policy in Mexico can be credited with achieving positive results. The general societal tendencies of the past have been reversed or contained. However, there is awareness in government and academic circles that on at least three counts population policy faces great challenges. Population programs need to move in the direction of specifically targeted (sub) populations. To advance effectively, more sophisticated research might be needed to shed light on more focused issues, specific social groups, and particular regions. Second, there is need for structural changes in spatial distribution patterns. Indications that adequate means have been found to bring about these changes await confirmation. Finally, population policy has to address more directly the issue of labor force absorption. This last issue is perhaps the most serious challenge to be confronted.

Notes

1. The infant mortality estimate corresponds to the 1979–1981 period (Camposortega 1987).

2. The law was formulated in 1973, but came into effect on January 7, 1974.

3. Of the institutions that compose the public health sector, the SSA and the IMSS are the two most important. Other specialized social security organizations serve employees of specific parastatal enterprises (like PEMEX) or the government itself (ISSSTE), or are charged with protecting and providing care for children (DIF).

4. This dual emphasis is embedded in the General Population Law of 1973, and has continually been reiterated in successive policy statements. The first document in which the population policy took shape states that "the demographic policy here presented integrates two fundamental objectives: on the one hand, to induce a fertility reduction, fully respecting individual freedom and, through it, a decrease of

population growth; on the other hand, to rationalize the distribution of migratory movements to achieve a settlement pattern conducive to a more balanced regional development." (See "Presentación," Consejo Nacional de Población, *Política demográfica nacional y regional: Objetivos y metas 1978–1982*.) The current National Population Program echoes this position. Although "the regulation of the rate of population growth" is a major objective of the program, the other equally important objective is "the rationalization of population distribution in the national territory within a framework of a more balanced rural, urban, and regional development" (Consejo Nacional de Población, *Programa nacional de población 1984–1988*).

5. The 104 million figure comes from the most recent "alternative" projection, under the hypothesis of a fertility trend higher than the "programmatic" one (Instituto Nacional de Estadística, Geografía e Informática and Consejo Nacional de Población 1985). Previously, the alternative projection figure was 109 million under an assumed higher fertility trend (Instituto Nacional de Estadística, Geografía e Informática et al. 1983).

6. There are important problems of comparability arising from variability in census dates, diversity of criteria for classification of sector of activity, lack of uniformity in enumerating unpaid family workers, etc. Based on an evaluation of these and other problems, the country's total active population in 1960 has been estimated at 10.2 million, instead of the 11.3 provided by the census (Altimir 1974). Regarding the 1980 census, the fact that 30 percent of the economically active population was counted as unspecified calls for great caution in the adjustments made. Total active population has been estimated as low as 17.3 million versus the count of 22 million (Rendón and Salas 1986).

7. The average length of stay outside Mexico has been estimated to be six months (Centro Nacional de Información y Estadísticas del Trabajo 1982).

8. Urban localities are defined as those with fifteen thousand or more inhabitants (Unikel et al. 1976).

9. Migration was measured between 107 regions (Cabrera 1976).

10. For a further discussion on these issues and the broader aspects of population and development, see Alba and Potter (1986).

References

Alba, Francisco, and Joseph E. Potter. 1986. "Population and Development in Mexico since 1940: An Interpretation." *Population and Development Review* 12:47–75.

Altimir, Oscar. 1974. "La medición de la población economicamente activa de México, 1950–1970." *Demografía y Economía* 8:55–83.

Benítez, Raúl, and Gustavo Cabrera. 1967. *Tablas abreviadas de mortalidad de la población de México 1930, 1940, 1950, 1960*. Mexico City: Colegio de México.

Cabrera, Gustavo. 1976. "Población, migración y fuerza de trabajo." In *Mercados regionales de trabajo*, pp. 241–248. Mexico City: Instituto Nacional de Estudios del Trabajo.

Cabrera, Gustavo, et al. 1973. "Tabla abreviada de la mortalidad en México 1969–1971." Mimeo. Mexico City: Colegio de México.

Camposortega, Sergio. 1987. "Mortality decline in Mexico, 1940–1980." Mimeo. Chicago: PPA Annual Meeting.

Casar, J. I., and J. Ros. 1981. "Reflexiones sobre el proceso de industrialización en México." Mimeo.

Centro de Estudios Económicos y Demográficos et al. 1974. "Proyecciones de la población de México." Mimeo. Mexico City.

Centro Nacional de Información y Estadísticas del Trabajo. 1982. *Los trabajadores mexicanos en Estados Unidos*. Mexico City: Secretaría del Trabajo y Previsión Social.

Consejo Nacional de Población. 1985a. *Programa nacional de planificación familiar 1985–1988*. Mexico City.

———. 1985b. *Programa nacional de población 1984–1988*. Mexico City.

———. N.d.a. *Resultados principales de la encuesta nacional demográfica de 1982*. Mexico City.

———. N.d.b. *La población de México en el año 2000*. Mexico City.

García y Griego, Manuel, and Francisco Giner de los Ríos. 1985. "Es vulnerable la economía mexicana a la aplicación de políticas migratorias estadounidenses?" In Manuel García y Griego and Gustavo Vega (eds.), *México–Estados Unidos 1984*, pp. 221–272. Mexico City: Colegio de México.

Gómez Oliver, Luis. 1978. "Crisis agrícola, crisis de los campesinos." *Comercio Exterior* 28:714–727.

Instituto Nacional de Estadística, Geografía e Informática, and Consejo Nacional de Población. 1985. *Proyecciones de la población de México y de las entidades federativas: 1980–2010*. Mexico City.

Instituto Nacional de Estadística, Geografía e Informática et al. 1983. *México: estimaciones y proyecciones de población 1950–2000*. Mexico City.

Núñez, Leopoldo, and Lorenzo Moreno. 1986. *México: proyecciones de población urbana y rural para 1980–2010*. Mexico City: Academia Mexicana de Investigación en Demografía Médica.

Passel, Jeffrey S., and Karen W. Woodrow. 1984. "Geographic Distribution of Undocumented Immigrants: Estimates of Undocumented Aliens Counted in the 1980 Census by State." *International Migration Review* 18:642–671.

Programa Regional del Empleo para América Latina y el Caribe. 1982. *Mercados de Trabajo en Cifras 1950–1980*. Santiago, Chile.

Pullum, Thomas W.; John B. Casterline; and Fátima Juárez. 1985. "Changes in Fertility and Contraception in Mexico, 1977–1982." *International Family Planning Perspectives* 11:40–47.

Rendón, Teresa, and Carlos Salas. 1986. "La población económicamente activa en el censo de 1980. Comentarios críticos y una propuesta de ajuste." *Estudios Demográficos y Urbanos* 1:291–309.

Unikel, Luis, et al. 1976. *El desarrollo urbano en México: diagnóstico e implicaciones futuras.* Mexico City: Colegio de México.

2.

The Central American Demographic Situation: Trends and Implications

Sergio Díaz-Briquets

In 1950 the combined population of the six Central American republics just exceeded 9 million, approximately double what it had been at the turn of the century (McEvedy and Jones 1978:289–290).[1] Over the next three and one half decades, the regional population tripled, reaching the 27 million mark by 1987. Throughout much of this period, very slowly at first, but with increasing momentum, strong demographic links—mainly the result of international migration—were being forged between Central America and the United States. How many Central Americans there are in the United States today is difficult to gauge. The 1980 census enumerated 331,219 persons of Central American birth; of these, 38.2 percent and 22.8 percent entered the United States between 1975–1980 and 1970–1974, respectively, with less than 14 percent arriving before 1960 (Peterson 1986). The actual number of Central Americans in the United States now, however, is believed to be much higher. Some of the migrants are likely to have been missed by the census, and many more are known to have entered since the 1980 enumeration. As many as 1.3 million Central Americans could be in the United States today, with about half of them residing in California alone (Wallace 1986:659–660).

The reasons for the uncertainty about the number of Central Americans in the United States are well known. We have a firm idea of the annual number of legally admitted Central American immigrants, thanks to the records kept by the Immigration and Naturalization Service, but the number of legal entries (369,924 between 1954 and 1985) cannot be equated with the current resident population, because of mortality, return migration, and undocumented immigration (Peterson 1986:70). The greatest uncertainty is associated with the magnitude of undocumented immigration. Whether pushed by political instability, violence, human rights violations, or poor economic prospects, Central Americans in increasing numbers have chosen to enter or to stay in the United States without legal authorization. Elusive in their movements, undocumented migrants are not easily counted, since they avoid official contact as much as possible.

Equally uncertain is the impact undocumented immigration, Central American immigration included, has on American political, social, and economic institutions. Very few analysts quarrel with many of the undesirable features associated with undocumented immigration or with how illegal immigration is at odds with certain aspects of our political and legal system. Far less certain are the social and economic consequences of undocumented immigration. Some analysts claim that the costs far exceed the benefits, whereas others hold the opposite view. The effects of the 1986 Immigration Reform and Control Act on future levels of undocumented immigration remain to be seen, but it seems likely that, at least in the short run, undocumented immigration rates ought to decline substantially. It is far more difficult to anticipate what will occur over the long term, since both the domestic and the international determinants of emigration from Latin America to the United States are many and work in intricate ways (Díaz-Briquets and Macisco 1986; Teitelbaum 1986).

The latest immigration legislation ensures that the United States will maintain its traditionally generous legal immigration policy. Therefore, it is reasonable to expect a continuation of Central American immigration, even if undocumented migration is effectively curtailed. Since 1954 the yearly number of legally admitted Central American immigrants has been rising in a nearly monotonical fashion, increasing from 3,359 in 1954 to 6,510 in 1960, to 8,924 in 1970, to 19,848 in 1980, and to 24,949 in 1985 (Peterson 1986:70). The legalization program and the family reunification provisions of the 1986 immigration legislation will give added momentum to the process. The annual number of legal admissions is still well below the combined permissible upper boundary for all Central American countries, and the number of immediate relatives who are permitted to enter does not fall under individual country quotas. Since Central Americans exhibit a strong tendency to concentrate in selected cities and states, as do other immigrant communities, the Central American presence will continue to be disproportionately felt in a few regions, including the Southwest.

That population growth in Central America is in one way or another linked to emigration to the United States is beyond dispute, although it would be erroneous to think that demographic factors alone account for increases in migratory flows. It is clear, however, that rapid population growth intensifies latent socioeconomic pressures in national environments characterized by poor economic prospects and political instability and in countries where economic development generally lags behind rapid social and cultural changes. These changes result in rising individual aspirations not likely to be satisfied in countries of origin, given limited domestic opportunities that stand in stark contrast to what emigrants can hope for in the far more tranquil and prosperous United States. Under some circumstances, like those prevailing in some of the Central American nations today, political, economic, and social tensions contribute to a climate of violence and instability many prospective migrants wish to leave behind. Demographic pressures are nonetheless a substantial element in the migratory equation, since they help aggravate some the internal tensions.

The Demography of Central America

It is appropriate to initiate a discussion of the main characteristics of the Central American population by noting the demographic diversity of the small countries of this region. Some of the Central American republics, Costa Rica and Panama in particular, are well along in their demographic transitions, whereas others have some of the least advanced demographic regimes in the Western Hemisphere. These differentials, not surprisingly, evidence a strong relationship with country-specific indicators of socioeconomic development. The most economically modern nations—and from a comparative perspective, the more socially equitable—tend to have the more favorable demographic indicators. These same countries also tend to be among the most politically stable Central American nations. Conversely, the more socioeconomically backward countries—whether in terms of income distribution, percentage of the population engaged in agricultural activities, or literacy—are also the more demographically backward. The specific demographic features of each country are reviewed in alphabetical order, beginning with Costa Rica.

Costa Rica

In most respects, Costa Rica has attained demographic characteristics typical of the developed world. With an estimated 1987 population of 2.8 million, or 10.4 percent of the total Central American population, it currently has one of the lowest crude birth rates (thirty-one births per thousand population) and the lowest crude death rate (four deaths per thousand population) in the region.[2] In one important respect, however, Costa Rica differs from the developed world: its estimated 1987 rate of natural increase (the difference between the birth and death rates) is a very high 2.7 percent, a typical developing-country characteristic. In the absence of international migration, the natural increase rate closely approximates the annual rate of population change. Such a growth rate implies a population doubling time (years necessary for the population to double in size) of only twenty-five years.

The rapid pace of population growth may come as a surprise to many nonspecialists, who have frequently heard that Costa Rica represents a demographic "success" story, which indeed it does. For instance, Costa

Table 2.1 Basic Demographic Indicators for 1987, Central America, Mexico, and the United States

	Pop. Estimate (millions)	Crude Birth Rate	Crude Death Rate	Nat'l Increase Rate (%)	Pop. Doubling Time (current)	Pop. Projected to 2020 (millions)	Infant Mortality Rate	Total Fertility Rate	% of Pop. under Age 15/65+	Life Expectancy at Birth (years)	Urban Pop. (%)	Per Capita GNP, 1985 (U.S. $)
Costa Rica	2.8	31	4	2.7	25	3.7	19	3.5	35/4	74	48	1,290
El Salvador	5.3	36	10	2.6	27	7.2	65	4.7	46/4	66	43	710
Guatemala	8.4	41	9	3.2	22	12.2	71	5.8	46/3	60	39	1,240
Honduras	4.7	39	8	3.1	22	7.0	69	5.6	47/3	63	40	730
Nicaragua	3.5	43	9	3.4	20	5.1	69	5.7	47/3	61	53	850
Panama	2.3	27	5	2.2	32	2.9	25	3.3	38/4	72	51	2,020
Mexico	81.9	31	7	2.5	28	104.5	50	4.0	42/4	67	70	2,080
U.S.	243.8	16	9	0.7	102	268.0	10	1.8	22/12	75	74	16,400

SOURCE: Population Reference Bureau, *1987 World Population Data Sheet*, Washington, D.C.

Rica has been able to reduce mortality to an extent matched by few other developing countries. The country's progress can best be described through the use of two mortality indicators whose levels are independent of cross-national variations in age structure, something that is not true for the crude rates.[3] Life expectancy at birth (for both sexes combined) in 1987 was around 74 years; at present, the infant mortality rate, one of the most sensitive barometers of socioeconomic conditions, is estimated to be in the range of 18 to 19 infant deaths per thousand live births. Both of these estimates lag somewhat behind those for Japan (77 and 5.5, respectively), the nation with the most favorable mortality indices.

The rate at which Costa Rican women are bearing children can be assessed by examining trends in the total fertility rate (TFR). This measure conveys how many children the average woman is likely to have over her reproductive life if she bears children according to the age-specific fertility pattern currently prevailing. The TFR is a useful summary measure, since it can be loosely interpreted as indicating average family size. Between 1950–1955 and 1980–1985, according to United Nations estimates (see tables A.1–A.4), the TFR was halved, from 6.7 to 3.3 children per woman, indicating unusually rapid fertility decline (United Nations 1980:238). There have been indications for some time now, however, and confirmed in 1986 by a new demographic survey, that the fertility decline in Costa Rica has leveled off. In fact, the latest survey shows an increase in the TFR from 3.4 in 1982, to 3.7 in 1986 (Population Reference Bureau 1986:4).

This leveling-off of the TFR in Costa Rica is not an isolated phenomenon, since comparable patterns are increasingly being reported in other developing countries. The most common explanation of the deceleration is that Costa Rican women are willing and capable of reducing their childbearing to levels congruent with their desired family size. Once desired family size is reached, women begin to rely on contraception to terminate childbearing rather than merely to control birth spacing (Rosero Bixby 1981:86–87). This is a crucial development, since it suggests that in some developing countries there might be a lower boundary beyond which fertility is not likely to decline unless women or couples internalize norms favoring smaller family sizes.

The Costa Rican case is a particularly revealing one, because in this country levels of knowledge, availability, and current and ever use of contraception are among the highest in the developing world. The present trend suggests that the Costa Rican population will continue to grow at high rates for the foreseeable future, the fertility decline only reasserting itself once desire for smaller family size is acquired. The 1986 survey found that nearly a third of the women with three children wanted additional children, whereas over half of those with two living children did not want any more (Population Reference Bureau 1986:4). Another factor possibly involved in the recent rise in Costa Rican fertility may be substantial immigration of higher-fertility women from the troubled neighboring nations of Nicaragua and El Salvador. This is a credible partial explanation for the reversal in the fertility trend, but the evidence for this interpretation is limited and largely inferential (Bogan 1981).

In Costa Rica, as noted, use of contraception is widespread. Approximately 70 percent of all women in unions are users, with the pill being the most favored method: about one of very five women using contraception chooses the pill. Female sterilization is the method of choice for 16.5 percent of the women, and only 10 percent rely on traditional methods (Population Reference Bureau 1986:4).

Costa Rica has served as a historical destination for many international regional migrants. The ongoing regional violence has transformed what used to be a moderate flow, particularly of temporary migrants, into a minor flood. It has been estimated that in the 1985–1986 period, between 4.5 and 7.4 percent of the resident population of Costa Rica was foreign-born (Peterson 1986:IX). Many of these immigrants are recent entrants who have arrived as refugees, the vast majority from Nicaragua, but a good many from El Salvador and Guatemala. Some analysts have tied the arrival of these migrants, as indicated earlier, with the rising fertility trend.

Internal migration from rural areas to the cities has helped transform the Costa Rican urban landscape. For several decades, urban population growth rates have hovered at around 4 percent per year. By 1985 about half of all Costa Ricans lived in cities, whereas in 1950 only about three out of ten did. It is projected that by 1990, San José, the capital, will be home to some nine hundred thousand persons (United Nations 1980:129). By then this city alone will account for about 70 percent of the total urban population of the country.

Several decades of declining fertility have had a noticeable impact on the country's population age structure. In 1985 less than 39 percent of the population was under age fifteen; in 1960 the corresponding percentage was 47.5. The expanding size of successive age cohorts, however, and increasing female labor force participation rates have helped to sustain high growth rates (over 3 percent per year) for the economically active population (EAP). According to estimates and projections prepared by the International Labour Office (ILO), the growth rate of the EAP peaked during the 1970–1980 period and has been on the decline since. Nevertheless, the EAP is projected to still be increasing by over 2 percent per annum by the first decade of next century (International Labour Office 1986:5).

The ILO has also documented the profound transformation the EAP is undergoing by sector of economic activity. Its share in agriculture declined from 57.6 percent in 1950 to 30.8 percent in 1980. The share in industry, meanwhile, increased from 16.7 to 23.2 percent, and in services from 25.8

to 46.1 percent during the same period. These changes are routinely associated with the process of socioeconomic development. Within Central America Costa Rica is the country with the lowest percentage of the EAP in agriculture and the highest in industry (International Labour Office 1986:123).

As in other Latin American countries, rapid growth of the labor force has not been translated into exceptionally high open unemployment rates. In terms of employment generation, in fact, Costa Rica did surprisingly well up to the late 1970s, when the impact of the several oil shocks began to exert an overpoweringly negative effect. Throughout most of the 1960s and 1970s, urban unemployment rates remained at or below 5 percent (Programa Regional de Empleo para América Latina y el Caribe 1982:99). Open unemployment rates did increase substantially during the early 1980s as the world and regional economic crisis intensified.

In developing countries underemployment is a more critical indicator of labor force subutilization than unemployment rates. In the Central American economies few poor workers can afford not to engage, even if only temporarily, in an occupation, no matter how poorly remunerated. Estimates of underemployment are hard to come by. A crude idea can be derived indirectly by assuming that the percentage of the population managing to survive under a locally determined poverty line is marginalized from full participation in the national economy. Based on this assumption, it can be estimated that in Costa Rica 24.8 percent of the total population in 1980 found itself in this dire circumstance. About a fourth of all Costa Ricans were living in extreme poverty or were unable to satisfy all of their basic needs. In urban and rural areas the corresponding percentages were 13.6 percent and 34.2 percent. Although the magnitude of these figures would be intolerable in a developed nation, the figures for Costa Rica compare rather well to those from other Central American countries. Throughout Central America 65.4 percent of the population lives below the poverty line (47.7 percent in urban areas and 69.4 percent in rural areas) (United Nations 1983:9). It is not unreasonable to assume that most Costa Ricans living below the poverty line do not have (or the persons they depend on do not have) access to sufficiently well paid employment opportunities, although other factors (such as family size) are involved as well. All of these considerations suggest that underemployment rates in Costa Rica are substantially lower than in most other Central American countries. Hence, it is not surprising that the distribution of income in Costa Rica, although significantly skewed, is less so than in the rest of the region (United Nations 1983:17).

Legal Costa Rican immigration to the United States, although not insignificant, seems to have been less intense than from other Central American nations. Since 1966 the number of annual admissions has fluctuated between a few hundred to less than 2,000. Between 1954 and 1985, 40,041 Costa Ricans were legally admitted as immigrants. This figure is equivalent to 1.5 percent of the total Costa Rican population in 1985. The 1980 U.S. census identified 29,639 Costa Ricans in the United States at the time of the enumeration, or 1.3 percent of the total Costa Rican population that year (Peterson 1986:238).

Costa Rica is not known to be a country from which large numbers of undocumented immigrants come to the United States. Only a few hundred undocumented Costa Ricans have been deported in each of the last several years. It appears, then, that the total number of Costa Rican natives in the United States is possibly not much higher than the number suggested by the census and legal immigration statistics.

El Salvador

War-torn El Salvador, the country with the second-largest population in the region (5.3 million in 1987), is viewed by many as Central America's demographic calamity. With a density of 694 inhabitants per square mile in 1985, a population density four to thirteen times higher than those of other countries in the area, it currently exhibits a growth rate well below its natural increase rate because of substantial emigration. El Salvador's relatively moderate natural increase rate—by regional standards—of 2.6 percent a year, is the result of a death rate above the regional average and an as-yet modest fertility decline. It appears that prior to the civil war El Salvador did somewhat better than some of its poorer neighbors in reducing mortality. As may be surmised, because of high fertility and mortality, El Salvador has a youthful age structure, with almost half of its population under age fifteen.

Evidence also exists that the TFR has been gradually declining since the early 1970s. United Nations estimates show it dropping from 6.6 children per woman in 1965–1970 to 6 in 1975–1980. The relatively high levels of contraceptive knowledge and use recorded in a 1978 survey are consistent with this trend (London et al. 1985). Almost every married woman surveyed indicated an awareness of contraceptive methods (44 percent of women in reproductive unions were current users of contraceptives). Female sterilization was the most favored contraceptive technique, and when questioned, almost half of the women replied that they did not want additional children.

The war, however, has disrupted the national family-planning efforts, and contraceptive use rates must have declined. Whether or not the declining fertility trend has been reversed, however, is open to question. The social disruptions (deaths, marital separations, need to postpone childbearing) associated with violent conflicts may more than compensate for a reduction in contraceptive use.

An important offshoot of the conflict is that it has helped to accelerate population redistribution, a trend well under way for many years. In 1980 El Salvador was about 40 percent urbanized, with urban population growth rates exceeding, but not by a very wide margin, the national population growth rate. The United Nations estimates that San Salvador, the capital, had yet to reach the half-million mark by 1980 (United Nations 1980:129). This state of affairs seems to have changed dramatically. Many press accounts speak of San Salvador (where more than a million people may live) as overflowing with refugees. According to estimates compiled by Peterson, in 1985–1986 there were about 535,000 internally displaced people in El Salvador, or about 11 percent of the total population. A further 9 to 24 percent of the people, depending on the estimate used, have either migrated to other countries within Middle America (4 to 18 percent), Mexico included, or to the United States (5 to 6 percent). In total, 20 to 35 percent of the population of El Salvador may have been displaced by the middle of the decade (Peterson 1986:VII, VIII).

Immigration and U.S. census statistics give some idea about the increasing pace of emigration from El Salvador. Between the early 1970s and 1985, the number of legally admitted immigrants to the United States rose by a factor of five, from under 2,000 in 1971 to more than 10,000 in 1985. Salvadorans constitute the most sizable contingent of Central Americans enumerated in the 1980 census: 94,447. Over half of these arrived between 1975 and early 1980. Many more Salvadorans have been reaching the United States clandestinely after an often-arduous overland journey across Guatemala and Mexico. Over 17,000 of these illegal migrants were apprehended by the border patrol along the U.S.-Mexico border in 1985. In 1977, the earliest date for which separate figures for Salvadorans are available, there were fewer than 8,000 apprehensions (Peterson 1986:70, 72, 74). It is widely assumed that a far greater number of Salvadoran illegal entrants are not detected at the border.

Figures such as the ones briefly reviewed above provide some indication of the social and economic upheaval caused by the civil war. With regard to employment, the dislocations are incalculable. In a country where underemployment levels were already exceptionally high, the underemployment rate today must be astronomical. Tens if not hundreds of thousands of displaced Salvadorans subsist thanks only to international assistance. Refugee camps in bordering countries, managed by the United Nations and private relief agencies, provide the only support available to many of the displaced workers and their families (United States Committee for Refugees 1982–1986). The widespread destruction of the productive infrastructure, a major economic blow, continues at a ferocious pace. Many years will have to pass, regardless of the military and political outcome of the conflict, before El Salvador's economic foundation can be rebuilt.

The short- to medium-term implications of this destruction for a country already troubled by major economic and structural problems and in which the economically active population is projected to be growing at nearly 3 percent per year are ominous. Emigration may well be the only viable alternative for many young workers entering the labor force. The ILO labor force projections estimate that between 1985 and 2010 the economically active population will more than double, increasing from 1.8 to 4 million workers (International Labour Office 1986:6).

Guatemala

The largest of the Central American countries, with 8.4 million people, or 31.1 percent of the regional population in 1987, Guatemala differs in one important respect from its neighbors: it is fragmented by cultural diversity. The most "indigenous" of the Central American nations, Guatemala has a large percentage of its population only partially or not at all integrated into the dominant Spanish-Guatemalan culture. Upwards of a million Guatemalans are totally marginalized from the cultural mainstream, hundreds of thousands of them not even able to speak Spanish, the national language (Mayer and Masferrer 1979:220–221).

Demographically speaking, Guatemala is one of the least advanced countries not only in Central America, but throughout the Western Hemisphere. Its 1987 natural increase rate (3.2 percent) is second only to that of Nicaragua (3.4 percent). The birth rate is still above 40 per 1,000 population, and it has some of the worst mortality indicators in the region. Life expectancy at birth is only sixty years (or fourteen years less than Costa Rica), and the infant mortality rate exceeds seventy. Recent years have seen the country's population growth rate reduced by voluntary emigration and the displacement of refugees. During the 1980–1985 period, the population growth rate was estimated by the United Nations to be 2.8 percent annually.

Guatemala has one of the youngest age structures in Central America, with a median age of 16.9 in 1986. Forty-six percent of the population is below age fifteen. The country is also one of the least urbanized in the region (40 percent in 1985), although Guatemala City is the largest urban agglomeration in Central America. Urban growth has been proceeding rapidly for several decades, with cities growing at an annual rate of 3.5 percent or higher since the early 1960s.

Fertility has been on the decline for several decades, but at a slow pace. The TFR has dropped from over 7 children per woman in the 1950s to about 5.8 today. A 1983 family-planning survey found contraceptive use rates to be rather modest, with only 25 percent of the women using effective methods (Asociación Pro-Bienestar de la Familia de Guatemala and Centers for Disease Control 1984). This is the lowest contraceptive prevalence rate recorded in a nationally representative survey in the recent past for a Central American country.

Contraceptive use rates are markedly different according to ethnic group and place of residence. The use rate in Guatemala City in 1983 approached 50 percent, but in the indigenous rural population it was less than 5 percent. Sterilization, particularly female sterilization, was the most prevalent method used, with 44 percent of all users reporting a sterilization. Despite the low use rates, knowledge of contraception is common, with four out of every five women indicating that they had heard of at least one method. Overall, 40 percent of women in unions did not want any more children, although the percentage was much lower among indigenous women. These findings are fully consistent with the underprivileged status of the indigenous segment of the population. These differentials—associated as they are with a host of socioeconomic variables (such as education)—suggest that it will take a long time before Guatemala can realistically expect to achieve much success in substantially reducing fertility.

During the years of revolutionary turmoil, Guatemala has been a recipient as well as a source of regional migrants. Some of these migrations, however, are seasonal in nature. Over a quarter million Guatemalans, or 3 to 5 percent of the country's population, may have been residing in foreign lands in 1985–1986. As many Salvadorans may have been or actually are in Guatemala, although a great deal of uncertainty is attached to this estimate (Peterson 1986:VII, VIII). The roots of some of the international migratory movements taking place today antedate the prevailing political disturbances. Salvadoran seasonal migrants, for instance, have been coming into Western Guatemala since the 1960s to harvest cotton, just as Guatemalans venture into Chiapas in Southern Mexico to pick coffee (Williams 1986:65). But many of the contemporary moves are of more recent origin and can be directly attributed to human rights abuses and violence. Mexico has established several refugee camps, some of which are taking on a permanent character (Orme 1987; Rohter 1987). Belize and Costa Rica have also offered haven to Guatemalan refugees.

Since 1980 the number of legally admitted immigrants to the United States has been on the rise, although the number of Guatemalans apprehended as they try to enter the country clandestinely along the Mexican border has been uncharacteristically stable (except for 1985, when a major increase was recorded, perhaps because of tighter enforcement). Of the sixty-three thousand Guatemalans enumerated in the 1980 census, 46 percent arrived in the 1975–1980 period, an unmistakable indication of a rise in the rate of entry (Peterson 1986:70, 72, 74). Proportionately, however,

Guatemala seems to send a smaller share of its population to the United States than any other Central American nation.

Guatemala is one of the most agricultural countries in the region. In 1980, 57 percent of the EAP was engaged in agricultural activities, almost twice the percentage as in Costa Rica or Panama. Guatemala is also a country where the growth rate of the EAP has yet to reach its peak; the ILO projects higher growth rates during the first decade of the next century, at 3.5 percent annually. Guatemala exhibits the lowest rates of female labor force participation in the region, one reason why growth rates of the EAP can be expected to rise significantly. The size of the EAP in Guatemala is expected to increase from 2.3 million in 1985 to 5.2 million in 2010, an increase of approximately 125 percent in a quarter of a century (International Labour Office 1986:6, 61).

An imperfect indication of the extent to which poor Guatemalans are excluded from full participation in the country's economy can be conveyed by noting that 63 percent of the population lives under conditions of extreme poverty or are unable to satisfy all of their basic needs. In rural areas this percentage is 66 percent, suggesting that the poverty problem is almost as serious in the cities as it is in the countryside (United Nations 1983:9).

Honduras

One of the poorest of the Central American nations, Honduras has many demographic characteristics akin to those found in Guatemala and Nicaragua. With 1987 birth and death rates estimated at 39 and 8 per thousand population, respectively, its population growth rate exceeds 3 percent per year. The United Nations, assuming a gradual and sustained fertility decline, projects an increase in population by 2010 at well over 100 percent from the 1985 population of 4.4 million. Infant mortality rates are high (in the high sixties) and life expectancy at birth (sixty-three years) is only slightly better than in Guatemala.

Fertility started to decline in Honduras during the early 1970s, later than in any other country in the region. During the mid-1980s, the TFR in Honduras may have been the highest in Central America, although estimates based on a 1984 health and family-planning survey suggest an abrupt fertility decline during the preceding years (Honduran Ministry of Health, Family Planning International et al. 1986). If the estimates obtained using data from this survey and another one conducted in 1981 are accurate—some skepticism is warranted—they would indicate a decline in the TFR of about 1 child in only three years, from 6.4 to 5.4, an exceptionally rapid change. The 1984 survey also provided estimates indicating very dramatic declines in infant mortality, particularly in urban areas.

Levels of contraceptive knowledge in Honduras are high, with about 90 percent of the women interviewed claiming to be familiar with the two most popular methods used in the country: the oral contraceptive (used by 12.7 percent), and female sterilization (12.1 percent). Overall level of current use by women in unions approached 35 percent in 1984, a contraceptive use rate substantially higher than in Guatemala but only about half the latest estimate available for Costa Rica. Honduran women appear to desire relatively large families. Almost 40 percent of the nonpregnant, fecund women in unions with three living children claimed to want more children, for instance. The figure for those women with two living children was 66 percent, and four to five children 26 percent.

Only 40 percent of the Honduran population lives in urban localities, but urbanization is occurring rapidly. The highest urban growth rates in Central America since the early 1950s, when less than 20 percent of the national population lived in cities, have been those of Honduras, averaging over 5 percent per year. In contrast to other Central American countries, where a single major city dominates the urban grid, Honduras has two major urban agglomerations, San Pedro Sula and Tegucigalpa, the capital. In 1980 the population of the latter (254,000) was over half again as large as that of the former (United Nations 1980:129).

As in other Central American countries, the population of Honduras will more than double in the next twenty-five–odd years. In Honduras the EAP has been growing at an exceptionally rapid rate: between 1980 and the end of the century the ILO projects that it will grow at a rate of about 4 percent annually. In absolute terms this translates into an increase of from 1.1 to 2.4 million. The challenge this will present in terms of employment generation is obvious. With over 60 percent of its EAP in agriculture, the country will be hard-pressed to accommodate the growth of its labor force. In 1980 Honduras had an even higher percentage (68.2 percent) of its population than Guatemala living below a locally determined poverty line, another indication of the adverse local employment picture and of the pervasiveness of underemployment in the economy. In the Honduran case, the percentage of rural poor (80 percent) is far greater than of urban poor (44 percent) (United Nations 1983:9).

Honduras has been heavily affected by the arrival of displaced persons from El Salvador and Nicaragua. It may be second only to Costa Rica in the number of regional migrants and displaced persons it has accepted. In 1985–1986 these migrants represented between 2 and 3 percent of the estimated population. Between 100,000 and 120,000 persons from El Salvador and Nicaragua have found refuge in Honduras. About one-fourth of these are Salvadorans; most of the others are from Nicaragua. About 1,000 Guatemalans, in addition, are in Honduras (Peterson 1986:IX).

Trends in Honduran emigration to the United States parallel somewhat those described earlier for some of the other countries. The number of Hondurans legally admitted has risen over time rather gradually, but more markedly since 1977. Almost fifty-four thousand Hondurans were admitted between 1954 and 1985. The 1980 census counted fewer than forty thousand Honduran-born residents, only about a quarter of these having come in the five years preceding the census (Peterson 1986:70, 72). Such a pattern suggests that the trend of rising Honduran immigration was far more gradual than the trends recorded in the more politically troubled countries of Guatemala and El Salvador. The Honduran pattern, coincidentally, is more similar to the one for Costa Rica.

Nicaragua

Torn by violence since the late 1970s, Nicaragua is perhaps the least demographically modernized Central American nation. Its 1987 estimated birth rate (forty-three births per thousand live births) is the highest for the region, as is its rate of natural increase (3.4 percent). Its mortality indicators are also unfavorable, with life expectancy at birth in the low sixties and the infant mortality rate in the sixties.[4] The population growth rates projected by the United Nations for the next several decades are second in magnitude only to those projected for Honduras. Were the present rates of growth to persist, the population would double every twenty years, a rather dubious distinction no other Central American country shares. It is anticipated that the population will increase from 3.3 million in 1985 to 6.8 million by 2010.

Available estimates suggest that the Nicaraguan TFR has been on the decline since the mid-1960s, when women were having, on the average, seven children. Today it is slightly less than six. No national representative family-planning survey has ever been conducted, so it is not possible to determine with precision the nature and extent of contraceptive use, although the U.S. Census Bureau reports a 1977 contraceptive prevalence rate of 9 percent (Bureau of the Census 1986:45). As in El Salvador, the many disruptions caused by the tense political situation are certain to have thrown into disarray whatever family-planning efforts were under way, just as a rise in mortality is one of the negative consequences of the continued state of military activity.

Although it is the least densely settled country in Central America, Nicaragua has been among the most urbanized. As early as 1975 half the population was living in urban places. The percentage today probably exceeds 60, Managua having grown very rapidly since the overthrow of Somoza.

Despite the relatively high urbanization level, Nicaragua is still a predominantly agricultural nation. In 1980, 47 percent of the EAP was engaged in agricultural activities, only 16 percent in industrial activities. As in other Central American nations with young age structures and high rates of rural to urban migration, the Nicaraguan urban informal sector is rapidly growing (Programa Regional de Empleo para América Latina y el Caribe 1982:67). In 1980, 62 percent of all Nicaraguans were classified as poor or very poor, rural poverty being especially oppressive. Eighty percent of the rural population was extremely poor or could not satisfy all of its basic needs; in the cities the figure was 46 percent (United Nations 1983:9).

In 1985–1986, Nicaragua, after El Salvador and Guatemala, accounted for the largest contingent of displaced persons in Central America. Peterson calculates that about half a million Nicaraguans, or between 15 and 18 percent, were displaced, the bulk of them (between 340,000 and 419,000) to other countries. Some of these people followed the footsteps of earlier Nicaraguan migrants who settled in Costa Rica. The latter, continues to be the preferred destination of Nicaraguans, having taken almost 60 percent of all Nicaraguans living in other Central American countries. Honduras accounts for almost all of the others, between 72,000 and 87,000. INS statistics show that between 1966 and 1977 Nicaragua sent fewest legally admitted immigrants to the United States (fewer than 1,000 a year). This trend changed by the close of the decade, as the number of Nicaraguan immigrants, as well as the number from the other nations in the region, began perceptibly to increase. The relative increase of Nicaraguan immigration, however, was above the regional average. Census figures on Nicaraguans enumerated in the United States in 1980 further reinforce the view of an increase in immigration from this country since the late 1970s: 45 percent of all the Nicaraguans identified by the census arrived here after 1975. The corresponding figures for Costa Rica, Honduras, and Panama, all relatively peaceful countries, were 25, 28, and 24 percent, respectively. For El Salvador and Guatemala, in contrast, they were 51 and 40 percent. Political violence and its sequel, economic uncertainty, seem to be associated, indeed, with emigration to the United States, a position to which many observers subscribe (Stanley 1987).

Panama

The smallest and most demographically advanced country in Central America, Panama accounts for less than 9 percent of the regional population. Together with Costa Rica, this southernmost Central American republic is in many ways worlds apart from its neighbors. Panama's natural increase rate of 2.2, the lowest in the region, is a product of a birth rate of twenty-seven and a death rate of five. In terms of mortality, Panama trails Costa Rica but only by a small margin. Life expectancy at birth is estimated to be in the low seventies and the infant mortality rate in the mid-twenties.

Because of lower fertility, the median age of the population is four to five years older than that of its neighbors (Costa Rica is the exception). This means that Panama has a relatively low percentage of the population under age fifteen, approximately 38 percent in 1987.

Although Panama had a relatively late onset of fertility decline, since about 1970 it has been rapid. According to United Nations estimates, the TFR went from 5.6 in 1970 to 3.5 in 1985, a decline of 2 children per woman in fifteen years. The United Nations assumes that this trend will continue, although, as in Costa Rica, there is some evidence suggesting that the decline has slowed (Panama Ministry of Health and Centers for Disease Control 1986:12). In 1984, according to a survey, 63 percent of the women currently in union used contraception. This rate is about 11 percent lower than in Costa Rica, the regional leader. The most common contraceptive methods used are the pill and female sterilization, the former particularly by younger women. Almost one-third of ever-married women in Panama are sterilized, the highest proportion in Central America. As can be imagined, knowledge about contraception is high, knowledge of the most effective methods generally exceeding, at least in urban areas, 90 percent (Panama Ministry of Health and Centers for Disease Control 1986). The 1979 World Fertility Survey found that as many as 62 percent of the women currently in union wished to have no more children (London et al. 1985:M–311).

Panama's EAP, although currently growing at a rate of almost 3 percent annually, should be increasing at less than 2 percent a year by the beginning of the twenty-first century. In Panama, as throughout the region, the female EAP is growing faster than the male, although female labor force participation rates are but a fraction of the male rate. Panama, with again the exception of Costa Rica, is the only Central American nation in which the EAP will not double in the next twenty-five years; it will increase by a more modest 77 percent by 2010 (International Labour Office 1986:7). Less than 32 percent of the Panamanian EAP is in agriculture, but over 50 percent hold jobs in the service sector. This pattern is congruent with the international service orientation of the national economy and with the increasingly urbanized character of Panama, with Nicaragua, the most urban country in Central America.

Despite many other positive indicators, over 50 percent of the Panamanian population is poor; extreme poverty affects almost one in every four Panamanians. The situation is much worse in rural areas (67 percent) than in urban areas (43 percent) (United Nations 1983:9).

Hardly affected by the voluminous population displacements in the region, Panama has received fewer than two thousand refugees, more than half of whom are from El Salvador. On the other hand, Panama has historically been one of the greatest contributors of legal migrants to the

United States, a migratory tradition related to the American presence in the Canal Zone. Emigration from Panama to the United States has been at a more or less stable level since the 1950s, although the yearly series show some occasional upturns in the number of arrivals (Peterson 1986:70, 72). As discussed earlier, the data on Central Americans enumerated in the 1980 U.S. census corroborate the constancy of the Panamanian immigration flow.

A Regional Perspective

The demographic prospect for Central America, as suggested by the preceding country-by-country examination, is for continued population and labor force growth well into the twenty-first century. Only two countries, Costa Rica and Panama, accounting for less than 20 percent of the regional population, are well into their demographic transitions to low birth and death rates. But even in these two countries future rapid demographic growth is unavoidable.

There are several reasons for this. One is that the number of young women reaching reproductive age will continue to increase uninterruptedly for several more decades given the triangular shape of these countries' age structures. Another, more elusive, reason, but one subject to change, is that the number of children women apparently desire to have seems to be consistent with their current average fertility. Average family size today is still well above what would be needed eventually to bring the population of these countries into a state of population equilibrium in which natural increase rates approach zero. A TFR of about 2.2 children per woman is needed if population equilibrium is to be attained, a process that even under the best of circumstances will take many, many years. In Costa Rica and Panama, in contrast, the TFR is resisting a drop below 3.2 to 3.4 children per woman, although in Costa Rica, at least, the better-educated women are capable of limiting their family size. However, even among highly educated young (under thirty-five years of age) Costa Rican women in union, the average number of children desired was 3.4 in 1981 (Rosero Bixby 1981:39, 48).

In the other four countries it is almost certain that population growth rates will accelerate even further, mainly because more mortality declines are possible, particularly among infants and children. These mortality improvements should be forthcoming—especially once peace is reestablished in Central America—as more efficient and inexpensive public health interventions, such as oral rehydration, become more widely available. Although in these countries fertility almost certainly will continue its downward course, mortality reductions should more than compensate for fertility declines. The young age structures of these countries will provide added momentum to population growth.

The United Nations medium variant projections, the set of projections most likely to portray a realistic future scenario, estimate that the Central American population will increase from 25.9 million in 1985, to 39.7 million in 2000, to 50.8 million in 2010, and 68.2 million by the year 2025, the end of the projection period. In relative terms this implies that the regional population will approximately double in twenty-five years, increasing by one and one-half times within the next four decades. The projection results, it should be emphasized, are based on assumptions that already presuppose rather substantial future fertility declines as well as mortality improvements. Whether or not these assumptions hold in years to come is, of course, impossible to anticipate. However, the rapid pace of social and economic change Central America has experienced and will continue to undergo, as well as renewed and intensified family planning efforts, could well bring about the assumptions used.

High and sustained population growth rates eventually translate into high and equally sustained growth rates for the EAP. All together in 1985 there were slightly over 8 million economically active workers in the region. The number of workers will increase by over 5 million in the next fifteen years, to 13.1 million by the end of the century, and to over 17.7 million by 2010. In 2025 the EAP may have a size of approximately 26.4 million workers, the regional labor force more than tripling in a forty-year period. As is often noted, over the short to medium term, projections of the EAP are far more dependable than population projections, since many future workers (those currently under age fifteen) are already alive at the time these projections are made.

A development of some significance is that the rate of growth of the EAP will exceed that of population, since in the future an increasing number of women are expected to seek paid employment. In Central America, as in Latin America generally, female labor force participation rates are among the lowest in the world, so there is a vast potential for growth in the EAP (Durand 1975). Whereas the regional population as a whole is expected to increase by 196 percent between 1985 and 2010, the economically active population is projected to increase by 221 percent. The kind of employment pressures this EAP growth will impose in the regional economy is unprecedented. These pressures will be particularly grave in the war-devastated economies of El Salvador and Nicaragua, but just as daunting in some of the other countries in which combined unemployment and underemployment rates may exceed 50 percent and where absolute poverty is rampant.

Population Trends in Central America and the American Southwest

It would be rather naive to attempt to establish direct linkages between Central American demographic trends and future developments in the Southwest or in the United States at large. Although many indirect links undoubtedly exist, these are mediated by an almost limitless number of socioeconomic and political variables operating in Central America, the United States, and globally. Some of the interconnections, although primarily of an economic nature and of only limited potential for the whole Southwest region, can theoretically have an inordinate impact in selected localities. International trade is a good example.[5] A more prosperous, politically stable, and populous Central America can in principle provide an enhanced market for American-produced goods and services. A bigger population, of course, would not add much to the equation if, as it happens today, a very large share of the Central American people continues to be excluded from the modern market economy due to low income and overwhelming poverty.

When the question of population growth in the Third World and U.S. interests is raised, more often than not two concerns come to mind. One is the degree to which population growth can lead to political instability by contributing to the erosion of economic development or by bringing to a head latent problems that would have remained under the surface under less formidable demographic pressures. Current wisdom suggests that the nature of these relationships is rather intricate and not always in the direction some of the more pessimistic observers believe them to be (Working Group on Population Growth and Economic Development 1986). Population growth should not be regarded as a simple one-edged sword that inexorably undermines the prospects for socioeconomic development. Instead, it should be seen as detrimental, neutral, or beneficial, depending on the specific circumstances under consideration.

The concern of most immediate relevance, however is emigration from Central America to the United States. Even in this most limited area the answers are not at all clear, despite the efforts of generations of scholars who have analyzed the linkages between population growth and emigration. Population growth can certainly enhance the potential for emigration, but seldom if ever, can it be said to determine it. Several indirect linkages can, nevertheless, be suggested when population growth is placed within the specific Central American context. The most conspicuous is the highly inequitable socioeconomic situation in Central America, which condemns a vast percentage of the population of most countries in the region to live in abject poverty. This poverty, in combination with rapid socioeconomic development, technical change, nonparticipatory political institutions, and rapid population growth, has given tremendous instability to the region. In rural areas these forces have resulted in rapidly evolving agrarian structures. Some of the changes in the agricultural sector can be used to partially explain not only political turmoil but also some international migration and the high rates of rural to urban migration prevalent in Central America. In turn, high rates of internal migration can fuel social tensions in cities, and this can contribute to political strife.

These phenomena are by no means unconnected to the regional crisis. Several researchers have suggested very specific ways in which the process of agrarian change, social and political tensions, and the contemporary crisis are linked (Durham 1979; Williams 1986). These events, to an extent, can eventually be casually related to emigration to the United States, as recent immigration increases (legal as well as refugee flows) attest. Disputes over access to agricultural land between modern and well-capitalized agricultural interests—both domestic and foreign—and the poor and politically weak Central American peasantry, these researchers suggest, are being settled today in a revolutionary arena. Continuously since the Second World War, the dynamism of modern agriculture—promoted by the United States and other well-intentioned nations and international development agencies—has forced a rapidly growing rural population into a shrinking agricultural frontier, to seek work or land in neighboring countries, or into the rapidly growing Central American cities.

Successful as these efforts to modernize Central American agriculture have been—they have resulted in a more diversified economic base and have helped generate increased amounts of foreign exchange—they have had the unintended effect of enhancing income distribution differentials: the rich have become richer and the poor, poorer. In this context all that was needed was a veritable spark. This came in the form of the economic crisis of the late 1970s, which threw the regional economy into a tailspin and made the already deplorable situation of the poorest truly desperate. In short order, violent outbreaks followed in several countries. The connections between political instability, violence, and economic crisis, on the one hand, and emigration, on the other, can easily be established.

Other developments took place mainly in the cities of the region that contributed to emigration. In this sense, it appears certain that rapid urbanization and a swift process of modernization are closely intertwined with emigration. Most U.S.-bound Central American migrants come from an urban background; they also tend to have educational and labor force characteristics above the regional average. Wallace, using 1980 census statistics, found that about half the Central Americans enumerated in California had completed high school, many had held white-collar occupations before emigrating, and few had been engaged in agricultural work (Wallace 1986). Other studies of emigration from different parts of the world have discovered that most international migrants are not the unemployed but rather employed but frustrated workers unable to satisfy their aspirations at home. Many Central American migrants seem to conform to this model. Very substantial educational improvements over the last few decades, better awareness of conditions in the United States, the establishment of successful ethnic enclaves, much improved and inexpensive means of transportation, and a devastating political and economic crisis have led many Central Americans to emigrate in order to fulfill aspirations they could not hope to meet in their countries. It is far from simple to determine whether population growth is associated with these developments.

The intent of this brief discussion is to illustrate how difficult it is to establish precise and direct links between demographic trends and other phenomena. The exercise is even more demanding when the assumed links extend beyond national frontiers and encompass such a wide range of social and economic parameters. Decision makers should be fully cognizant of the complexities of socioeconomic-demographic interactions before recommending specific policies.

Appendix

Table 2A.1 **Estimated and Projected Population (thousands), Central American Countries, 1950–2025**

	Costa Rica	El Salvador	Guatemala	Honduras	Nicaragua	Panama
1950	858	1,940	2,969	1,401	1,098	893
1960	1,236	2,574	3,964	1,943	1,493	1,148
1970	1,732	3,582	5,246	2,639	2,053	1,531
1975	1,965	4,143	6,023	3,093	2,408	1,748
1980	2,279	4,797	6,917	3,691	2,771	1,956
1985	2,600	5,552	7,963	4,372	3,272	2,180
1990	2,937	6,484	9,197	5,105	3,871	2,418
1995	3,271	7,531	10,621	5,953	4,539	2,659
2000	3,596	8,708	12,222	6,978	5,261	2,893
2010	4,239	11,188	15,827	9,394	6,824	3,324
2020	4,827	13,769	19,706	11,972	8,435	3,701
2025	5,099	15,048	21,668	13,293	9,219	3,862

SOURCE: United Nations, Department of International Economic and Social Affairs 1986: 238, 242, 244, 247, 251, 252.

Table 2A.2 **Vital Rates, Central American Countries, 1950–1955 to 2020–2025**

	Costa Rica	El Salvador	Guatemala	Honduras	Nicaragua	Panama
			Birth Rate			
1950–55	47.6	48.8	51.3	51.3	54.1	40.3
1960–65	45.3	47.4	47.8	50.9	50.3	40.8
1965–70	38.3	44.9	45.6	50.0	48.4	39.3
1970–75	31.0	43.2	44.6	48.6	46.8	35.7
1975–80	30.7	42.1	44.3	47.1	45.6	31.0
1980–85	30.5	40.2	42.7	43.9	44.2	28.0
1985–90	28.5	37.9	40.8	39.4	41.8	26.7
1990–95	25.7	35.9	38.7	37.9	38.7	24.9
1995–00	23.3	34.2	36.3	38.0	35.4	22.8
2000–05	21.9	31.1	33.9	36.4	32.4	20.9
2010–15	19.4	26.7	28.7	30.4	27.2	18.0
2020–25	17.0	22.9	24.2	25.8	22.9	16.1
			Death Rate			
1950–55	12.3	20.4	22.4	21.7	22.7	13.2
1960–65	9.1	15.3	18.3	17.7	17.1	9.6
1965–70	7.2	12.8	15.9	15.9	14.7	8.4
1970–75	5.8	11.1	13.4	13.7	12.7	7.3
1975–80	4.6	9.4	12.0	11.8	11.8	6.0
1980–85	4.2	8.1	10.5	10.1	9.7	5.4
1985–90	4.2	7.0	8.9	8.4	8.0	5.2
1990–95	4.2	6.0	7.7	7.2	6.7	5.2
1995–00	4.4	5.2	6.7	6.3	5.7	5.2
2000–05	4.7	4.9	6.0	5.7	5.2	5.4
2010–15	5.4	4.9	5.3	4.9	4.8	6.0
2020–25	6.4	5.2	5.3	4.9	5.1	7.1
			Natural Increase			
1950-55	35.2	28.4	28.9	29.6	31.5	27.1
1960–65	36.2	32.1	29.5	33.2	33.3	31.3
1965–70	31.1	32.1	29.7	34.1	33.7	30.9
1970–75	25.2	32.1	31.1	34.9	34.1	28.4
1975–80	26.1	32.6	32.3	35.2	33.8	25.0
1980–85	26.3	32.1	32.2	33.8	34.5	22.6
1985–90	24.4	31.0	31.8	30.9	33.8	21.5
1990–95	21.5	29.9	31.0	30.6	32.0	19.8
1995–00	18.9	29.0	29.7	31.7	29.7	17.6
2000–05	17.2	26.1	27.9	30.8	27.2	15.5
2010–15	14.1	21.8	23.4	25.5	22.3	12.0
2020–25	10.6	17.8	19.0	20.9	17.8	9.1

SOURCE: See table A.1.

Table 2A.3 **Total Fertility Rate, Life Expectancy at Birth (both sexes), and Infant Mortality Rate, Central American Countries, 1950–1955 to 2020–2025.**

	Costa Rica	El Salvador	Guatemala	Honduras	Nicaragua	Panama
		Total Fertility Rate				
1950–55	6.72	6.46	7.09	7.05	7.34	5.68
1960–65	6.95	6.85	6.85	7.36	7.34	5.92
1965–70	5.80	6.62	6.60	7.42	7.09	5.62
1970–75	4.26	6.33	6.46	7.38	6.70	4.94
1975–80	3.73	6.01	6.40	7.13	6.31	4.06
1980–85	3.50	5.56	6.12	6.50	5.94	3.46
1985–90	3.26	5.10	5.77	5.59	5.50	3.14
1990–95	3.05	4.74	5.36	5.14	5.01	2.87
1995–00	2.85	4.45	4.90	5.00	4.50	2.65
2000–05	2.68	3.97	4.43	4.73	4.01	2.48
2010–15	2.40	3.32	3.56	3.95	3.20	2.24
2020–25	2.21	2.80	2.92	3.20	2.68	2.12
		Life Expectancy (both sexes)				
1950–55	57.3	45.3	42.1	42.2	42.3	55.3
1960–65	63.0	52.3	47.0	47.9	48.5	62.0
1965–70	65.6	55.9	50.1	50.9	51.6	64.3
1970–75	68.1	59.1	54.0	54.1	54.7	66.3
1975–80	71.4	62.2	56.4	57.1	56.3	69.2
1980–85	73.0	64.8	59.0	59.9	59.8	71.0
1985–90	73.7	62.1	62.0	62.6	63.3	72.1
1990–95	74.2	69.2	64.8	65.3	66.2	72.8
1995–00	74.4	71.3	67.2	67.8	68.5	73.3
2000–05	74.6	72.1	69.2	69.4	70.1	73.6
2010–15	75.0	72.8	71.3	71.5	71.9	74.1
2020–25	75.2	73.1	72.3	72.2	72.6	74.3
		Infant Mortality Rate				
1950–55	94	175	141	169	167	93
1960–65	81	131	119	136	131	63
1965–70	66	112	108	123	115	52
1970–75	51	97	95	110	100	43
1975–80	30	82	82	95	93	32
1980–85	20	70	70	82	76	26
1985–90	18	59	59	69	62	23
1990–95	17	48	48	57	50	21
1995–00	16	40	40	46	41	19
2000–05	16	34	34	40	35	19
2010–15	15	27	27	32	29	17
2020–25	14	24	24	29	27	17

SOURCE: See table A.1.

Table 2A.4 **Distribution of Population by Broad Age Groups, Central American Countries, 1950–2025**

	Costa Rica	El Salvador	Guatemala	Honduras	Nicaragua	Panama
			Age 0–14			
1950	43.5	42.2	44.1	44.7	44.6	41.0
1960	47.5	45.1	46.0	45.6	48.0	43.5
1970	46.1	46.1	45.9	47.5	48.3	44.2
1975	42.0	45.7	45.7	48.0	47.9	43.1
1980	38.5	45.2	45.9	47.8	47.4	40.5
1985	36.7	44.6	45.9	46.9	46.7	37.5
1990	36.3	43.4	45.4	45.2	45.8	35.0
1995	34.9	42.0	44.3	43.4	44.6	33.2
2000	32.5	40.7	42.9	42.3	42.7	31.5
2010	28.5	37.0	39.3	41.1	38.0	27.5
2020	25.9	32.7	34.8	36.5	33.3	24.3
2025	24.5	30.8	32.6	34.1	31.1	23.2
			Age 15–64			
1950	53.1	54.9	53.4	53.3	52.9	55.1
1960	49.5	52.0	51.3	52.2	49.7	52.5
1970	50.7	50.7	51.3	50.1	49.3	51.7
1975	54.6	51.0	51.5	49.4	49.7	53.0
1980	58.0	51.4	51.3	49.4	50.1	55.4
1985	59.5	52.0	51.2	50.2	50.7	58.0
1990	59.5	53.1	51.4	51.7	51.5	60.3
1995	60.6	54.3	52.2	53.4	52.5	61.8
2000	62.5	55.5	53.3	54.4	54.2	63.1
2010	65.6	59.0	56.8	55.5	58.5	66.1
2020	66.3	62.4	60.7	59.5	62.2	67.4
2025	66.1	63.6	62.5	61.5	63.8	67.2
			Age 65+			
1950	3.4	2.9	2.5	1.9	2.5	3.9
1960	3.0	2.9	2.6	2.1	2.3	4.0
1970	3.2	3.2	2.8	2.4	2.4	4.1
1975	3.4	3.3	2.8	2.6	2.4	3.9
1980	3.6	3.4	2.9	2.7	2.4	4.1
1985	3.8	3.4	2.9	2.9	2.5	4.5
1990	4.1	3.5	3.2	3.1	2.7	4.8
1995	4.5	3.7	3.5	3.2	2.9	5.1
2000	4.9	3.8	3.7	3.3	3.1	5.4
2010	5.8	4.1	3.9	3.5	3.5	6.5
2020	7.8	4.9	4.5	4.0	4.5	8.3
2025	9.4	5.6	4.9	4.4	5.2	9.6

SOURCE: See table A.1.

Table 2A.5 **Median Age and Dependency Ratio, Central American Countries, 1950–2025**

	Costa Rica	El Salvador	Guatemala	Honduras	Nicaragua	Panama
			Median Age			
1950	18.2	18.7	17.7	17.5	17.6	19.6
1960	16.4	17.6	17.0	17.2	16.0	18.3
1970	16.8	16.9	16.9	16.2	15.8	17.8
1975	18.3	17.0	17.0	15.9	15.9	18.3
1980	19.7	17.2	16.9	16.0	16.2	19.3
1985	21.1	17.5	16.9	16.4	16.5	20.6
1990	22.3	18.1	17.1	17.2	16.9	22.0
1995	23.3	18.7	17.6	17.9	17.5	23.5
2000	24.2	19.4	18.2	18.5	18.3	25.0
2010	26.9	21.4	19.9	19.4	20.6	28.0
2020	29.9	23.9	22.5	21.4	23.5	31.0
2025	31.3	25.3	23.9	22.8	24.9	32.5
			Dependency Ratio			
1950	68.3	82.1	67.4	87.4	89.0	81.5
1960	101.9	92.2	94.9	91.4	101.3	90.5
1970	97.2	97.2	95.1	99.7	102.9	93.3
1975	83.3	96.1	94.3	102.6	101.4	88.8
1980	72.5	94.6	95.1	102.3	99.4	80.6
1985	68.1	92.2	95.5	99.2	97.1	72.5
1990	68.0	88.4	94.6	93.2	94.3	65.9
1995	65.0	84.2	91.6	87.2	90.6	61.9
2000	60.0	80.1	87.5	83.8	84.5	58.5
2010	52.4	69.6	76.1	80.3	70.8	51.3
2020	50.8	60.2	64.8	68.0	60.7	48.4
2025	51.3	57.2	60.1	62.6	56.9	48.8

Source: See table A.1.

Table 2A.6 **Population Size in Selected Age Groups, Central American Countries, 1950–2025**

	Costa Rica	El Salvador	Guatemala	Honduras	Nicaragua	Panama
	Population 15–24 yrs. (thousands)					
1950	164	390	600	279	217	162
1960	214	455	721	363	269	207
1970	337	661	1,008	479	397	287
1975	427	805	1,182	577	486	338
1980	520	956	1,344	706	556	401
1985	561	1,105	1,541	864	656	460
1990	555	1,287	1,790	1,038	775	508
1995	586	1,505	2,120	1,233	907	527
2000	676	1,738	2,479	1,433	1,066	536
2010	773	2,202	3,217	17,775	1,408	590
2020	791	2,665	3,937	2,421	1,658	599
2025	812	2,799	4,228	2,680	1,752	593
	Female Population 15–49 yrs. (thousands)					
1950	197	465	682	328	258	199
1960	262	574	874	440	327	250
1970	377	775	1,163	570	448	331
1975	463	906	1,333	657	528	388
1980	569	1,058	1,517	788	615	455
1985	665	1,244	1,737	953	735	535
1990	749	1,490	2,029	1,154	882	619
1995	845	1,778	2,401	1,398	1,055	694
2000	947	2,100	2,836	1,675	1,257	763
2010	1,109	2,801	3,870	2,270	1,716	887
2020	1,221	3,560	5,073	3,039	2,199	955
2025	1,289	3,920	5,677	3,445	2,429	970

Source: See table A.1.

Table 2A.7 **Urban Percentage and Population Density, Central American Countries, 1950–2025**

	Costa Rica	El Salvador	Guatemala	Honduras	Nicaragua	Panama
			% Urban			
1950	33.5	36.5	30.5	17.6	34.9	35.8
1960	36.6	38.3	33.0	22.7	39.6	41.2
1970	39.7	39.4	35.7	28.9	47.0	47.6
1975	42.2	39.4	37.1	32.3	50.3	49.1
1980	46.0	39.3	38.5	36.1	53.4	50.5
1985	49.8	39.1	40.0	40.0	56.6	52.4
1990	53.6	39.8	42.0	44.0	59.8	54.8
1995	57.3	41.3	44.5	48.0	62.9	57.5
2000	60.8	43.6	47.5	52.0	65.9	60.4
2010	67.0	50.6	54.6	59.2	71.3	66.6
2020	72.3	57.9	61.4	65.5	75.9	71.9
2025	74.6	61.2	64.5	68.3	77.9	74.3
			Population Density			
1950	17	91	27	13	8	12
1960	24	120	36	17	11	15
1970	34	167	48	24	16	20
1975	39	194	55	28	19	23
1980	45	224	64	33	21	26
1985	51	260	73	39	25	29
1990	58	303	84	46	30	32
1995	65	352	98	53	35	35
2000	71	407	112	62	40	38
2010	84	523	145	84	52	44
2020	95	644	181	107	65	49
2025	101	703	199	119	71	51

Source: See table A.1.

Table 2A.8 **Rate of Annual Population Change, Central American Countries, 1950–1955 to 2020–2025 (%)**

	Costa Rica	El Salvador	Guatemala	Honduras	Nicaragua	Panama
			Total			
1950–55	3.53	2.68	2.89	3.19	3.03	2.49
1960–65	3.63	3.09	2.84	3.41	3.19	2.89
1965–70	3.11	3.52	2.77	2.72	3.19	2.88
1970–75	2.52	2.91	2.76	3.18	3.20	2.65
1975–80	2.96	2.93	2.77	3.53	2.81	2.26
1980–85	2.64	2.93	2.82	3.39	3.32	2.17
1985–90	2.44	3.10	2.88	3.10	3.36	2.07
1990–95	2.15	2.99	2.88	3.07	3.19	1.90
1995–00	1.89	2.90	2.81	3.18	2.95	1.69
2000–05	1.72	2.62	2.68	3.08	2.72	1.48
2010–15	1.41	2.18	2.30	2.56	2.24	1.14
2020–25	1.05	1.78	1.90	2.09	1.78	0.85
			Urban			
1950–55	4.4	3.2	3.7	5.8	4.3	3.9
1960–65	4.5	3.4	3.6	5.9	4.7	4.4
1965–70	3.9	3.8	3.5	5.1	5.1	4.3
1970–75	3.7	2.9	3.5	5.4	4.5	3.2
1975–80	4.7	2.9	3.5	5.7	4.0	2.8
1980–85	4.2	2.9	3.6	5.4	4.5	2.9
1985–90	3.9	3.4	3.9	5.0	4.5	2.9
1990–95	3.5	3.7	4.0	4.8	4.2	2.9
1995–00	3.1	4.0	4.1	4.8	3.9	2.7
2000–05	2.8	4.0	4.1	4.5	3.6	2.5
2010–15	2.2	3.6	3.6	3.6	2.9	2.0
2020–25	1.7	2.9	2.9	2.9	2.3	1.5
			Rural			
1950–55	3.1	2.4	2.5	2.6	2.3	1.6
1960–65	3.1	2.9	2.4	2.6	2.1	1.8
1965–70	2.6	3.4	2.4	1.8	1.6	1.7
1970–75	1.7	2.9	2.3	2.2	1.9	2.1
1975–80	1.6	3.0	2.3	2.4	1.5	1.7
1980–85	1.2	3.0	2.3	2.1	1.9	1.4
1985–90	0.9	2.9	2.2	1.7	1.8	1.1
1990–95	0.5	2.5	2.0	1.6	1.6	0.7
1995–00	0.2	2.1	1.7	1.6	1.3	0.2
2000–05	0.0	1.5	1.3	1.5	1.0	-0.2
2010–15	-0.3	0.6	0.7	0.9	0.5	-0.6
2020–25	-0.7	0.1	0.2	0.4	0.0	-0.9

SOURCE: See table A.1.

Table 2A.9 **Distribution of Economically Active Population by Sector, Central American Countries, 1950–1980 (%)**

		Agriculture	Industry	Service
Costa Rica	1950	57.6	16.7	25.8
	1960	51.2	18.4	30.4
	1970	42.6	20.0	37.5
	1980	30.8	23.2	46.1
El Salvador	1950	65.4	15.4	19.2
	1960	61.4	17.2	21.4
	1970	56.0	14.4	29.6
	1980	43.2	19.4	37.4
Guatemala	1950	68.4	13.8	17.8
	1960	66.6	13.4	20.0
	1970	61.3	17.0	21.6
	1980	56.8	17.0	26.1
Honduras	1950	72.3	8.9	18.8
	1960	70.4	10.6	19.0
	1970	64.9	14.1	21.0
	1980	60.5	16.2	23.4
Nicaragua	1950	67.9	15.2	17.0
	1960	61.8	16.0	22.2
	1970	51.6	15.4	33.0
	1980	46.6	15.8	37.6
Panama	1950	56.4	13.6	30.0
	1960	51.0	14.0	35.0
	1970	41.6	17.6	40.8
	1980	31.8	18.2	50.2

SOURCE: International Labour Office 1986: Table 3, pp. 123–125.

Notes

1. For the purposes of this paper, Central America is defined as Costa Rica, El Salvador, Guatemala, Honduras, Nicaragua, and Panama. Belize, although geographically located within the region, is excluded, since culturally it has more in common with the former British West Indies than with the other Central American nations.

2. Throughout this essay the 1987 demographic estimates cited in the text have been drawn from the *1987 World Population Data Sheet* of the Population Reference Bureau, Inc., of Washington, D.C. Other estimates used have been culled from several United Nations sources and other private organizations. Many of these estimates are shown in the appendix tables.

3. A comparison of crude rates can be misleading, since variations in age structure can have a major effect on the levels of rates. The 1987 crude death rate for the United States, for example, is more than double that for Costa Rica. This does not mean that mortality is lower in Costa Rica than in the United States; the opposite is in fact the case. A higher percentage of the Costa Rican population is in the younger age groups, in which age-specific mortality rates are lower.

4. Some observers have claimed that primary health care programs introduced in Nicaragua by the Sandinistas have had a dramatic impact on health conditions and, presumably, on mortality. The war, on the other hand, may have negated many of the potential beneficial effects of these programs. For one of the most detailed examples of this type of literature, see Donahue (1986). An expansion of primary health care programs in Honduras may also be behind the avowedly rapid infant mortality declines identified by the 1984 health and family-planning survey conducted in that country (Honduran Ministry of Health, Family Health International et al., 1986). It is still too early to accept these claims; further evidence needs to be analyzed. The public health technology is now available, however, to bring about rapid mortality changes in developing countries with high mortality if sufficient financial resources and personnel are assigned for those purposes.

5. In 1986 the United States exported $2.3 billion of goods and services to Central America (International Trade Administration 1987).

References

Asociación Pro-Bienestar de la Familia de Guatemala and Centers for Disease Control. 1984. "Family Planning and Maternal/Child Health Survey: Guatemala 1983." Final English-Language Report, Atlanta, December.

Bogan, Marcos. 1981. *Los impactos de la migración internacional en la fecundidad*. San José: Asociación Demográfica Costarricense.

Bureau of the Census, U.S. Department of Commerce. 1986. *World Population Profile: 1985*. Washington, D.C., October.

Díaz-Briquets, Sergio, and John J. Macisco. 1986. "Population Growth and Emigration in Latin America: What Is the Nature of the Relationship?" In John Saunders (ed.), *Population Growth in Latin America and U.S. National Security*, pp. 308–336. Bethesda: Adler and Adler.

Donahue, John M. 1986. *The Nicaraguan Revolution in Health.* South Hadley, Mass.: Bergin and Garvey Publishers.

Durand, John D. 1975. *The Labor Force in Economic Development.* Princeton: Princeton University Press.

Durham, William H. 1979. *Scarcity and Survival in Central America.* Stanford: Stanford University Press.

Honduran Ministry of Health, Family Planning International et al. 1986. *Maternal-Child Health and Family Planning Survey: Honduras, 1984.* Tegucigalpa, December.

International Labour Office. 1986. *Economically Active Population: Estimates, 1950–1980 and Projections, 1985–2025.* Vol. 3, Latin America, Geneva.

International Trade Administration, U.S. Department of Commerce. 1987. *1986 U. S. Foreign Trade Highlights.* Washington, D.C., March.

London, Kathy A., et al. 1985. "Fertility and Family Planning Surveys: An Update." *Population Reports*, Series M, No. 8 (September–October).

McEvedy, Colin, and Richard Jones. 1978. *Atlas of World Population History.* New York: Penguin Books.

Mayer, Enrique, and Elio Masferrer. 1979. "La población indígena de América en 1978." *America Indígena* 39, no. 2 (April–June).

Orme, William A. Jr. 1987. "Guatemalans take Root in Mexico." *Washington Post,* pp. A19 and A24, January 5.

Panama Ministry of Health, and Centers for Disease Control. 1986. *Maternal-Child Health/Family Planning Survey, Panama 1984.* Atlanta, August.

Peterson, Linda S. 1986. *Central American Migration: Past and Present.* Washington, D.C.: U.S. Bureau of the Census, Center for International Research, November.

Population Reference Bureau, Inc. 1986. "Survey Report: Costa Rica." *Population Today* 14, no. 12 (December): 4.

Programa Regional de Empleo para América Latina y el Caribe. 1982. *Mercado de trabajo en cifras: 1950–1980.* Santiago, Chile.

Rohter, Larry. 1987. "In Maya Land, Refugees Who Stay." *New York Times,* March 27, p. 3.

Rosero Bixby, Luis. 1981. *Fecundidad y anticoncepción en Costa Rica 1981.* San Jose: Westinghouse Health Systems/Asociación Demográfica Costarricense.

Stanley, William D. 1987. "Economic Migrants or Refugees from Violence? A Time Series Analysis of Salvadoran Migration to the United States." *Latin American Research Review* 21, no. 1:132–152.

Teitelbaum, Michael S. 1986. "Intersections: Immigration and Demographic Change and Their Impact on the United States." In Jane Menken (ed.), *World*

Population and U.S. Policy: The Choices Ahead, pp. 133–174. W. W. Norton and Company, New York.

United Nations, Department of International Economic and Social Affairs. 1980. *Patterns of Urban and Rural Population Growth*. Population Studies, no. 68. New York.

———. 1986. *World Population Prospects: Estimates and Projections as Assessed in 1984*. Population Studies, no. 98. New York.

United Nations, Comisión Económica para América Latina. 1983. *Satisfacción de las necesidades básicas de la población del Istmo Centroamérica* (E/CEPAL/MEX/1983/L.32). Mexico City, November.

United States Committee for Refugees. 1982–1986. *World Refugee Survey*. New York.

Wallace Steven P. 1986. "Central American and Mexican Immigrant Characteristics and Economic Incorporation in California." *International Migration Review* 20 (Fall):657–671.

Williams, Robert G. 1986. *Export Agriculture and the Crisis in Central America*. Chapel Hill: University of North Carolina Press.

Working Group on Population Growth and Economic Development, Committee on Population. 1986. *Population Growth and Economic Development: Policy Questions*. Washington, D.C.: National Academy Press.

3.

The Spanish-Origin Population in the American Southwest

Frank D. Bean, W. Parker Frisbie, B. Lindsay Lowell, and Edward E. Telles

The demography of the American Southwest cannot easily be separated from the story of the Hispanic population in the United States, and especially from the story of the Mexican-origin population. Over the past two decades the population of Hispanic origin has had an increasing impact on the ethnic, socioeconomic, and demographic features of the United States (Bean and Tienda 1987). Persons who have emigrated (or migrated) from Mexico, Puerto Rico, Cuba, or from any of the Central or South American or other Hispanic countries—from any of some twenty-three nations altogether—have increasingly received attention as the public policy issues of immigration, population growth, and bilingual education have assumed more prominent places on political agendas. The regional concentration of the Mexican-origin population in the five Southwestern states—which continues to the present day—has made it relatively easy in the past for the rest of the country to overlook even this largest and oldest of the Spanish-speaking populations. However, the social consciousness of the 1960s gave renewed emphasis to both the cultural diversity and the disadvantaged economic position of most Hispanic groups. Thus, as Latino immigration to already-growing Sunbelt states increased during the 1970s, the national visibility of the Hispanic population grew substantially.

If the Hispanic population has become a part of the national demographic landscape, the Hispanic population in the Southwest (which we will define as Arizona, California, Colorado, New Mexico, and Texas) has become even more important. Following conventional practice (see Bean and Tienda 1987: chap. 2), we will define Hispanics as persons who identify themselves in recent decennial censuses as being of Spanish origin. In the southwestern states, such persons are largely of Mexican origin (82.3 percent in 1980). Hence, the study of the Hispanic population in the Southwest is, for the most part, the study of the Mexican-origin population.

A discussion of the recent demographic situation in the American Southwest would involve, of course, more than an assessment of the features and trends of the Hispanic or Mexican-origin populations. For example, the phenomenon of migration to the Sunbelt from other parts of the United States is an important recent demographic characteristic of the region. However, perhaps an even more important demographic feature of the Southwest involves the growth of the Hispanic and Mexican-origin populations. Because it is this aspect of the demographic situation of the Southwest that is viewed in many quarters as being relevant to United States population policy vis-à-vis Mexico and Central America, we will focus our attention here on the demographic behavior of the Mexican-origin population. In many places, we will present data for the entire Mexican-origin population in the United States rather than merely for the regional group. But just as most Hispanics in the Southwest are of Mexican origin, so too are most persons of Mexican origin in the country residents of the Southwest (82.9 percent). Hence, the demographic story of the Mexican-origin population in the United States is virtually synonymous with the story of the Mexican-origin population in the Southwest.

Size and Growth of the Population

The two most basic questions that can be asked about any population are How many persons are there? and Who are they? In 1980, the Census Bureau enumerated 14.6 million persons of Hispanic origin residing in the continental United States. An additional 3.2 million people—most of them Hispanics—resided on the island of Puerto Rico in 1980. Of 226 million enumerated in 1980, Hispanics represented 6.4 percent of the U.S. population, up from 4.5 percent in 1970 (table 1). The 1980 enumeration represents an increase of 61 percent over the 1970 count of 9.1 million, a rise almost seven times greater than the 9 percent growth registered for non-Hispanics during the period.

The fastest growth, by far, is observed in the *near doubling* of the number of Mexican-origin persons counted in the 1980 census as compared to the 1970 enumeration. Some fraction of this increase no doubt results from the Census Bureau's concerted effort to enumerate the Hispanic population in 1980, which resulted in many undocumented aliens being included in the census. Since current research indicates that approximately 1.1 million undocumented immigrants from Mexico were counted in that year (Warren and Passel 1987), and since there is no reason to believe that large numbers of *indocumentados* were included in earlier censuses, part of the increased count must be due to improved coverage. However, the largest part of the increase was obviously due to "real growth," especially through natural increase.

Table 3.1 **Population by Race/Ethnicity in the United States, 1970–1980**

	1970		1980		1970–1980
	Population	%[a]	Population	%[a]	% Change
Total	203,210,158	100.0	226,545,805	100.0	11.5
White	178,119,221	87.4	189,035,012	83.5	6.4
Black	22,549,815	11.1	26,482,349	11.7	17.4
Hispanic origin	9,072,602	4.5	14,603,683	6.5	61.0
Mexican origin	4,532,435	2.2	8,678,632	3.8	92.8
Puerto Rican	1,429,396	0.7	2,004,961	0.9	40.9
Cuban	544,600	0.3	806,223	0.4	47.5
Other Spanish	2,566,171	1.3	3,113,867	1.4	18.9

SOURCE: U.S. Bureau of the Census:
 1970: "Persons of Spanish Origin," *Subject Reports* PC(2)-1-C (June 1973): Table 1; "Negro Population," *Subject Reports* PC(2)-1B (May 1973): Table 1; "General Social and Economic Characteristics," *United States Summary* PC(1)-C1 (June 1972): Table 68.
 1980: "Persons of Spanish Origin by State: 1980," *Supplementary Report* PC80-S1-7 (August 1982); p. 2; "General Social and Economic Characteristics," *United States Summary* PC80-1-C1 (December 1983): Tables 72, 74, 75.

[a]Percentages do not sum to 100, since persons of Hispanic origin may be of any race. However, well over 90% of Hispanics are white by conventional census definitions.

The data in table 1 reveal an extraordinary growth in the Hispanic population over the 1970–1980 period. Even discounting the effects of certain underenumeration problems encountered in 1970 (Bean and Tienda 1987), there is no doubt that the growth rate of the Hispanic population, which averaged 6.1 percent on an annual basis during the seventies, far exceeded that of blacks (1.8 percent) and other whites (0.6 percent).

Two factors stand out in accounting for the phenomenal growth of the Hispanic population since 1960: an increased immigration from Latin America, on the one hand, and relatively higher fertility among Hispanic origin women, on the other (U.S. Bureau of the Census 1984). In the sections that follow we consider the relative importance of each of these factors in contributing to changes in the size and composition of the Hispanic population during the 1970s.

Before addressing this question, it is useful first to note the concentration of the Mexican-origin population in the five southwestern states (table 2). As noted above, 82.7 percent of all Mexican origin persons in 1980 resided in these five states. That the Hispanic presence in the Southwest is overwhelmingly Mexican is indicated by the that fact 82.3 percent of all southwestern Hispanics were Mexicans. Only in New Mexico were less than half of the Hispanics of Mexican origin; in Texas over 92 percent of the Hispanics were Mexican in origin. It is also interesting to note that growth in the

Table 3.2 **Total Hispanic-Origin and Mexican-Origin Population by State, Southwestern States, 1980**

State	Hispanic Origin (1)	Mexican Origin (2)	% Mexican Origin [(2)/(1) x 100]
Arizona	440,701	396,410	89.9
California	4,544,331	3,637,466	80.0
Colorado	337,717	207,204	61.4
New Mexico	477,222	233,772	49.0
Texas	2,985,824	2,752,487	92.2
Total in Southwestern states	8,785,795	7,227,339	82.3
Total in U.S.	14,608,673	8,740,439	59.8
% in Southwestern states	60.1	82.7	

SOURCE: Same as table 1.

Mexican-origin population accounted for 45.5 percent of the total growth in the populations of these states between 1970 and 1980 (table 3), even though persons of Mexican origin constituted only 10.9 percent of these states' total populations in 1970. By 1980, however, this percentage had increased to 16.1 percent. The Mexican-origin population accounted for over half of Texas' and California's growth, with other Hispanics contributing nontrivial components of growth in New Mexico and California.

Differing rates of immigration and fertility among Hispanics have diversified the national origin composition of the population and will probably continue to do so for some time. Of the 14.6 million Hispanics enumerated in 1980, approximately 60 percent were of Mexican origin, 14 percent of Puerto Rican origin, 6 percent of Cuban origin, 7 percent of Central or South American origin, and 14 percent of other Hispanic origin (fig. 1). The last group includes not only part-Hispanics, that is, offspring from Hispanic and non-Hispanic parents, but also persons of mixed Hispanic origin, that is, offspring of marriages between members of different Hispanic subgroups, and Hispanos, the long-term residents of the Southwest whose origins are traced to Spanish and Mexican/Indian stock (Hispanic Policy Development Project 1984).

Although few would deny that the Hispanic population increased rapidly during the 1970s, it is highly unlikely that a 61 percent change for the total population, or a 93 percent increase for the Mexican-origin population, represents real growth over the ten-year period. Even with high levels of legal and illegal immigration, and with fertility levels 35 to 40 percent above those of Anglos, a near doubling of the Mexican-origin population

Table 3.3 **Increase in Mexican-Origin and Hispanic-Origin Population as Percentage of Total Increase by State, Southwestern States, 1970–1980**

	% of Total Increase Due to Increase in Mexican-Origin Population	% of Total Increase Due to Increase in Hispanic-Origin Population
Arizona	25.3	18.6
California	50.1	58.6
Colorado	15.2	16.4
New Mexico	41.5	58.9
Texas	53.4	37.7
Total Southwest	45.5	43.6

SOURCE: Same as table 1.

between 1970 and 1980 seems highly implausible. Therefore, in the following section we discuss in very general terms the relative importance of measurement error, immigration, and natural increase in producing the large intercensal increase in the Mexican-origin population.

Components of Growth: An Approximation

Besides natural increase and net migration, which are the only true sources of growth of a population, the measured change in the size of the Mexican-origin population reflects coverage and classification errors in both time periods. The existence of such errors complicates the task of sorting out the natural increase and net immigration components of growth for this population (Siegel and Passel 1979). Thus, although there is no way to know precisely the "true" intercensal population growth rate (Willette et al. 1982), information about the demographic structure of the Mexican-origin population, together with official statistics about the volume of immigration from Mexico during the 1970s, provides a general idea about the relative importance of immigration and natural increase in producing the observed growth of the Mexican-origin population. Since rapid growth is one of the distinguishing features of the Mexican-origin population, it is essential to develop a knowledgeable interpretation of the published statistics that imply very high growth rates.

A major reason for elaborating on the components of growth, even if in a highly approximate way, stems from popular and often unfounded conceptions about how much immigration has contributed to the rapid growth of the Hispanic population. Immigration from Mexico, the Spanish-speaking Caribbean, and Latin America increased substantially during the 1970s. Its impact is manifested in the age structure and national origin composition of

Figure 3.1 **Hispanic-Origin Population in the United States, 1980**

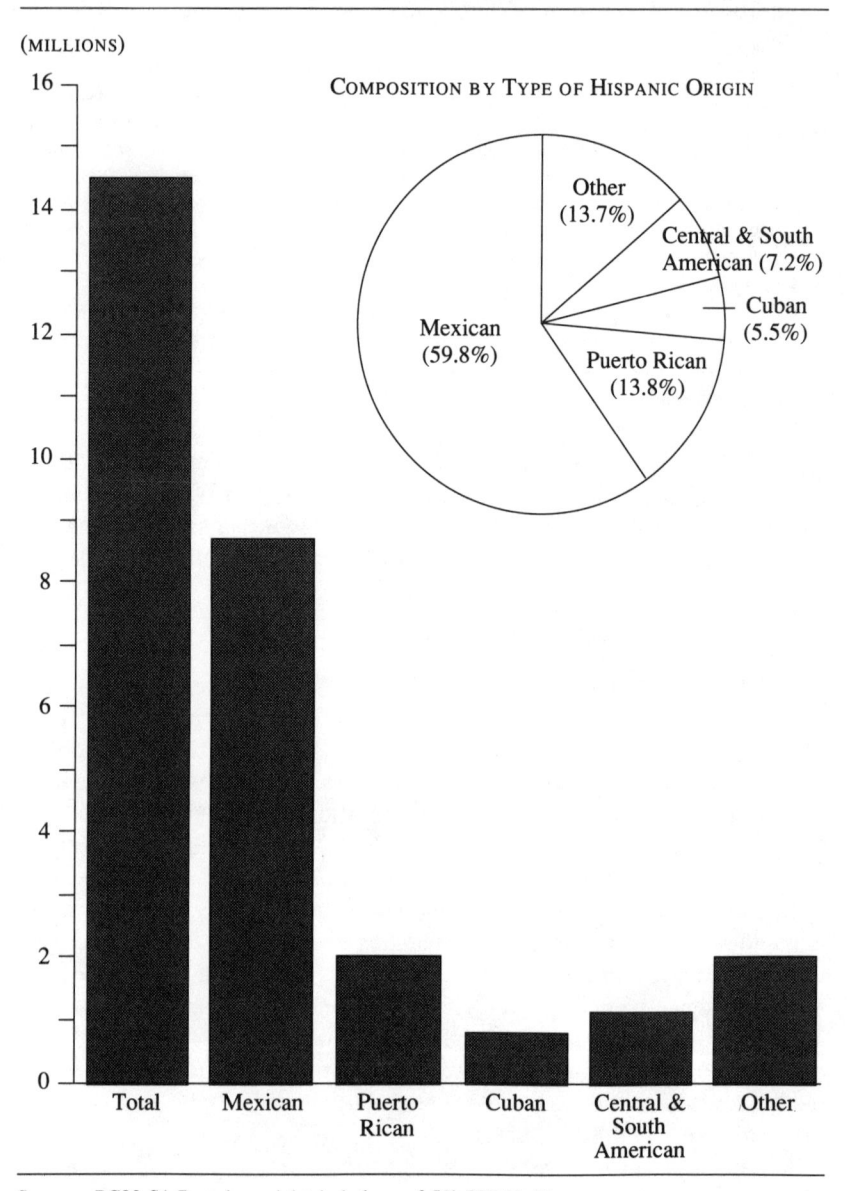

(MILLIONS)

COMPOSITION BY TYPE OF HISPANIC ORIGIN

- Mexican (59.8%)
- Other (13.7%)
- Central & South American (7.2%)
- Cuban (5.5%)
- Puerto Rican (13.8%)

SOURCE: PC80-S1-7, and special tabulations of 5% PUMS file.

the Mexican-origin population. Based on the data we present here, however, we find little evidence to support the claim that immigration accounts for more than half of the growth of the Mexican-origin population.

The issue of immigration has become increasingly controversial because of the attention devoted to the problem of illegal immigration. As the data and computations in table 4 show, the question of assessing the growth of the Mexican-origin population during the decade is a complicated one. First of all, the 1980 enumeration includes a large number of persons who misclassified themselves as being of Mexican origin, a large number of illegals, and some "extra" number of persons who were enumerated because of coverage improvements in 1980 compared to 1970 (rows B, C, and D) (Warren and Passel 1987). Also, the 1970 enumeration gave low results in comparison to totals from Current Population Surveys taken just before and after the census (row G). Taking all of these factors into account, we find that a more "accurate" amount of increase over the decade would be about

Table 3.4 **Estimated Components of Change in Mexican-Origin Population (1970–1980) and Change Due to Immigration (thousands)**

Row Label	Description	Formula	Count or %
A	Mexican-origin population: 1980 census	(X)	8,740
B	Misreporting of Mexican origin: 1980 census[a]	(X)	200
C	Estimated number of undocumented Mexicans included in 1980 census[b]	(X)	1,130
D	Coverage improvement: 1980 census over 1970 census	(X)	100
E	Adjusted 1980 legal Mexican-origin population	A–B–C–D	7,310
F	Mexican-origin population: 1970 census	(X)	4,530
G	Estimate of 1970 classification error[c]	(X)	500
H	Adjusted 1970 Mexican-origin population	F+G	5,030
I	1970–1980 legal increase	E–H	2,280
J	Number of Mexican legal immigrants as of April 1, 1980[b]	(X)	575
K	Number of Mexican illegal immigrants in 1980 who entered 1970–1980[b]	(X)	902
L	1970–1980 total increase	I+K	3,182
M	Total immigration as a % of total increase	J+K/L	46.4
N	Legal immigration as a % of legal increase	J/I	25.2

[a]U.S. Bureau of the Census 1982.
[b]Warren and Passel 1987.
[c]Passel, personal communication 1986.
(X): Not applicable.

2.3 million rather than 4.2 million persons (row I), assuming we base our calculations only on legal persons. The figure would be about 3.2 million persons (row L) if we based our calculations on legal and illegal persons. Row I represents an increase of 45.3 percent over the decade, and row L, an increase of 63.3 percent. Certainly the former is more consistent with "plausibility" than is the 93 percent increase that is obtained if none of these complicating factors are taken into consideration. Finally, when we calculate immigration as a percentage of increase, we obtain figures of 46.4 percent and 25.2 percent (rows M and N), depending on whether we include estimates of the number of illegal immigrants coming to the United States during the decade in our calculations (Warren and Passel 1987). In either case, however, measured immigration represents less than half of the measured population increase from 1970 to 1980.

Our contention that immigration was responsible for less than half (and substantially less than half in the case of legal immigration) of the growth of the Mexican-origin population finds further support in figures 2 and 3, which show how immigration between 1970 and 1980 and that prior to 1970 altered the age-sex pyramid of the Mexican-origin population. The wide base of the Mexican-origin population (fig. 3) shows the influence of high fertility during the 1960s and before. When compared to the base of the total U.S. population pyramid (fig. 2), that of Mexicans is much wider. Moreover, at ages fourteen and below, the foreign-born never reach one-fifth of the age-sex population segment; for ages fifteen to forty-four, the foreign-born make up anywhere from 22 percent to 41 percent of the respective age-sex segment. As a result of the changing age structure of recent immigrants and the aging of earlier immigrants, the foreign-born Mexican-origin population became more youthful between 1960 and 1980, with the median age declining from forty-two years in 1960 to twenty-nine years in 1980 (Bean and Tienda 1987). Mexican immigration in the period under discussion largely involved young adults, but women participated more than they had before 1970.

Assessment of Components of Growth

On balance, these numerical exercises are useful in illustrating that, although the Mexican-origin population grew rapidly during the 1970s, a nontrivial amount of the net change reflects improved coverage of the population in the 1980 census. Although this is no longer a disputed point (Siegel and Passel 1979), our general discussion of the components of growth has attempted to put into perspective interpretations of the measured increase in the size of the Mexican-origin population. Many users of census data, although acknowledging an undercount problem in the case of 1970 census data on Hispanics, nevertheless present growth rates based on

THE SPANISH-ORIGIN POPULATION IN THE AMERICAN SOUTHWEST   73

Figure 3.2 **Age-Sex Composition of the Total U.S. Population, 1980**

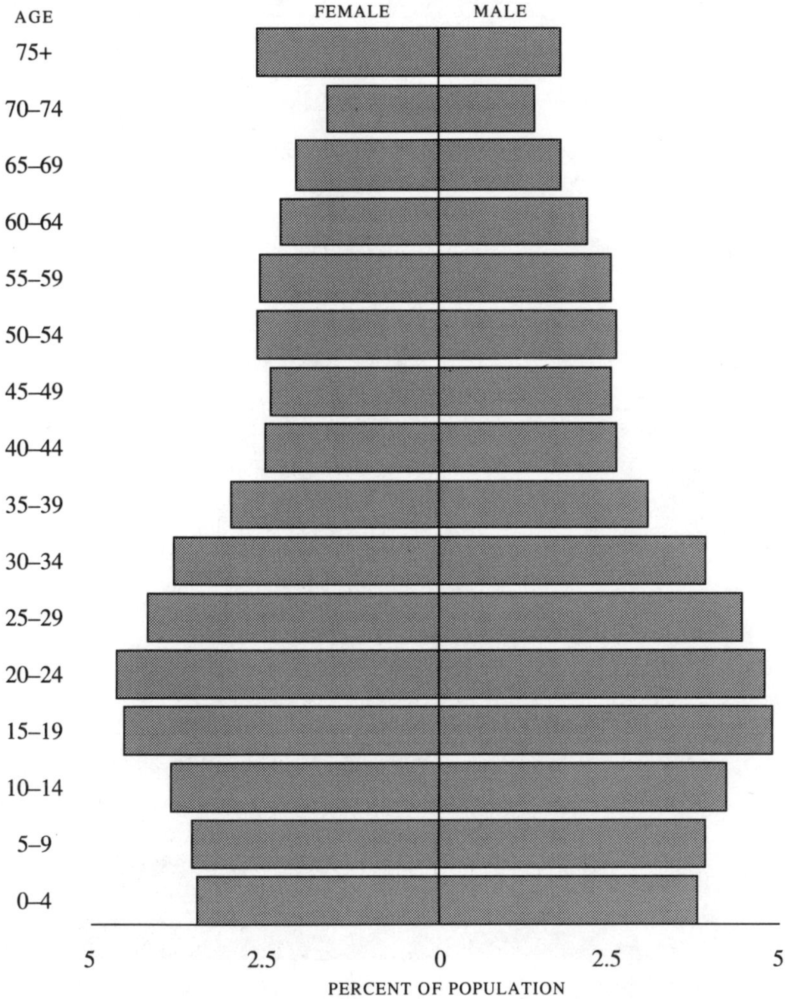

SOURCE: U.S. Bureau of the Census, 1980 Census of Population, "Age, Sex, Race and Spanish Origin of the Population by Regions, Divisions, and States: 1980." *Supplementary Report* PC80-S1-1, 1981.

net change as though the reported increase represented "true" growth. Even more serious misunderstandings concerning the future size of the Mexican-origin population result from basing population projections on the changes in the size of the Mexican-origin or Hispanic population measured between 1970 and 1980, as some usually credible organizations have done.

The impact of immigration on intercensal growth has also been misunderstood. What seems clear from the evidence presented above, how-

Figure 3.3 **Age-Sex Composition of the Mexican-Origin Population in the U.S., by Nativity, 1980**

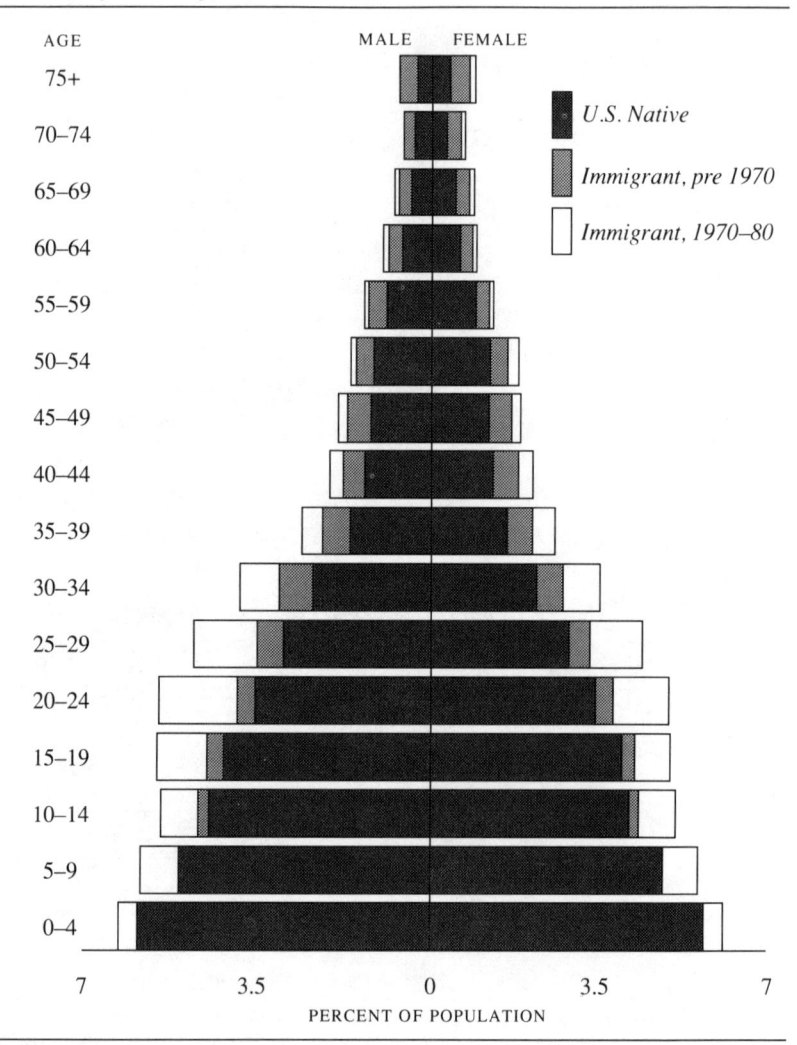

[Population pyramid with age groups from 0-4 to 75+ on vertical axis, Male on left and Female on right, Percent of Population from 7 to 0 to 7 on horizontal axis. Legend: U.S. Native (black), Immigrant, pre 1970 (gray), Immigrant, 1970–80 (white).]

SOURCE: 1980 PUMS, A Sample.

ever, is that immigration probably was *not* the major source of growth for the Mexican-origin population during the 1970s, although its impact was quite significant. That other sources of growth were often more important even when the volume of immigration from Mexico was increasing during the 1970s only underscores the need to exercise caution in attributing the major causes of growth for the Mexican-origin population during the 1970–1980 intercensal period to immigration.

Geographical Distribution and Internal Migration

One of the factors affecting the volume and character of immigration, as well as settlement patterns among immigrants after they arrive in the United States, is the existence of social networks consisting of family and friends, which facilitate the settlement process and the location of employment (Massey 1985). This being the case, we would expect to find a greater geographical concentration among foreign-born Hispanics than among the native-born. Evidence for this emerges from the data presented in table 5, which shows the regional distributions of the Hispanic and Mexican-origin populations by nativity in 1980. In the cases of the Mexican-origin population, a higher fraction of the foreign-born population is found in the regions where the greatest concentration of these populations occurs. For example, 65 percent of foreign-born Mexicans as opposed to only about 50 percent of the native-born live in the West, the region of greatest concentration among Mexican Americans.

As interesting as such figures on patterns of regional concentration are, they suffer at least two limitations that hamper inferences about whether the Hispanic and Mexican-origin populations are becoming more dispersed throughout the United States over time. First, regional groupings of states are so large that they do not enable the detection of dispersal within regions. Second, they do not reveal whether the shifts in the distribution of the Hispanic and Mexican-origin populations over time are distinct from regional shifts occurring in the population at large. A clearer picture about the tendency for these populations to have distributed themselves more widely throughout the United States can be obtained from the state distributions of the populations in 1960, 1970, and 1980. Because population shifts in general—such as the tendency for movement to have occurred out of Northeastern and North Central states into Sunbelt states during the 1970s

Table 3.5 **Percentage Distribution of the Hispanic-Origin Populations, by Region and Nativity, 1980**

	Northeast	North Central	South	West
Total Hispanic-origin				
Foreign-born	17.3	7.9	29.3	45.5
Native-born	18.1	9.0	31.1	41.8
Mexican				
Foreign-born	0.9	9.9	24.1	65.0
Native-born	1.1	9.1	39.5	50.3

SOURCE: Bureau of the Census, "General Social and Economic Characteristics" PC80-1-C2 through C52, Table 100, Washington, D.C.: Government Printing Office and 1980 PUMS-A.

(Biggar 1979)—affect the distribution by state both of the total population and of the population of Hispanic origin, it is desirable to compute a measure of distributional concentration for the populations of Hispanic and Mexican origin in each of the three census years that is free of such general population shifts. A measure of distributional difference that serves this purpose—the index of dissimilarity—was thus computed between the state distribution of each of the Hispanic-origin groups and the distribution of the general population in each of the census years (Massey 1979). This index varies from a minimum of 0 to a maximum of 100 and can be interpreted as the percentage of the Mexican-origin population that would have to change its state residence in order to result in the same population distribution as that occurring in the total population.

The picture that emerges from examining the values for this index for Mexican Americans indicates a clear pattern of deconcentration, with the value of the dissimilarity index decreasing from a high of about 80 in 1960, to 77 in 1970, to about 65 in 1980. Although Mexican Americans in 1980 remained highly concentrated in certain states, this concentration was considerably less pronounced than it was in 1960.

Further insight into this tendency of Mexican immigrant groups to settle among their own kind can be obtained by comparing indexes of dissimilarity computed between the state distribution of native-born Mexican Americans and the state distributions of Mexican immigrants classified according to when they entered the United States. In the case of Mexican immigrants who entered the United States before 1970, for example, the index yields a value of 20.4, indicating that slightly more than 20 percent would have to change their state of residence in order to yield the same state distribution that is characteristic of the native-born Mexican American population in 1980. By contrast, those immigrants who entered after 1970 show an index value of 29.4, indicating that a substantially higher fraction would have to change their state of residence to achieve the same population distribution characterizing native-born Mexican Americans. In short, the more recent Mexican immigrants are more concentrated in a few states of residence, whereas those who have been in this country for a longer period reveal a state distribution more similar to that of native-born Mexican Americans.

Metropolitanization and Urbanization

Historically, European immigrants to the United States settled in the large cities of the Northeast, thus concentrating in urban areas to a greater degree than was the case with the native-born population (Zelinsky 1973). To a considerable extent, this pattern has been repeated in the case of Puerto Ricans, Cubans, and Central/South Americans, whose places of settlement have tended to be in the metropolitan areas in and around New York and Miami.

Early Mexican immigrants, however, were much more likely than these groups to be employed in mining, railroads, and agriculture, all nonurban industries. For this reason, as well as because the Southwest was to a considerable degree a rural region before World War II, Mexican Americans during the first half of the twentieth century were a rural population to a much greater degree than were other immigrant populations. For example, in 1920 only about 45 percent of the Mexican foreign-stock population lived in urban areas in the United States, whereas this percentage for most of the populations of European stock was about 75 (Hutchinson 1956).

After World War II, however, the Mexican population urbanized more rapidly than the rest of the population (Grebler, Moore, and Guzmán 1970). By 1960 the total Hispanic-origin population in the United States, including persons of Mexican origin, was more metropolitan in character than the non-Hispanic white population (table 6). Moreover, the tendency toward metropolitanization persisted during the 1960s, when large areas of the United States were experiencing a decrease in the percentage of the population living in metropolitan areas (Brown and Beale 1981). In 1980, all of the Hispanic and Mexican-origin groups showed a higher concentration of persons living in metropolitan areas than was the case for the non-Hispanic white population.

The tendency of immigrants to settle in places where there exists the highest concentration of persons of similar national origin is also revealed in the figures in table 6. The percentage of the foreign-born within the Hispanic and Mexican-origin groups residing in metropolitan areas in each of

Table 3.6 **Percentage of the Hispanic-Origin Population Living in Metropolitan Areas, by Nativity, 1960, 1970, 1980**

	1960	1970	1980
Total White	62.8	67.8	73.3
Total Hispanic-origin	79.7	86.8	84.4
Foreign-born	87.5	93.2	91.6
Native-born	76.0	83.7	80.3
Mexican	73.6	83.1	80.9
Foreign-born	75.5	88.1	87.1
Native-born	73.2	81.9	78.6

SOURCE: 1960 PUS, 1970 PUS, AND 1980 PUMS; U.S. Bureau of the Census, 1960 Census of Population, "Standard Metropolitan Statistical Areas" PC(3)-1D; 1970 Census of Population, "General Population Characteristics" PC(1)-B1; 1980 Census of Population, "General Population Characteristics" PC80-1-B1.

the three census years is greater than it is in the case of the native-born. Hence, consistent with the earlier immigration patterns involving Europeans, the foreign-born Mexican-origin populations tend to be even more highly concentrated in metropolitan areas than is the case with the native-born population.

Which of the country's metropolitan areas (SMSAs) contain the largest concentrations of Hispanics? Table 7 lists the SMSAs in the United States containing one hundred thousand or more Hispanic-origin persons in 1980, ranked in order of the number of such persons in the SMSA. If considered only in and of themselves, the Hispanic populations in at least two of

Table 3.7 **Standard Metropolitan Statistical Areas with 100,000 or More Hispanic-Origin Persons, 1980**

SMSA	Total Persons	Hispanic Origin Pop.	%
Los Angeles–Long Beach, Cal.	7,477,503	2,066,103	27.6
New York, N.Y.–N.J.	9,120,346	1,493,148	16.4
Miami, Fla.	1,625,781	580,994	35.7
Chicago, Ill.	7,103,624	580,609	8.2
San Antonio, Tex.	1,071,954	481,511	44.9
Houston, Tex.	2,905,353	424,903	14.6
San Francisco–Oakland, Cal.	3,250,630	351,698	10.8
El Paso, Tex.	479,899	297,001	61.9
Riverside–San Bernardino–Ontario, Cal.	1,558,182	290,280	18.6
Anaheim–Santa Ana–Garden Grove, Cal.	1,932,709	286,339	14.8
San Diego, Cal.	1,861,846	275,177	14.8
Dallas–Fort Worth, Tex.	2,974,805	249,614	8.4
McAllen–Pharr–Edinburg, Tex.	283,229	230,212	81.3
San Jose, Cal.	1,295,071	226,611	17.5
Phoenix, Ariz.	1,509,052	199,003	13.2
Denver–Boulder, Colo.	1,620,902	173,773	10.7
Albuquerque, N.Mex.	454,499	164,200	36.1
Brownsville–Harlingen–San Benito, Tex.	209,727	161,654	77.1
Corpus Christi, Tex.	326,228	158,119	48.5
Fresno, Cal.	514,621	150,790	29.3
Jersey City, N.J.	556,972	145,163	26.1
Newark, N.J.	1,965,969	132,372	6.7
Philadelphia, Pa.–N.J.	4,716,818	116,280	2.5
Oxnard–Simi Valley–Ventura, Cal.	529,174	113,192	21.4
Tucson, Ariz.	531,443	111,418	21.0
Nassau–Suffolk, N.Y.	2,605,813	101,975	3.9
Sacramento, Cal.	1,014,002	101,694	10.0

SOURCE: U.S. Bureau of the Census, 1980 Census of Population and Housing, "General Population Characteristics" PC80-1-B1, Table 70, Government Printing Office: Washington, D.C.

these—Los Angeles-Long Beach and New York—would rank among the largest Spanish-speaking cities in the world. For example, Los Angeles-Long Beach contained over two million persons of Hispanic origin, about 28 percent of the total population of the SMSAs in 1980. New York contained nearly a million and a half persons of Hispanic origin, about 16 percent of that city's total population.

Table 8 shows these same metropolitan areas with their total Hispanic-origin populations broken down by type. It is evident that most SMSAs with large numbers of Hispanic-origin persons are predominantly "Mexican." For example, about 80 percent of the Hispanic-origin population of Los Angeles is of Mexican origin. Not surprisingly, anywhere from 80 to well over 90 percent of the Hispanic-origin populations of most of the California and all of the Texas SMSAs listed are of Mexican origin. Even in the case of Chicago, which is outside the Southwest, nearly two-thirds of the Hispanic-origin population is Mexican. Only two SMSAs—New York and Philadelphia—contain a majority of Puerto Ricans in their Hispanic-origin populations, although Nassau-Suffolk and Newark come close to 50 percent. Finally, Miami represents the only SMSA whose Hispanic-origin population is predominantly Cuban, and Albuquerque the only SMSA whose Hispanic-origin population contains a majority of persons of other Hispanic origin.

Internal Migration

Historically, the United States has been characterized by three major population movements (Biggar 1979). The first of these was the movement of people from east to west, a pattern of migration that was still evident during the 1970s. The second was a movement of persons from rural to urban areas, a trend that has been even more characteristic of Mexican Americans than of non-Hispanic whites since World War II. The third involved the movement of people out of the South to other regions of the country, a trend that reversed itself during the 1970s as regional economic development increased the attractiveness of "Sunbelt" states as destinations for migrants (Berry and Silverman 1980).

Between 1975 and 1980, the dominant pattern of regional migration in the United States involved the net movement of people out of the Northeast and North Central census regions into the Southern and Western regions. This can readily be seen in table 9, which presents net migration totals for the major census regions both for non-Hispanic whites and for the total Hispanic-origin population, as well as for the population of Mexican origin. For purposes of the present analysis, migrants are defined as those who changed their residence from one state to another between 1975 and 1980. Among non-Hispanic whites, for example, nearly 1.5 million more persons

Table 3.8 **Standard Metropolitan Statistical Areas with 100,000 or More Hispanic-Origin Persons, by Origin Type, 1980**

SMSA	Hispanic-Origin Persons	Mexican Pop.	%
Los Angeles–Long Beach, Cal.	2,066,103	1,650,934	79.9
New York, N.Y.–N.J.	1,493,148	26,332	1.8
Miami, Fla.	580,994	13,238	2.3
Chicago, Ill.	580,609	368,981	63.6
San Antonio, Tex.	481,511	447,416	92.9
Houston, Tex.	424,903	374,510	88.1
San Francisco–Oakland, Cal.	351,698	189,742	54.0
El Paso, Tex.	297,001	282,001	94.9
Riverside–San Bernardino–Ontario, Cal.	290,280	252,513	87.0
Anaheim–Santa Ana–Garden Grove, Cal.	286,339	232,472	81.2
San Diego, Cal.	275,177	227,943	82.8
Dallas–Fort Worth, Tex.	249,614	223,105	89.4
McAllen–Pharr–Edinburg, Tex.	230,212	221,971	96.4
San Jose, Cal.	226,611	176,838	78.0
Phoenix, Ariz.	199,003	177,546	89.2
Denver–Boulder, Colo.	173,773	108,697	62.6
Albuquerque, N.Mex.	164,200	71,617	43.6
Brownsville–Harlingen–San Benito, Tex.	161,654	138,509	85.7
Corpus Christi, Tex.	158,119	151,126	95.6
Fresno, Cal.	150,790	140,976	93.5
Jersey City, N.J.	145,163	1,385	1.0
Newark, N.J.	132,372	3,677	2.8
Philadelphia, Pa.–N.J.	116,280	8,535	7.3
Oxnard–Simi Valley–Ventura, Cal.	113,192	100,629	88.9
Tucson, Ariz.	111,418	100,085	89.8
Nassau–Suffolk, N.Y.	101,975	3,354	3.3
Sacramento, Cal.	101,694	78,597	77.3

SOURCE: U.S. Bureau of the Census, 1980 Census of Population and Housing, "General Population Characteristics" PC80-1-B1, Table 70, Government Printing Office: Washington, D.C.

aged five years and older in 1980 left the Northeast for other regions than left these regions for the Northeast. Net movement out of the North Central region occurred on a nearly comparable scale. By contrast, the South gained nearly 1.75 million movers and the West over a million.

Among the total Hispanic and Mexican-origin groups, a similar pattern of geographic mobility occurred. Because these groups are so much smaller than the group of non-Hispanic whites, it is difficult to compare the former with the latter using raw numbers of migrants. It is thus of interest to calculate migration rates and compare them to those of non-Hispanic whites in order to ascertain whether the magnitude as well as the direction of move-

Puerto Rican		Cuban		Other Hispanic	
Pop.	%	Pop.	%	Pop.	%
36,662	1.8	44,289	2.1	334,218	16.2
892,375	59.8	71,203	4.8	503,238	33.7
44,656	7.7	407,253	70.1	115,847	19.9
126,713	21.8	17,780	3.1	67,135	11.6
3,639	0.8	1,044	0.2	29,412	6.1
4,397	1.0	6,376	1.5	39,620	9.3
19,700	5.6	3,988	1.1	138,268	39.3
2,846	1.0	420	0.1	11,734	4.0
4,886	1.7	1,750	0.6	31,131	10.7
5,734	2.0	4,820	1.7	43,313	15.1
6,007	2.2	1,531	0.6	39,696	14.4
2,882	1.2	3,060	1.2	20,567	8.2
267	0.1	204	0.1	7,770	3.4
6,266	2.8	1,610	0.7	41,897	18.5
2,152	1.1	545	0.3	18,760	9.4
2,067	1.2	1,169	0.7	61,840	35.6
748	0.5	396	0.2	91,439	55.7
271	0.2	180	0.1	22,694	14.0
379	0.2	230	0.1	6,384	4.0
705	0.5	128	0.1	8,981	6.0
55,828	38.5	45,719	31.5	42,231	29.1
62,236	47.0	21,073	15.9	45,386	34.3
79,564	68.4	4,648	4.0	23,533	20.2
1,239	1.1	486	0.4	10,838	9.6
955	0.9	351	0.3	10,027	9.0
49,919	49.0	6,692	6.6	42,010	41.2
2,232	2.2	410	0.4	20,455	20.1

ment was similar among these groups. These rates, together with the rates for non-Hispanic whites, which are indexed to a value of 100, are presented in table 9 under each of the regional headings. It is evident that the total Hispanic and Mexican-origin groups left the Northeast and North Central regions for the South and West, as was also true of non-Hispanic whites. Although the regional direction of movement was the same for Mexican Americans as for non-Hispanic whites, the magnitude was not nearly so great for the former group.

Although these figures indicate the patterns of net gain or loss for the major census regions, they reveal neither the origins of persons going to regions that gained movers nor the destinations of persons going to regions that lost movers. Insight into the former is provided from figure 4, which

Table 3.9 **Total Net Migration and Rates for Census Regions by Type of Hispanic Origin, Indexed to Non-Hispanic Whites, 1980**

Group	Net Migration[a]	Migration Rate[b]	Index[c]	Net Migration[a]	Migration Rate[b]	Index[c]
	Northeast			North Central		
Non-Hispanic whites	-1,478	-38	100	-1,279	-27	100
Total Hispanic	-106	-45	118	-31	-28	104
Mexicans	-6	-77	203	-14	-20	74
	South			West		
Non-Hispanic whites	1,754	33	100	1,003	34	100
Total Hispanic	106	27	82	30	5	15
Mexicans	18	7	21	2	1	3

SOURCE: U.S. Bureau of the Census, 1980 Census of Population and Housing, "General Social and Economic Characteristics" PC80-1-C2 through C52, Table 100, Government Printing Office: Washington, D.C.

[a]In thousands, for persons 5 years and older in 1980.
[b]Net migration per 1,000 population 5 years and older in 1980.
[c]Indexed to the non-Hispanic white net migration rate, which was set equal to 100.

shows the directions and relative magnitudes of all net positive cross-regional flows for the total Hispanic and Mexican-origin groups. In general, the overall directional pattern for the total Hispanic and Mexican-origin groups is similar to that of non-Hispanic whites, with the South gaining movers from each of the other three regions, the West gaining from the North Central and the Northeast regions, and the North Central gaining from the Northeast region.

Socioeconomic Conditions and Trends

Education

Education is a key socioeconomic attribute in assessing the ease and degree of participation of any group in American society. In the first place, it serves as a mechanism of acculturation. Although cultural assimilation does not necessarily give rise to structural assimilation, the knowledge and skills acquired through formal education obviously play a major part in determining opportunities for obtaining higher status in general and more highly rewarded occupations in particular. The disadvantaged position of

THE SPANISH-ORIGIN POPULATION IN THE AMERICAN SOUTHWEST   83

Figure 3.4 **Interregional Net Migration Flows, 1975–1980**

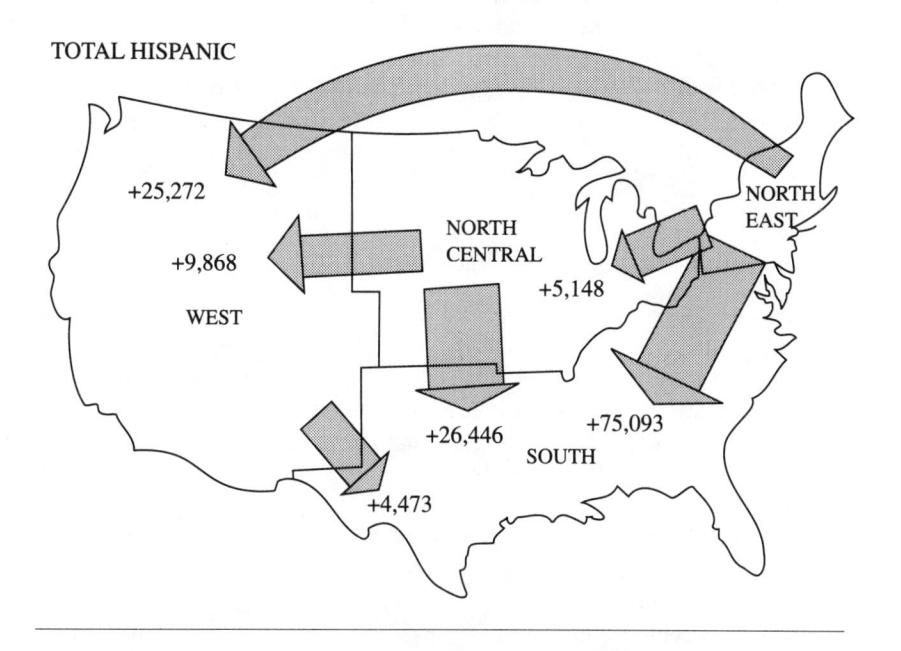

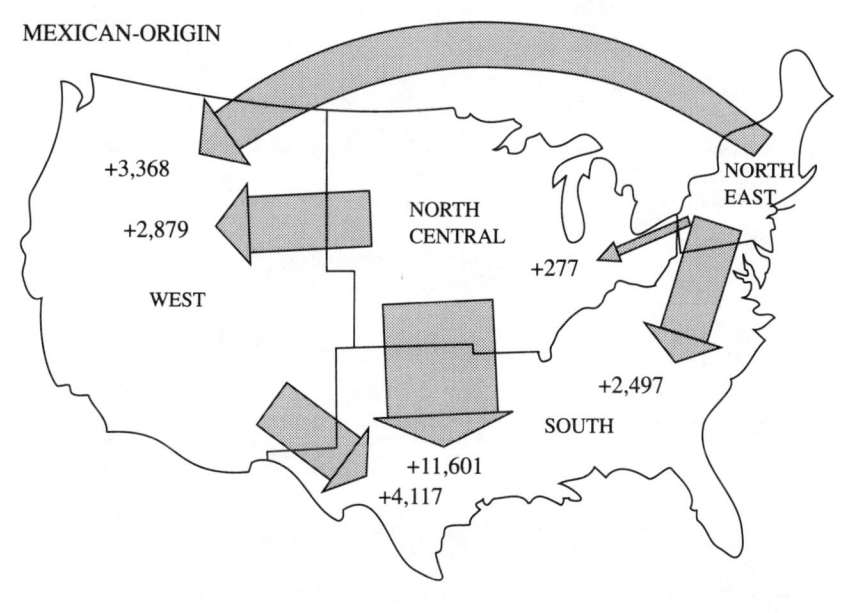

TOTAL HISPANIC

+25,272
+9,868
WEST
NORTH CENTRAL
+5,148
NORTH EAST
+26,446
+75,093
SOUTH
+4,473

MEXICAN-ORIGIN

+3,368
+2,879
WEST
NORTH CENTRAL
+277
NORTH EAST
+2,497
SOUTH
+11,601
+4,117

NOTE: Arrows are proportional within figures, but not across figures.

the Mexican-origin population is revealed in its lower levels of education as compared to those of the total population.[1] For example, table 10 shows that, in 1980, only about 38 percent of Mexican Americans aged twenty-five years and older had completed high school, and, that on the average, education for this group was terminated after only a year or two of schooling beyond the elementary grades. The figures for 1980 represent a substantial improvement over 1970 levels; nonetheless, Mexican Americans and Puerto Ricans lag well behind the general population.

Labor Force Participation

Because a large proportion of the Mexican-origin population consists of migrants to the United States and because, in recent decades, migration has been largely a movement of labor (Portes 1979; Portes and Bach 1985), labor force participation should be a useful indicator of the reception encountered by recent Mexican-origin immigrants, as well as of the subsequent accessibility of the American economic system to them. Of course, factors other than the structure of majority-minority group relations will impinge on labor force trends. Economic decline may reduce the number of available jobs, and the rapid growth in the number and proportion of female workers may directly or indirectly produce a decline in male participation rates. Despite these complications, however, substantial variation in labor force participation by ethnicity would certainly indicate differences in the degree of structural assimilation.

Table 3.10 **Educational Attainment, by Type of Hispanic Origin and Race, United States, 1970 and 1980**

Origin	% High School Graduates (Persons 25+) 1970	1980	Median Years of School Completed 1970	1980
Mexican American	24.2	37.6	8.1	9.6
Black[a]	31.4	51.2	9.8	12.0
Total	52.3	66.5	12.1	12.5

SOURCE: U.S. Bureau of the Census.
  1970: "Persons of Spanish Origin," *Subject Reports* PC(2)-1C (June 1973): Table 4; "General Social and Economic Characteristics," *United States Summary* PC(1)-C1 (June 1972): Table 88.
  1980: "General Social and Economic Characteristics," *United States Summary* (December 1983): Table 166.

[a] All blacks in 1970. Blacks not of Hispanic origin in 1980.

At least two important conclusions are suggested by the data on labor force participation rates in table 11. First, the small increase observed among Mexican Americans runs counter to the trend among other male workers, which involves a decline in labor force participation in the 1970–1980 interval. In sharp contrast, participation of women in the work force grew substantially between 1970 and 1980. The increase is particularly marked among Mexican-origin women, who recorded a double-digit (12.6 percent) increment. Interestingly, race or ethnicity per se does not seem either to greatly stimulate or seriously stifle participation. Mexican American males have the highest rates at both points in time, and the same is true for black females. Thus, except for the gains among Mexican Americans and the overall comparatively low rates among black males, no major racial/ethnic differentials emerge from the figures in table 11.

However, there is evidence of more substantial ethnic variation, if one tracks labor force data from 1960 onward (Cooney and Warren 1979; Ortiz n.d.), and particularly if one focuses attention on workers who are household heads (Frisbie 1985: chap. 5). In table 12 are found data on labor force participation by race/ethnicity for two types of household heads between 1960 and 1980. The two household types, female-headed and intact (never disrupted) male-headed, are important because, in a very real sense, they represent the range of economic characteristics related to household and family structure. Households containing a head and spouse with no history of marital disruption and with children present have typically been found to be better off economically than "non-couple households" (Bianchi 1981; Frisbie 1985). In addition, if there is an ideal or traditional household type in the United States, it would likely be one composed of a married couple neither of whom has ever experienced marital dissolution, and both of

Table 3.11 Civilian Labor Force Participation Rates of Persons Aged 16 and Over, by Hispanic Origin, Race, and Sex, United States, 1970 and 1980

	Males			Females		
Origin	1970	1980	1970–80	1970	1980	1970–80
Mexican American	77.4	79.7	2.3	36.4	49.0	12.6
Black[a]	69.8	66.7	-3.1	47.5	53.3	5.8
Total	76.6	75.1	-1.5	41.4	49.9	8.5

Source: U.S. Bureau of the Census.
　1970: "Persons of Spanish Origin": Table 7; "General Social and Economic Characteristics": Table 90.
　1980: "General Social and Economic Characteristics": Table 168.

[a]All blacks in 1970. Blacks not of Hispanic origin in 1980.

Table 3.12 **Labor Force Participation Rates of Household Heads, by Household Type, Hispanic Origin, and Race, United States, 1960–1980 (%)**

	Household Type							
	Never Disrupted with Spouse and Children				Female-Headed			
	1960	1970	1980	1960–80	1960	1970	1980	1960–80
Mexican American[a]	97.8	95.3	95.5	-2.8	50.7	55.6	64.6	16.7
Black[b]	95.5	93.7	93.5	-2.0	63.9	60.7	64.1	0.2
Anglo[c]	98.2	97.6	97.0	-1.2	68.8	72.9	76.5	7.7

SOURCE: Adapted from Frisbie 1985: Table 5–3.

[a]In 1960, Mexican Americans are identified as whites of Spanish surname. In 1970 and 1980, Mexican Americans are defined as those who self-identify as of Mexican origin.
[b]Non-Hispanic blacks.
[c]Non-Hispanic whites.

whom reside with their child or children. Although such a traditional arrangement has become less and less normative over time, it remains the modal type for the groups, except for blacks, included in this analysis (Frisbie 1985: chap. 4). Thus, household heads in this category would seem to be a logical baseline against which to draw comparisons.

One of the most salient of other comparisons involves female-headed households, which in the past two decades have grown several times faster than the number of households containing both a husband and wife (Ross and Sawhill 1975; Glick 1984). Second, female-headed households constitute such a growing and disproportionately large share of low-income households that many observers have begun to speak of the "feminization of poverty" (Auletta 1982). In addition to the importance of these two household types for analytical and policy-related purposes, their comparison makes clear the case for marital status as a predictor of progress toward structural assimilation by Hispanics over the next several decades. As can be seen in table 12, allowing for illness and disability, participation in the labor force is virtually universal among male heads of intact families where children are present. (Other research [Bianchi 1981:89] suggests that it may be more the presence of children per se, rather than number of children, that is associated with stable participation in the labor force among male heads.)

The low levels of labor force participation among female heads contrast markedly with those of married male heads. Again, female heads in all the groups recorded minor (0.2 percent among blacks) to large (16.7 percent among Mexican Americans) increases in rates. The propensity of Mexican

Americans to settle in the Southwest, which has figured prominently in the Sunbelt economic boom, may partially explain the overall improvement in their labor force participation (table 11), including the major rise in rates among female heads (table 12). The rapid increase in rates among Mexican American females, however, cannot continue indefinitely. Nevertheless, one is forced toward the conclusion that obtaining a desirable economic niche in the U.S. economy may be a brighter hope for Mexican Americans than it is for blacks.

Income

Income data yield many of the same conclusions in regard to the economic niche of the Mexican-origin population in American society as does information on other socioeconomic characteristics. Both in hourly wages and median income, Mexican American males show a level below that of Anglo males and one that more nearly approximates that of blacks (table 13). Hourly wages of females are especially low among Mexican Americans. It is interesting to note that, whereas there is a tendency for hourly wages of blacks to exceed those of Mexican Americans, median income is higher for the latter group. A plausible explanation of this seeming

Table 3.13 **Average Hourly Wage and Median Annual Income, by Sex, Race, and Hispanic Group**

Origin	Average Hourly Wage, 1975[a]	Median Annual Income, 1979[b]
Mexican American		
Males	$4.31	$8,858
Females	2.88	4,556
Black		
Males	4.65	7,835
Females	3.46	4,676
Anglo		
Males	5.97	13,029
Females	3.67	5,378

SOURCES:
 National Commission for Employment Policy, *Hispanics and Jobs: Barriers to Progress*, table 8.
 U.S. Census of Population and Housing: 1980. "General Social and Economic Characteristics," *U.S. Summary*, table 170.
 Adapted from Bean et al. 1984: Table 11.

[a] Persons 14 years or older, working for a wage or salary.

[b] Persons 15 years or older with income.

anomaly is that Mexican Americans, who are concentrated in a region where wages are relatively low, simply work more hours than do blacks.

Table 14 presents trends in occupational and income distributions by type of household headship. The table indicates that, in the case of both husband-wife and female-headed households, the proportion employed in white-collar jobs has increased faster in the Mexican-origin population than in the Anglo population. On the other hand, comparisons such as the latter mask the fact that minorities may be concentrated in lower-paying jobs within the broader occupational categories (McLemore 1980:328). Thus, for most comparisons, the income (in constant dollars) of Mexican-origin

Table 3.14 Economic Characteristics of Household Heads, by Household Type, Hispanic Origin, and Race, United States, 1960–1980

	\% White Collar	Never Disrupted with Spouse and Children Mean Personal Income[d]	Ratio to Anglo Income	\% White Collar	Female-Headed Mean Personal Income[d]	Ratio to Anglo Income
Mexican American[a]						
1960	18.3	$4,126	.68	27.6	$1,444	.63
1970	19.6	5,009	.64	28.7	1,955	.64
1980	27.7	4,886	.66	44.8	2,360	.73
Δ1960–80	9.4	760		17.2	1,093	
Black[b]						
1960	12.6	$3,040	.50	12.8	$1,232	.54
1970	19.6	4,499	.57	27.0	1,791	.59
1980	27.7	4,865	.65	45.7	2,373	.73
Δ1960–80	15.1	1,825		32.9	1,141	
Anglo[c]						
1960	41.0	$6,108	1.00	58.9	$2,293	1.00
1970	46.1	7,847	1.00	62.9	3,058	1.00
1980	46.5	7,451	1.00	69.4	3,254	1.00
Δ1960–80	5.5	1,343		10.5	961	

SOURCE: Adapted from Frisbie 1985: Table 5-4.

[a]In 1960, Mexican Americans are identified as whites of Spanish surname. In 1970 and 1980, Mexican Americans are defined as those who self-identify as of Mexican origin.
[b]Non-Hispanic blacks.
[c]Non-Hispanic whites.
[d]In 1960 dollars.

household heads, relative to their Anglo counterparts, did not rise appreciably in the twenty years between 1960 and 1980, and in many cases the Mexican-origin ratios actually declined.

Although female heads are more apt to have obtained white-collar jobs than are male heads of families, on the average they earn much less. This may be the result of (1) the concentration of females in the lower ranks of white-collar employment, (2) gender differentials in seniority, full-time employment, and wage levels, and/or (3) discrimination. Our interest here is not primarily in gender stratification, but it should be noted that, whatever the reasons for the differences, the trend for all workers over the twenty-year interval was in the direction of growing gender inequality. Only among Mexican Americans was income growth (in constant 1960 dollars) between 1960 and 1980 not greater for male heads than for female heads.

Returning to our focus on differentials, we find that the income data in table 14 tell a familiar story. Once again, Mexican Americans, in their level of economic achievement, fall between blacks and Anglos. Although characterized by lower levels of education than blacks, Mexican American male heads of intact households have higher mean income than black heads at each of the three points in time covered in table 14.

One interesting contrast within categories of headship is that the ratio of black to Anglo income increased by fifteen points. Income improvements of blacks in these years is a result in part of the civil rights movement and intervention of the government. Among female heads, the ratio for blacks and Mexican Americans also increased, although the overall advantage of Anglo women was preserved in absolute dollar terms.

Fertility and Household and Family Structure

The most important questions that might be asked about the reproductive behavior of the Mexican- and Hispanic-origin populations are (1) Do the groups of Mexican- and Hispanic-origin women have more (or fewer) children than non-Hispanic Anglo women? and (2) How different are they in this respect from women who belong to other racial/ethnic minority groups in the United States? Table 15 presents data that provide at least rough answers to these questions. It contains information on the number of children ever born per one thousand women aged fifteen to forty-four for various racial/ethnic groups, including the Hispanic- and Mexican-origin groups for each of the three most recent census years. The figures enable only rough comparisons to be drawn, because the groups and time periods may differ with respect to their age, sociodemographic, and socioeconomic composition. Such differences can affect the magnitude of the fertility differences observed among the groups. Despite this limitation, the data in table 15 are useful in one very important respect: they represent actual numbers of children born to actual numbers of women.

The data reveal that by 1980 Hispanic-origin women had indeed borne larger numbers of children than had non-Hispanic Anglo women (1,591 per thousand versus 1,232 per thousand). This difference is considerable, representing a Hispanic-origin level of childbearing more than 29 percent higher than that of non-Hispanic Anglo women. The differential is also greater than it was in 1970, when Hispanic-origin fertility was 21 percent higher than non-Hispanic–origin fertility.

Turning to our second question concerning how the fertility levels of the Hispanic-origin groups compare with those of other racial/ethnic groups in the United States, we find that the data in table 15 provide considerable support for the idea that the Mexican- and Hispanic-origin groups are characterized by relatively high fertility. Most strikingly, women of Mexican origin show a higher rate of childbearing in 1980 than any of the other groups, including Native Americans. Also, the fertility of Mexican-origin women exceeds that of black women by nearly 9 percent, and it surpasses that of non-Hispanic Anglo women by 39 percent. As has been determined from other research, much of this difference cannot be accounted for by differences among these groups in such factors as age, age at marriage, and education (Bean and Tienda 1987).

The data in table 15 also provide dramatic confirmation of the reduction in fertility occurring in the United States since the beginning of the 1960s, the approximate time when the "baby boom" ended. As with other women, Hispanic-origin women participated in the decline, although not quite to the degree that non-Hispanic Anglo women did. Moreover, because women of Mexican origin especially were starting the decline from a higher level of childbearing to begin with, and because their fertility had not gone down as much on a percentage basis as that of non-Hispanic Anglo women, relative fertility differentials between this group and non-Hispanic Anglos actually increased from 1970 to 1980 (in the case of Mexican-origin women, for example, fertility increased from 33 percent higher in 1970 to 39 percent higher in 1980).

As we shall see, the high fertility of the Mexican-origin population affects certain aspects of household structure within this population. Household structure, in turn, influences economic well-being. It has been well documented, for example, that households in which both husband and wife are present fare better economically than other types (Bianchi 1981; Frisbie 1985). That this difference is not merely a function of the number of earners is evident from the data examined comparing the personal income of heads of household. In particular, female-headed households constitute a

Table 3.15 **Children Ever Born per 1,000 Women Aged 15–44, by Race, 1960–1980**

Origin	1960	1970	1980	% Change 1960–1970	% Change 1970–1980
Total	1,746	1,621	1,302	-7.2	-19.7
Non-Hispanic					
Anglo	1,712	1,589	1,232	-7.2	-22.5
Black	2,016	1,862	1,575	-7.6	-15.4
Native American[a]	2,405	2,116	1,701	-11.0	-19.6
Asian[b]	1,521	1,421	1,184	-6.6	-16.7
Other[c]	1,984	1,550	1,164	-21.9	-24.9
Hispanic					
Total	—	1,919	1,591	—	-17.1
Mexican	2,290	2,114	1,715	-7.7	-18.9

SOURCES:
1960: U.S. Census, "Women by Number of Children Ever Born" PC2(3A): Tables 8, 9, 10.
1970: U.S. Census, "Women by Number of Children Ever Born" PC2(3A): Tables 8 and 13.
1980: U.S. Census, "General Social and Economic Characteristics" PC80-1C-1: Table 166.

[a] 1960, 1970: American Indian. 1980: American Indian, Eskimo, and Aleut.

[b] 1960: Japanese and Chinese. 1970: Japanese, Chinese, Filipino, Hawaiian, and Korean. 1980: Asian and Pacific Islander.

[c] 1960: Filipinos, Koreans, Hawaiians, Asian Indians, Eskimos, Aleut, Malayans, etc. 1970: Those not included in other categories (e.g., Eurasian, Cosmopolitan, Interracial). 1980: Those not of other categories.

disproportionate share of households living in poverty (Auletta 1982; McEaddy 1976).

There is no single, unambiguous explanation of why traditional families tend to be more financially secure. A complete understanding of the issue would involve multiple determinants, including the overall disruptive effects of marital dissolution, constraints on the earning power of women as related to gender inequalities, and difficulties associated with active attempts to pursue a career while maintaining sole responsibility for rearing children. Whatever the case, it appears necessary to take into account trends in household structure and marital status in assessing the future chances of the Mexican-origin population for socioeconomic advancement.

Size, as well as stability, of households is an important consideration. Large household sizes that arise from high fertility may create an obstacle to socioeconomic achievement, since time and monetary resources that might otherwise be used for the advancement of careers and business enterprise must be diverted to the support of dependent children. The fertility literature is replete with references to the fact that, as satisfying and fulfilling as bearing and raising children may be, in the modern world, children tend to be economic liabilities. To illustrate, Preston (1974) has demonstrated the negative impact of high fertility on chances of intergenerational upward mobility for blacks, and there is no apparent reason why the effects should be substantially different in the case of the Mexican-origin population.

Table 16 shows that the Mexican- and Hispanic-origin populations have both advantages and disadvantages in regard to household size and structure. As is to be expected based on their high fertility, Mexican Americans were characterized by much larger than average household size in 1960, 1970, and 1980. In fact, in 1980, the mean household size among Mexican Americans (3.8) was a half-person larger than was the case for all households two decades earlier (Frisbie 1985).

Turning to marital status, we can see that the Mexican-origin population followed the national pattern of marital dissolution between 1960 and 1980. However, even though the prevalence of marital disruption increased from 1960 to 1980, and although the proportion of never-disrupted families declined across the board, Mexican Americans continue to have a majority of households with no history of marital disruption. Currently, about one-fifth of Mexican American households are headed by a person whose spouse is absent due to divorce, separation, or widowhood. This compares to about one-quarter of Anglos and 40 percent of blacks in the disrupted status in 1980. Research taking individuals as the units of analysis and focusing only on the dissolution of marriage because of divorce or separation has produced similar findings for these groups, net of controls for age at marriage, education, and current age (Frisbie 1986). The conclusion is that, to the extent that household structure and marital status influence the quest of the Mexican-origin population for full participation in the socioeconomic system of the United States, Mexican Americans might be expected to move forward at a somewhat faster pace than blacks. The potential for Mexican Americans may be even greater than the figures in table 16 suggest, since the mean number of children per household declined more sharply between 1970 and 1980 among Mexican Americans than among any of the other groups under consideration (Frisbie 1985: table 4-2).

Acculturation/Language Use

Acculturation, or cultural assimilation, might be conceived as a determinant of an ethnic minority's ability to become structurally assimilated.

Table 3.16 **Household and Family Structure, by Race/Ethnicity, 1960, 1970, 1980**

	Total			Anglo			Black			Mexican American[a]		
	1960	1970	1980	1960	1970	1980	1960	1970	1980	1960	1970	1980
Mean household size	3.3	3.1	2.8	3.2	3.0	2.7	3.8	3.5	3.1	4.4	4.2	3.8
Mean number of adults per household	2.1	2.0	2.0	2.1	2.0	1.9	2.2	2.0	1.9	2.2	2.2	2.2
Current marital status												
% Never married	6.1	7.6	12.2	6.0	7.4	11.3	6.2	9.7	17.9	4.8	7.0	10.5
% Never disrupted	60.2	55.1	47.1	62.1	57.0	49.0	41.7	37.7	30.1	61.4	58.3	54.9
% Disrupted	19.2	23.4	27.0	17.8	21.8	25.4	32.8	37.8	40.6	18.8	21.1	22.6
% Remarried	14.6	13.9	13.8	14.1	13.8	14.3	19.4	14.7	11.4	15.0	13.6	12.0

SOURCE: Frisbie 1985: Table 4-1.

[a]The Mexican American population is defined in terms of the white Hispanic surname identifier in 1960 and in terms of the self-identification item in 1970 and 1980.

It seems indisputable that cultural assimilation does not ensure structural assimilation (van den Berghe 1967), but it is possible that certain features of a minority group's culture may impede easy entry into majority-dominated economic and political spheres. To a large extent, the issue with respect to Hispanics comes down to the concern by a number of scholars and policymakers that retention of Spanish may negatively affect structural integration.

It has been noted that the "one issue unique to Hispanics . . . is that they share a common language" (Davis, Haub, and Willette 1983:21), and Grenier suggests that, "although Hispanics are not a homogeneous group of people, they have some characteristics in common, the most important one being their language" (1984:537). Although it is clear that Spanish use is a prominent manifestation of Hispanic cultural heritage, this observation, in itself, certainly does not constitute evidence of a detrimental effect. To the contrary, fluency in more than one language is an asset, not a liability. What then might be the problem?

Mirowsky and Ross, in their investigation of Spanish-language networks among Mexican Americans, suggest one possibility. These authors posit that, to a rather large extent, individuals depend on others for information and resources needed for advancement. Specifically (Mirowsky and Ross 1984:552),

> Language carries the vast majority of this information, and is itself information about social origins and social position. When one language group is economically dominant, as is the case with English-speaking whites in the United States, then having friends, family, and acquaintances who speak the language provides the information, common experiences, and social contacts that facilitate upward mobility. In order to move into the middle classes in the United States, it helps a great deal to speak English and to be embedded in an English-speaking network (Fishman et al. 1966; Olmedo 1979; López 1978).

If retention of Spanish has, in the past, impeded social mobility because of its channeling of Hispanics away from English-speaking networks, the problem appears to be of declining significance. Data from the 1976 Survey of Income and Education show that, among those who spoke Spanish as a child, only 48 percent of Mexican-origin persons have retained Spanish as their primary language of communication, as compared to about 57 percent of Puerto Ricans and 68 percent of Cubans (Grenier 1984:541–542). Moreover, these figures indirectly give rise to a counterargument. Cubans have the highest level of Spanish retention, and yet they "outpace other Hispanics in high school achievement tests and college entrance" (Davis, Haub, and Willette 1983:33). Cubans also lead the way in occupational and income attainment. Since a large number of Cuban immigrants came from the better-educated and more affluent strata of Cuban society, it is entirely likely that it is lack of English proficiency and other class-related phenomena, rather than Spanish use per se, that impedes structural assimilation. Mirowsky and Ross reach a somewhat similar conclusion regarding the class-related basis of the current status of Mexican Americans (1984:561–562).

Substantial support for this interpretation emerges from Tienda and Neidert's study of Mexican, Puerto Rican, Central/South American, and other Hispanic-origin males. These authors conclude that "retention of Spanish does not hinder the socioeconomic achievements of Hispanic-origin groups, provided that a reasonable level of proficiency in English is acquired" (1984:533). An exception to this general conclusion is the case of immigrants from Mexico, "for whom Spanish bilingualism and monolingualism exert independent negative effects on the occupational achievement of adult men" (1984:533).

Finally, there is evidence that Mexican Americans take advantage of opportunities to become fluent in English and that, as would be expected, English proficiency varies by immigrant generation and increases over time. For example, fully 90 percent of Mexican Americans born in the United States speak English well, although only about 30 percent use English exclusively. Among recent Mexican immigrants (arrived in 1975 or later), about 70 percent speak English poorly or not at all (Bean et al. 1984).

Immigration

Any analysis of the demographic situation in the American Southwest cannot be complete without considering Mexican immigration to the United States. Furthermore, it is difficult to understand the volume and impact of both legal and illegal immigration without understanding the social and historical context within which they have occurred. Both the amount and composition of immigration to the United States have changed considerably since the early 1960s, largely as the result of three developments (Massey 1981). The first was the passage of the 1965 Amendments to the Immigration and Nationality Act. These at once abolished the restrictive provisions of the national origins quota system, raised the annual ceiling on the number of immigrants from 158,000 to 270,000, and increased the number of categories of persons who could enter exempt from numerical limitations. The second was the passage of legislation that made it much easier for political refugees, particularly those from Cuba and Indochina, to enter the country. The third was an apparent increase in undocumented immigration to the United States, a phenomenon that was part of the worldwide emergence during the 1960s of labor migration from less-developed to more-developed countries (Keely and Elwell 1981).

The Social and Historical Context

In the years since 1970 (two years after the 1965 amendments took effect), annual immigration to the United States has averaged over 462,000 persons a year, as compared to 252,000 per year during the 1950s (Immigration and Naturalization Service 1983). Moreover, the ethnic composition of legal immigrants has changed substantially as well, shifting away from a preponderance of Europeans to a preponderance of Asians and Latin Americans. For example, during the 1950s Europeans still made up over half (52.7 percent) of all immigrants, whereas in the years since 1970 they have made up only 17 percent of legal entrants. By contrast, persons of Latin American origin have increased their share of total immigration during this same time span from 24.6 percent to 40.2 percent (Immigration and Naturalization Service 1983). Asians also have shown a sizable increase in their fraction of immigrants.

The ethnic composition of immigrant streams to the United States also changed in the late nineteenth and early twentieth centuries. The increase in the proportion of Southern and Eastern European immigrants fueled a growing antiforeign sentiment at the time among native-born Americans, which was a factor contributing to the passage in 1924 of the restrictive legislation that set quotas for the numbers of new immigrants based on the national origins of the U.S. population in 1920 (Higham 1971). The changes in law adopted since 1965 have similarly resulted in larger numbers of immigrants and a changed ethnic composition. For example, including the 132,781 refugees granted lawful permanent resident status in the United States in 1978, a total of 601,442 new lawful entrants arrived in that year, the second highest number in any year since 1921, which was the peak year for the number of immigrants coming to this country after World War I (Immigration and Naturalization Service 1983). Not only has the volume of immigration been increasing, but relatively more immigrants have been coming from Third World countries, over one-third of whom are Hispanic in origin. Moreover, the Hispanic element in the immigration flows has been and continues to be supplemented by sizable numbers of refugees from Cuba and by an uncertain but not trivial number of undocumented migrants from Mexico. Legal immigrants are thus not only greater in number than at any time since the early 1920s, but perhaps also more visible than at any time in the nation's history. As in the early twentieth century, all of this may have fueled the recent drive to modify immigration policy, a drive that ironically has been aimed more at halting illegal migration than at changing legal immigration (Bean and Sullivan 1985).

A preoccupation on the part of policymakers with undocumented immigration has also manifested itself in a number of other ways. Among these is the work of special commissions established to address immigration reform. For example, in 1978, the president of the United States implemented legislation passed by Congress to create the Select Commission on Immigration and Refugee Policy. The commission was charged with the twin responsibilities of making a thorough assessment of the consequences for the country of current immigration and refugee laws and of developing recommendations concerning future law. The members and staff of the Select Commission—whose work received considerable public attention—held numerous hearings, examined the results of empirical studies, and sponsored research projects when there existed a special need for information otherwise unavailable. In its final report, the commission noted: "One issue has emerged as most pressing—*the problem of undocumented/illegal migration*" (Select Commission on Immigration and Refugee Policy 1981:35; emphasis added). Because by far the largest national-origin group of illegal migrants to the United States comes from Mexico (Heer 1979; Siegel, Passel, and Robinson 1980; Warren and Passel 1987), the volume and consequences of Mexican immigration have become of particular significance.

A number of factors have contributed to the emergence of the viewpoint that undocumented migration in general and undocumented Mexican migration in particular are critical problems. Not the least of these is a rising fear about the future employability of Mexico's youthful population, which included 33.3 million persons (44 percent) still under the age of fifteen in 1983 (Population Reference Bureau 1983). With Mexico continuing to confront a severe economic crisis brought about in part by a global decline in oil prices, the prospect of a still larger number of its citizens seeking employment opportunities in the United States seems a very real possibility (Teitelbaum 1985). And, for many observers, the fact that undocumented immigration is illegal itself constitutes a sufficient basis for concern, if for no other reason than that it appears to make a mockery of those who wait for years (and often in vain) for legal permanent residence visas.

The Size of the Undocumented Population

The perception that illegal immigration is a "problem" is reflected in the speculations put forth concerning the size of this population. Early conjectures were that anywhere from eight to twelve million such persons resided in the country at any given point in time (Chapman 1975). What does the evidence about the size of the undocumented population reveal? The most systematic and careful analyses have concluded that it is improbable that more than three to six million undocumented aliens resided in the United

States in 1980 (Siegel, Passel, and Robinson 1980), and that it is possible that many fewer were here. Moreover, analysis of the one data source that permits an assessment of the number who have come since 1980 indicates that by April 1983 the size of the illegal population probably had not grown appreciably (Passel and Woodrow 1984).

Because a majority of illegals are Mexican in origin, and because no other single group constitutes more than a small fraction of this population, questions about the number of illegals residing in the United States must be viewed in large part as queries concerning the size of the illegal Mexican population. Even in this case, however, almost every new piece of evidence that has emerged in recent years points to a smaller number residing in the country than many persons have thought were here. As shown in table 17, for example, demographic analysis of 1980 Mexican census data has shown that no more than about 1.5 to 3.8 million Mexican nationals could have been living in the United States in 1980 (Bean, King, and Passel 1983), with the figure probably closer to the lower end of that range (Bean, Lowell, and Taylor 1986). Other research has concluded that about 1.1 million undocumented Mexicans were included in the 1980 U.S. census (Warren and Passel 1987).

Taken together, these two sets of analyses may be viewed as providing estimates of an upper and lower boundary to the number of undocumented Mexicans in the country in 1980. The analyses of the Mexican census data suggest that it is very unlikely that more than 3.8 million were here in 1980; the analyses of the U.S. census data tell us that at least the 1.1 million included in the 1980 census were here. In addition, an unknown number not included in the U.S. census were also here. Although there is no way to know this latter number with certainty, the burden of expert opinion and other evidence suggest that the 1980 census included at least half of all undocumented Mexicans in the United States in 1980. For example, Keely

Table 3.17 **Selected Alternative Estimates of the Number of Illegal Migrants of Mexican Origin Living in the United States in 1980 (thousands)**

Data Source for Estimates	Males	Females	Total
Mexican census data (Bean, King, and Passel 1983)			
High	2,289	1,511	3,800
Low	913	608	1,521
U.S. census data (Warren and Passel 1987)	620	510	1,131

SOURCE: Bean and Tienda 1987: Table 4.7.

believes that the 1980 census had "an undercount of one-third to one-half of the undocumented aliens in the country" (1983:17), and others have also argued that it was probably within this range (Passel 1986; Slater 1985). Moreover, based on an examination of school enrollment data, Muller (1984) concludes that the 1980 U.S. census probably counted most of the illegals living in Los Angeles County, a large fraction of whom were Mexican. In fact, it seems reasonable to think that a minimum undercount rate for illegal Mexicans in 1980 might not be appreciably greater than the highest rate measured in the United States for any given group, which was about 20 percent for black males aged twenty to twenty-nine in 1980 (Passel, Siegel, and Robinson 1982). Moreover, if it is unlikely that fewer than 1.5 million Mexican undocumenteds were living in the United States, as the analyses of Mexican census data suggest, then a minimum undercount rate of about 25 to 30 percent is implied (e.g., the 1.1 million included in the 1980 U.S. census is about 73 percent of the 1.5 million figure).

In light of these considerations, table 18 presents an indication of the number of undocumented Mexicans in the United States in 1980 under a range of assumptions about the undercount rate for undocumented Mexicans. The range is based on the expert opinions noted above, but makes no allowance for differential undercount by sex. An undercount rate of about 25 percent would imply that about 1.5 million undocumented Mexicans were living in the United States in 1980; an undercount rate of 33 percent, that about 1.7 million were here; and an undercount rate of 50 percent, that about 2.3 million were here.[2] If the last figure were correct, and if Mexicans made up about 60 percent of all illegals, as the evidence seems to suggest, then one would expect there to have been an additional 1.5 million non-Mexican illegals here in 1980, for a total of about 3.8 million illegals. If one of the smaller figures were correct, the total number of undocumenteds here in 1980 would, of course, have been even less.

In sum, the results of recent research on the question point to numbers of

Table 3.18 **Estimates of the Size of the Illegal Mexican Population Living in the United States in 1980 under Alternative Assumptions about Undercount Rates for Illegal Mexicans (thousands)**

Undercount Rate (%)	Males	Females	Total
50[a]	1,240	1,020	2,262
33[b]	1,013	675	1,688
25[c]	905	603	1,508

[a]As based on Keely (1983).
[b]As based on Slater (1985).
[c]As based on Passel, Siegel, and Robinson (1982).

illegal aliens living in the United States in 1980 that are in the lower portions of the ranges of the best estimates that have been made. This conclusion is consistent with the report on immigration statistics of the National Academy of Sciences, which states that "the size and growth of the illegal alien population may not be problems of the magnitude sometimes suggested" (Hill 1985).

The Labor Market Implications of Undocumented Immigration

Even if many fewer undocumenteds are in the United States than was once thought, the number is nonetheless considerable. This has led to another major question on which the legislative debate on undocumented immigration has turned. This concerns the economic impact of undocumented immigration, particularly undocumented Mexican immigration. As with the question of the size of the undocumented population, when the legislative debate began, little if any research had been conducted that provided a basis for assessing the validity of such assertions. Most of the available evidence dealt with the effects of legal rather than undocumented immigration. Relevant data for undocumented immigration were unavailable until recently, forcing researchers interested in addressing questions about the economic effects to assume that such effects could be extrapolated from the study of the effects of legal immigration. Two developments occurring around 1980, however, changed this. One was the inclusion for the first time of substantial numbers of undocumented persons in the census in 1980; the other was the development of appropriate methodologies for estimating the numbers included (Warren and Passel 1987).

Given these developments, it is useful to examine research results, some only recently available, concerning the labor market impact of undocumented immigration. Two types of research are relevant. The first involves research based on empirically based designs that seek to assess the impact of immigration either on unemployment rates or on earnings. The second involves studies that are more model-based. Many have relied on aggregate production functions involving combinations of labor inputs as a basis for specifying estimable equations. The results from this second kind of approach provide a way to assess the degree to which various labor groups are complements or substitutes in the labor market.

Cross-cutting both of these types of studies is their reliance on either of two kinds of data: (1) data on immigrants (in some cases, only legal immigrants, in other cases, both legal and undocumented) from which the effects of undocumented immigrants might be extrapolated, or (2) data on undocumented immigrants. These two research approaches and the reliance on two different types of data may be viewed as constituting a fourfold classification of studies conducted on the effects of undocumented immigration. Below we present a review of the results of these studies organized in terms of this classification. Table 19 presents a summary of the design and empirical results of each study discussed.

Empirical studies based on data for both legal and undocumented immigrants. Two studies that have received a great deal of attention are those by Muller and Espenshade (1985) and by McCarthy and Valdez (1986). Both have been published in paper version, by the Urban Institute and the Rand Corporation, respectively. They are not limited to the examination of labor market impacts but analyze a broad set of economic effects on natives caused by immigration. However, both consider a restricted population, namely, Mexican immigrants in California. Although the studies make no effort to distinguish legal and undocumented immigrants, it is widely recognized that a high proportion of immigrants in California are undocumented. Both hypothesize that the Los Angeles labor market would be especially affected by immigration, because recent immigrants in that city make up a larger share of the labor force than in other urban areas of California and the United States.

McCarthy and Valdez find little effect on the wages of the native work force, except in the case of Latino workers, whose wages grew at less than the national average between 1970 and 1980. They suggest that Mexican immigration served to improve the conditions and employment opportunities of native workers by providing a boost to otherwise failing, low-wage industries. Their analysis is admittedly inferential and limited to a rough examination of quite general industry-level categories and employment and earnings growth in the United States, California, and Los Angeles. It does not control for other factors that might affect native earnings. Furthermore, it is not clear whether Latinos are disaggregated by nativity. The results of this type of analysis should be regarded as speculative in light of the methodology used.

Muller and Espenshade reach similar findings through a regression approach designed to depict the functioning of the labor market. They focus especially on differences in black family income due to differences in immigration across labor markets. The variables they choose to explain such differences are percentage Hispanic in 247 U.S. labor markets (or percentage Mexican-born in the analysis of 51 southwestern SMSAs); population growth from 1970 to 1980; percentage income in construction and durable goods manufacturing; percentage black who have completed twelfth grade; and white income, which they view as a control for local economic factors affecting all workers. Percentage Hispanic (percentage Mexican-born) is meant to serve as an indicator of Mexican immigration under the assumption that such immigration is directly related to the Hispanic (Mexican-born) population of geographic labor markets. For the United States, the

Table 3.19 **Studies That Assess the Impact of Undocumented Immigration on U.S. Labor Markets**

Source	Data	Method
McCarthy and Valdez 1986	1970 and 1980 U.S. census	Examination of earnings growth
Muller and Espenshade 1985	1970 and 1980 U.S. census	Regression analysis
Simon and Moore 1984	Unemployment data (UI), current population surveys, INS *Annual Report*	Regression analysis
Grossman 1982	1970 U.S. census	Translog production function
Borjas 1984	1970 1/100 PUS and 1980 1/20 PUMS-A U.S. census	Generalized Leontief production function
Borjas 1985	1980 1/20 PUMS-A U.S. census sample	Generalized Leontief production function
Borjas 1986	1970 1/100 PUS and 1980 1/20 PUMS-A U.S. census	Generalized Leontief production function
King, Lowell, and Bean 1986	1970 PUS 1/100 U.S. census sample	Regression equ. based on human cap. & Leontief production function
Bean, Lowell, and Taylor 1988	1980 U.S. census	Generalized Leontief production function

[a]Endogeneity controls account for the fact that the labor supply may be endogenous rather than exogenous.

Control for Skill Level	Endo-geneity Controlled[a]	Control for Capital	Results	
No	No	No	Latino wage growth was less than the national average in areas with large Mexican immigrant population	
No	No	No	Mexican immigrants increase black family income and decrease black unemployment	
No	No	No	No observed increase in unemployment due to total legal immigration in the U.S.	
No	No	Yes	Total foreign-born persons:[b]	
			second-generation wages	-0.2%
			third-generation wages	-0.3%
Yes	Yes	Yes	Total immigrant males: (1980)[b]	
			young white male earnings	-1.2%
			old white male earnings	+0.6%
			young black male earnings	+2.7%
			old black male earnings	+1.5%
			native females	-1.5%
Yes	Yes	Yes	Total Hispanic immigrants:[b]	
			white native wage	0.0%
			black native wage	+0.1%
			Hispanic native wage	+0.2%
Yes	Yes	Yes	Total immigrant males have almost no effect on white males and are slightly complementary to black males[b]	
Yes	No	No	Foreign-born Hispanics have little effect on the earnings of natives	
Yes	Yes	No	Undocumented Mexican males:[b]	
			Mexican native U.S. males	0.0%
			black males	-0.1%
			white males	+0.1%
			total females	

[b]Results expressed as the effect of a 10% increase on the number of (proxy) immigrants.

Hispanic population has a small negative effect on black family income, but in the Southwest a positive relation is found for percentage Mexican-born. The authors conclude that, positive or negative, the effect on black family income is very small.

Model-based studies using data on legal immigrants. Other approaches have been adopted that analyze labor market impacts using a more formal model of how that market is believed to operate. Using the basic theory of labor demand and assuming that firms seek to maximize profits, these studies have employed a model of the labor market in order to provide a basis for assessing the degree of substitutability/complementarity among labor force aggregates. Such a methodology involves estimating how the earnings of native workers are affected by the numbers of immigrant workers across labor markets. (For further information on the theory and choice of methodologies, see Hamermesh and Grant 1979.) To our knowledge, only five studies have employed an aggregate production function to analyze the impact of legal immigrants on the native labor force: Grossman (1982); Borjas (1984, 1985, 1986); King, Lowell, and Bean (1986). The consensus that has emerged from this research is that there are only slight substitution effects between the immigrant and native labor forces when both groups are considered in their entirety. The only substantial negative effects observed are on the earnings of the immigrants themselves.

Model-based studies using data on undocumented immigrants. The only research that, to our knowledge, is based on data on *undocumented* immigrants is a study conducted by Bean, Lowell, and Taylor (1988). This study focuses on the impact of the undocumented portion of Mexican immigrants on legal U.S. workers in southwestern metropolitan labor markets. Enumerations of Mexican undocumenteds in SMSAs from the 1980 census are used to estimate earnings elasticities based on a Leontief model of earnings determination (Bean, Lowell, and Taylor 1988).[3] The most general result of the study is that undocumented workers exert little impact on the earnings of individuals in each of five other labor force groups. Of considerable interest is the finding that different effects occur for the undocumented and legal Mexican populations. For example, the supply of legal Mexican workers exhibits a negative impact on female earnings, whereas undocumented Mexican workers show a positive effect on female earnings. As shown in table 19, a 10 percent increase in the supply of Mexican undocumenteds is estimated to increase female earnings by about five-tenths of one percent.

The earnings of black as well as native Mexican workers do not appear to be significantly affected by the relative quantity of undocumented workers in local labor markets. The finding of nonsignificance is especially interesting because black and native Hispanic minorities are thought to work in industries most affected by undocumented workers. Neither does there appear to be a significant effect from increases in the supply of undocumented workers on the earnings of white workers, although, interestingly, the direction of the effect is positive. It is interesting to note that the findings of small complementarities between undocumented Mexicans and some other groups, together with the finding of small substitutions between legal immigrants and some groups, are more consistent with the argument advanced by some observers that undocumenteds may hold jobs that few others want to do than they are with the view that undocumenteds compete with native (especially) minorities for jobs and wages.

The Discrepancy between Public Perceptions and Research Results

The size of the undocumented population in the United States has increasingly proven to be smaller than many observers have speculated. Also, studies of labor market impacts have consistently found small effects of immigrants (both legal and undocumented) on the wages and earnings of other labor force groups. Ironically, however, public perceptions often have run in the opposite direction. How can this discrepancy be explained? We think at least four factors have contributed to the development of such a gap between perception and evidence.

First, observers have often failed to specify the population to which an estimate (or speculation) refers. Estimates of the kind discussed above usually refer to the population "stock," or the size of the population in residence in the country at a particular point in time (Passel 1986). The "flow" of persons into and out of the country over a given period of time may be much larger, especially if the stay of many of the persons involved is relatively brief or if they make repeated trips to the United States. Under these circumstances, the flow of undocumented immigrants may exceed the stock substantially and create the impression that the stock is larger than it really is.

Second, distinctions have not been drawn among different types of undocumented immigrants. Some undocumenteds come intending to establish permanent settlement. This type of immigrant thus has been referred to as "settlers" (Passel 1986; Sullivan 1986). Others come intending to stay only a short while, and thus have been called "sojourners." Persons in the latter category often gradually move into the former, often with the assistance of social networks, which enable them to solve the problems of finding employment and suitable housing (Massey 1985). It is likely that the census has included a higher proportion of settlers than sojourners and that estimates of the size of the undocumented population are better for the former than for the latter group.

A third major factor contributing to confusion is that legal immigrants, as noted above, have been growing in number. Since many of these persons speak only limited English, their increasing presence in the country may have fostered the impression that the undocumented population has been larger and has been growing faster than actually has been the case. Moreover, legal immigrants have been found in many instances to exert a small negative effect on the wages and earnings of other groups, thus inviting the generalization that undocumented immigrants might have the same effect. However, as Bean, Lowell, and Taylor (1988) have found, undocumented Mexican immigrants generate small increases in the earnings of some other groups.

Fourth, the ethnic composition of legal immigrants has changed over the past twenty years to include higher proportions of Hispanics and Asians. Since most undocumenteds are of these national origins, the growing presence of legal immigrants may again have contributed to confusion about differences between the size and growth of the legal and illegal populations.

It is impossible to say with certainty that it is these circumstances that have generated the apparent gap between perception and evidence concerning the undocumented population in the United States. Xenophobic forces and ethnic prejudice may also have played a role, although it is difficult to document the influence of these factors. Whatever the case may be, the results of recent research cast doubt on two common perceptions about the undocumented population: that a large and damaging undocumented labor force resides in the United States; and that it is impossible to verify any conclusion to the contrary about this population. Many who firmly believe the first are hard-pressed to find acceptable data to support a pessimistic viewpoint about the consequences of undocumented immigration, as well as reluctant to accept contrary data derived from the close study of any "clandestine population." Recently developed numerical estimates and statistical analyses dispel the notion that no such evaluations can be drawn.

Conclusions

This chapter has assessed the demographic situation of the American Southwest by examining population characteristics and trends involving the Mexican-origin population in that region. It is this population that is especially relevant for U.S. population policies concerning Mexico, because the Mexican-origin population is in many instances likely to be both cause and consequence of such policies. The extent to which the Mexican-origin population has reached high levels of structural assimilation (i.e., high levels of educational and occupational attainment) is likely to affect the nation's views about the costs and benefits associated with legal and undocumented Mexican immigration to the United States.

Hence, the results of social science research in general and of demographic research in particular will continue to be salient for public policy formulations. Nowhere is this interplay between research and policy better illustrated than in the case of recent research on the size and effects of undocumented immigration. The results of this research have clear policy implications and illustrate the usefulness of empirical investigation. That recent legislative efforts designed to curtail a presumably damaging undocumented immigration have often been justified by arguments that seem to run counter to research results might appear to suggest, however, that research has little bearing on policy formulation. Such a conclusion is premature. To be sure, the justifications given for the legislation seem to have exposed the ways in which implicit theory shapes public policy. However, it is difficult to know what legislation might have been passed, or what its content might have been, in the absence of the results of social science research. This interplay between research and policy ultimately demonstrates the strengths and weaknesses of both theory and research, as well as their inherent inseparability. The results of immigration research clearly have implications for public policy, just as public policy issues have affected the direction and focus of immigration research. Both future research and the evolution of policy are likely to provide further demonstration of this interdependence.

Notes

Portions of this chapter are adapted from the following: Frank D. Bean and Marta Tienda, *The Hispanic Population of the United States* (New York: Russell Sage, 1987); Frank D. Bean; Lindsay Lowell; and Eduardo Telles, "Illegal Immigration to the United States: Myth and Reality," paper presented at the annual meetings of the Population Association of America, Chicago, Illinois, May 1987; Parker Frisbie, "Trends in Ethnic Relations: Hispanics and Anglos," Texas Population Research Center Papers, no. 8.005, University of Texas, Austin, 1986.

1. In the discussion that follows, comparisons are sometimes drawn with the total population and at other times with the Anglo population, depending on data availability and comparability over time. Since Anglos make up such a large proportion of the total, it is not surprising that, where both types of comparison are possible, conclusions reached are exactly the same. As is to be expected, the differentials are slightly greater when the contrast is with respect to Anglos as opposed to the total population.

2. That is, if 1.13 million were included in the 1980 census, but 25 percent of the total population was *not* included, then this implies a total population of 1.5 million

(of which approximately 0.37 million would not have been included).

3. The technology parameters of the Leontief model were estimated for 1980 metropolitan areas (SMSAs) in the Southwest, or the labor markets with most of the undocumented population. An estimate of the legally resident Mexican population was made using alien registration (I-53) data for 1980 from the Immigration and Naturalization Service and data on legally admitted aliens. This estimate was subtracted from the total Mexican alien population enumerated in the 1980 census. Various corrections and adjustments were made and are described in detail in previous work (Passel and Woodrow 1984; Warren and Passel 1987). For the estimated impact to be substantially different, the distribution of nonenumerated undocumented workers across local labor markets would have to be implausibly at variance with the enumerated population.

It was first established that a system that disaggregates undocumented and legal immigrants is significantly different from a system that lumps together the undocumented and legal. A disaggregation of the undocumented and legal population was therefore considered. And because the Leontief model preferably includes the wages of each group considered—note that the identification of undocumented individuals is problematic in the census—several alternative systems were analyzed. Controls for individual skill levels, as well as a correction for the endogeneity of labor supply, were introduced in the statistical models.

References

Auletta, K. 1982. *The Underclass*. New York: Random House.

Bean, Frank D.; Allan G. King; and Jeffrey S. Passel. 1983. "The Number of Illegal Migrants of Mexican Origin in the United States: Sex Ratio Based Estimates for 1980." *Demography* 20:99–109.

Bean, Frank D.; H. L. Browning; and W. P. Frisbie. 1984. "The Sociodemographic Characteristics of Mexican Immigrant Status Groups: Implications for Studying Undocumented Migrants." *International Migration Review* 18 (Fall):672–691.

Bean, Frank D. et al. 1984. "Generational Differences in Fertility among Mexican Americans: Implications for Assessing Immigration Effects." *Social Science Quarterly* 65 (June):573–582.

Bean, Frank D., and Teresa Sullivan. 1985. "Immigration and Its Consequences: Confronting the Problem." *Society* 22 (May/June):67–73.

Bean, Frank D.; Allan G. King; and Jeffrey S. Passel. 1986. "Estimates of the Size of the Illegal Migrant Population of Mexican Origin in the United States: An Assessment, Review and Proposal." In H. Browning and R. de la Garza, eds., *Mexican Immigrants and the Mexican American People*. Austin: Center for Mexican American Studies, University of Texas, pp. 13–36.

Bean, Frank D., and Marta Tienda. 1987. *The Hispanic Population in the United States*. New York: Russell-Sage.

Bean, Frank D.; B. L. Lowell; and L. Taylor. 1988. "Undocumented Mexican Immigrants and the Earnings of Other Workers in the United States." *Demography* 25:35–52.

Berry, Brian J., and Lester P. Silverman, eds. 1980. *Population Redistribution and Public Policy*. Washington, D.C.: National Academy of Sciences.

Bianchi, Suzanne M. 1981. *Household Composition and Racial Inequality*. New Brunswick, N.J.: Rutgers University Press.

Biggar, Jeanne. 1979. "The Sunning of America: Migration to the Sunbelt." *Population Bulletin* 34, no. 1.

Borjas, George J. 1984. "The Impact of Immigrants on the Earnings of the Native-Born." In V. M. Briggs, Jr. and M. Tienda, eds., *Immigration: Issues and Policies*. Salt Lake City, Ut.: Olympus Publishing, p. 84.

———. 1985. "Immigrants, Minorities, and Labor Market Competition." Unpublished paper.

———. 1986. "The Sensitivity of Labor Demand Functions to the Choice of Dependent Variable." *Review of Economics and Statistics* 68:56–66.

Brown, David L., and Calvin Beale. 1981. "Diversity in Post-1970 Population Trends." In Amos Hawley and Sara Nulls Mazie, eds, *Nonmetropolitan America in Transition*. Chapel Hill: University of North Carolina Press.

Chapman, Leonard F., Jr. 1975. "Illegal Aliens—A Growing Population." *Immigration and Naturalization Reporter* 24:15–18.

Cooney, Rosemary S., and Alice E. C. Warren. 1979. "Declining Female Participation among Puerto Rican New Yorkers: A Comparison with Native White Non–Spanish New Yorkers." *Ethnicity* 6:281–297.

Davis, Cary; Carl Haub; and JoAnne Willette. 1983. "U.S. Hispanics: Changing the Face of America." *Population Bulletin* 38:1–43.

Fishman, Joshua, et al. 1966. *Language Loyalty in the United States*. The Hague: Mouton.

Frisbie, W. Parker. 1985. *Household and Family Demography of Hispanics, Blacks and Anglos*. Final NICHD Report. Austin: University of Texas Population Research Center.

———. 1986. "Variations in Patterns of Marital Instability among Hispanics." *Journal of Marriage and the Family* 48:99–106.

Glick, Paul H. 1984. "Marriage, Divorce and Living Arrangements." *Journal of Family Issues* 5:7–26.

Grebler, Leo; Joan W. Moore; and Ralph C. Guzmán. 1970. *The Mexican American People*. New York: The Free Press.

Grenier, Giles. 1984. "Shifts to English as Usual Language by Americans of Spanish Mother Tongue." *Social Science Quarterly* 65:537–550.

Grossman, Jean B. 1982. "The Substitutability of Natives and Immigrants in Production." *Review of Economics and Statistics* 54:596–603.

Hamermesh, Daniel S., and James Grant. 1979. "Econometric Studies of

Labor–Labor Substitution and Their Implications for Policy." *The Journal of Human Resources* 14 (Summer):518–542.

Heer, David M. 1979. "What Is the Annual Net Flow of Undocumented Mexican Immigrants to the United States?" *Demography* 16 (3):417–423.

Higham, John. 1971. *Strangers in the Land: Patterns of American Nativism, 1860–1925*, 2d ed. New York: Atheneum.

Hill, Kenneth. 1985. "Illegal Aliens: An Assessment." In Daniel B. Levine, Kenneth Hill, and Robert Warren, eds., *Immigration Statistics: A Story of Neglect*. Washington, D.C.: National Academy Press.

Hispanic Policy Development Project, 1984. *The Hispanic Almanac*. Lebanon, Pa.: Sowers Printing Company.

Hutchinson, E. P. 1956. *Immigrants and Their Children, 1850–1950*. New York: John Wiley and Sons.

Immigration and Naturalization Service. 1983. *Statistical Yearbook of the Immigration and Naturalization Service*. Washington, D.C.: U.S. Department of Justice.

Keely, Charles. 1983. Affidavit submitted for plaintiffs in Cuomo et al. v. Baldrige et al., U.S. District Court, Southern District of New York, 80 Div. 4550(JES).

Keely, Charles B., and Patricia J. Elwell. 1981. "International Migration: Canada and the United States." In Mary M. Kritz, Charles B. Keely and Silvano M. Tomasi, eds., *Global Trends in Migration: Theory and Research on International Population Movements*. New York: Center for Migration Studies, pp. 181–207.

King, Allan G.; B. L. Lowell; and Frank D. Bean. 1986. "The Effects of Hispanic Immigrants on the Earnings of Native Hispanic Americans." *Social Science Quarterly* 67:672–689.

López, David. 1978. "Chicano Language Loyalty in an Urban Setting." *Sociology and Social Research* 62:267–279.

Massey, Douglas S. 1979. "Residential Segregation of Spanish Americans in the United States Urbanized Areas." *Demography* 16:553–564.

———. 1981. "Dimensions of the New Immigration to the United States and the Prospects for Assimilation." *Annual Review of Sociology* 7:57–85.

———. 1985. "The Settlement Process among Mexican Migrants to the United States: New Methods and Findings." In Daniel B. Levine, Kenneth Hill, and Robert Warren, eds., *Immigration Statistics: A Story of Neglect*. Washington, D.C.: National Academy Press, pp. 255–292.

McCarthy, Kevin F., and R. Burciaga Valdez. 1986. *Current and Future Effects of Mexican Immigration in California*. Santa Monica, Cal.: Rand Corporation.

McEaddy, Beverly J. 1976. "Women Who Head Families: A Socioeconomic Analysis." *Monthly Labor Review* 99:3–9.

McLemore, S. Dale. 1980. *Racial and Ethnic Relations in America*. Boston: Allyn and Bacon.

Mirowsky, John, and Catherine E. Ross. 1984. "Language Networks and Social Status among Mexican Americans." *Social Science Quarterly* 65:551–564.

Muller, T. 1984. *The Fourth Wave: California's Newest Immigrants*. Washington, D.C.: Urban Institute Press.

Muller, T., and T. Espenshade. 1985. *The Fourth Wave*. Washington: Urban Institute Press.

Olmedo, Esteban L. 1979. "Acculturation: A Psychometric Perspective." *American Psychologist* 34:1061–1070.

Ortiz, Vilma. N.d. "Changes in the Characteristics of Puerto Rican Migrants from 1955 to 1980." Madison: University of Wisconsin Center for Demography.

Passel, Jeffrey S. 1986. "Undocumented Immigration." *The Annals* 487 (September):181–200.

Passel, Jeffrey S.; J. S. Siegel; and J. G. Robinson. 1982. "Coverage of the National Population by Age, Sex, and Race in the 1980 Census: Preliminary Estimates by Demographic Analysis." *Current Population Reports*, P-23, No. 115. Washington, D.C.: U.S. Government Printing Office.

Passel, Jeffrey S., and Karen A. Woodrow, 1984. "Geographic Distribution of Undocumented Immigrants: Estimates of Undocumented Aliens Counted in the 1980 Census by State." *International Migration Review* 18(3):642–671.

Population Reference Bureau. 1983. *World Population: Toward the Next Century*. Washington, D.C.: Population Reference Bureau.

Portes, Alejandro. 1978. "Migration and Underdevelopment." *Politics and Society* 8:1–48.

―――. 1979. "Illegal Immigration and the International System: Lessons from Recent Legal Mexican Immigrants to the United States." *Social Problems* 26:425–438.

Portes, Alejandro and Robert L. Bach. 1985. *Latin Journey: Cuban and Mexican Immigrants in the United States*. Berkeley and Los Angeles: University of California Press.

Preston, Samuel H. 1974. "Differential Fertility, Unwanted Fertility, and Racial Trends in Occupational Achievement." *American Sociological Review* 39:492–506.

Ross, Heather and Isabel V. Sawhill. 1975. *Time of Transition: The Growth of Families Headed by Women*. Washington, D.C.: Urban Institute.

Select Commission on Immigration and Refugee Policy. 1981. *U.S. Immigration Policy and the National Interest*. Washington, D.C.: U.S. Government Printing Office.

Siegel, Jacob S., and Jeffrey S. Passel. 1979. "Coverage of the Hispanic Population of the United States in the 1970 Census: A Methodological Analysis." *Current Population Reports*, P-23, No. 82. Washington, D.C.: U.S. Government Printing Office.

Siegel, J.; J. Passel; and G. Robinson. 1980. *Preliminary Review of the Existing Studies of the Number of Illegal Residents in the United States*. Report to the Commission on Immigration and Refugee Policy. Washington, D.C.: U.S. Bureau of Census.

Slater, Courtenay. 1985. "The Illegals." *American Demographics* 7(1):26–29.

Sullivan, Teresa A. 1986. "Stratification of the Chicano Labor Market under Conditions of Continuing Mexican Immigration," In Harley L. Browning and Rodolfo O. de la Garza, eds., *Mexican Immigrants and Mexican Americans: An Evolving Relation*. Austin: Center for Mexican American Studies, University of Texas, pp. 55–73.

Teitelbaum, Michael S. 1985. *Latin Migration North: The Problem for U.S. Foreign Policy*. New York: Council on Foreign Relations.

Tienda, Marta, and Lisa J. Neidert. 1984. "Language, Education and the Socioeconomic Achievement of Hispanic Origin Men." *Social Science Quarterly* 65:519–536.

U.S. Bureau of the Census. 1971. *A Public Use Sample of Basic Records from the 1960 Census: Description and Technical Documentation*. Washington, D.C.: U.S. Government Printing Office.

———. 1982. *Persons of Spanish Origin by State: 1980*. PC80-S1-7. Washington, D.C.: U.S. Government Printing Office.

———. 1983. *Public Use Microdata Samples Technical Documentation*. Washington, D.C.: U.S. Government Printing Office.

———. 1984. *The Condition of Hispanics in America Today*. Washington, D.C.: U.S. Government Printing Office.

U.S. Department of Justice. 1983. *Statistical Yearbook of the Immigration and Naturalization Service, 1983*. Washington, D.C.: U.S. Government Printing Office.

van den Berghe, Pierre L. 1967. *Race and Racism*. New York: Wiley.

Warren, Robert, and Jeffrey S. Passel. 1987. "A Count of the Uncountable: Estimates of Undocumented Aliens Counted in the 1980 United States Census." *Demography* 24:375–393.

Willette, Joanne, et al. 1982. "The Demographic and Socioeconomic Characteristics of the Hispanic Population in the United States: 1950–80." Report prepared by Development Associates, Inc., and the Population Reference Bureau for the U.S. Department of Health and Human Services. Washington, D.C.: Development Associates.

Zelinsky, Wilbur. 1973. *Immigration Settlement Patterns: The Cultural Geography of the U.S*. Englewood Cliffs, N.J.: Prentice-Hall.

4.

Growing Imbalances between Labor Supply and Labor Demand in the Caribbean Basin

Thomas J. Espenshade

Unemployment and underemployment are spreading—an overriding social and economic problem in [El Salvador, Honduras, Nicaragua, Guatemala, and Costa Rica]. The high rate of population growth magnifies these problems. Job opportunities are vanishing, even as a quarter of a million young people are entering Central America's job markets each year. In a region where half of the population is below the age of 20, the combination of youth and massive unemployment is a problem of awesome—and explosive—dimensions.
—The Kissinger Commission (1984:385)

Introduction and Overview

By virtue of its high rates of population growth and close physical proximity to the United States, the Caribbean Basin holds a place of special significance to this country and to U.S. foreign policy.[1] Indeed, as pointedly demonstrated by the events surrounding the civil strife in Nicaragua and El Salvador, the concern over the servicing and repayment of Latin American foreign debt, and the large international movements of refugees and undocumented migrants throughout the Western Hemisphere, the United States is not immune to the consequences of important economic, social, and political developments in Mexico, Central America, and other parts of the region.[2] Interdependence between the United States and Latin America seem certain to grow in coming years.

The Caribbean Basin's estimated population of 164 million in 1980 was groughly three-fourths as large as the U.S. population. But according to middle-series projections prepared by the United Nations (1986) and the U.S. Bureau of the Census (1984), the Caribbean Basin is expected to draw even with the United States, at about 275 million people in less than twenty years. These same sources project a population for the Caribbean Basin in 2025 that is nearly 25 percent larger than the U.S. population (372 versus 301 million). Over the same period the labor force in the Caribbean Basin is expected nearly to triple in size, growing from 53 million in 1980, to a projected 150 million by 2025. Signs of strain have already started to appear. For example, Mexico led the list of the world's countries sending both legal and undocumented migrants to the United States in the early 1980s, and other Caribbean Basin nations figured prominently in the top ten.

Partly in response to these demographic developments, the U.S. Congress passed the Immigration Reform and Control Act of 1986 (IRCA) in October 1986, and President Reagan signed the bill into law on November 6, 1986. A major objective of this legislation, which represents the most sweeping revision of U.S. immigration laws since 1965, is to control the flow of undocumented migration into the United States. One of the principal means of enforcement is through employer sanctions—a system of fines and other penalties on employers who knowingly hire undocumented workers.[3]

Whether IRCA achieves the aims its supporters intended will depend on a number of domestic considerations, including U.S. employers' needs for low-skill, low-wage labor and their willingness to risk fines and jail sentences for hiring illegal workers, the shortfall among native workers as members of the baby-bust generation begin entering the labor market, and the extent to which business perceives that the INS is determined to enforce the new law.[4] In addition, however, the success of IRCA will depend on international factors, including the strength of external demand for illegal entry into the United States, which is in turn largely a function of the imbalance between labor supply and job availabilities in the Caribbean Basin.[5] It is likely that IRCA will have to contend with mounting pressures on U.S. labor markets from outside the country unless major and simultaneous efforts are undertaken to accelerate the process of job creation in those countries of Latin America closest to the United States.

As a first step in assessing the likely effectiveness of IRCA, this chapter examines push factors underlying migration northward from the Caribbean Basin to the United States. It assumes that much of this migration is motivated by a desire to improve one's economic circumstances and that keys to the strength of this motivation are the availability of jobs and associated rates of pay in one's own country compared with opportunities in the United States (Portes 1982; Bradshaw and Frisbie 1983). Rising numbers and rates of unemployed dampen the chances of finding satisfactory domestic employment and cause people to look elsewhere for work. The next section of this paper examines the growing imbalance between labor supply and labor demand in the Caribbean Basin by utilizing alternative assump-

Figure 4.1 **The Caribbean Basin**

[Map of the Caribbean Basin showing United States, Gulf of Mexico, Atlantic Ocean, Bahamas, Cuba, Haiti, Dominican Republic, Mexico, Belize, Jamaica, Guatemala, Honduras, El Salvador, Nicaragua, Caribbean Sea, Pacific Ocean, Costa Rica, Panama, Venezuela, and Colombia.]

tions about how rapidly labor demand is likely to increase in the future. The implications of rising unemployment for migratory pressures are then discussed. Following that we examine how many additional jobs would have to be created, beyond those that might be generated by the continuation of present policies, to achieve a variety of postulated policy targets. The projected cost of creating these additional jobs is also estimated.

My analysis shows that, to prevent the number of unemployed persons from rising above their 1980 levels in any of the four regions of the Caribbean Basin between 1980 and 2010, eleven million additional jobs need to be created at a total cost (in 1982 dollars) of more than $400 billion. A less stringent policy target is to aim to prevent unemployment rates from rising more than 50 percent above their 1980 levels in any of the regions of the Caribbean Basin between 1980 and 2010. This objective necessitates nearly four million additional jobs at a total estimated cost of almost $120 billion. An intermediate scenario that tries to maintain a ceiling on unemployment rates at their 1980 levels would require more than seven million extra jobs and cost an added $270 billion. Whether any of these projected levels of investment can be achieved will influence the pattern and strength of legal and undocumented migration to the United States in the next two decades.

Labor Supply and Labor Demand Projections for the Caribbean Basin

Let me begin this section by briefly describing population trends in the Caribbean Basin because population growth is a major determinant of subsequent growth in the labor force.[6] The specific population outlook for Mexico and Central America is reviewed in other chapters in this volume. The Caribbean Basin generally shares the demographic features of these two constituent regions. Between 1950 and 1980, population in the Caribbean Basin grew from 71 million to 164 million, an increase of about 130 percent in just thirty years. A further increment of roughly the same relative magnitude is expected during the next forty-five years, with the population reaching a total projected size of 372 million by 2025. Average annual rates of population growth for the Caribbean Basin fluctuated between 2.6 and 2.9 percent in the three decades separating 1950 and 1980, with rates in individual regions reaching as high as 3.3 percent in the Southern Rim (Columbia, Venezuela, Guyana, and Suriname) during the 1950s, and 3.2 percent in Mexico in the 1960s. It is commonly known that such high rates of population growth were due to the unprecedented declines in death rates that began before World War II and accelerated between the war's end and the early 1960s, without a corresponding reduction in birth rates.[7]

In making its medium-variant projections for the Caribbean Basin population, the United Nations (1986) assumed that birth rates throughout the region would gradually fall, thereby lowering future rates of population growth. Average annual growth rates for the entire Caribbean Basin are expected to drop below 2.0 percent in the first decade of the next century and continue declining to 1.2 percent by 2025. Projected rates are lowest for the Caribbean Islands and consistently highest in Central America. As a result, the population in Central America increases as a share of the total, rising from 13 percent in 1950 to 18 percent by 2025. Slower growth in the Caribbean Islands is expected to reduce its share from 24 percent in 1950 to 16 percent by 2025. Mexico and the Southern Rim had the largest populations in the region in 1980, with 69 and 42 million people, respectively. By 2025 their respective shares of the total are projected to reach 41 and 25 percent, just slightly ahead of their 1950 levels.

Labor Supply: 1950–2020

The labor force is an important channel by which population trends affect the economy, because changes in the size and composition of the labor force are key factors in determining rates of economic growth. At the same time, increases in the size of the labor force, which outstrip the capacity of the economy to create useful employment, may have adverse demographic as well as other consequences. People in rural areas who are unable to find employment may migrate to nearby cities, adding to already overcrowded conditions and putting additional demands on public services.[8] Insufficient numbers of jobs in either rural or urban areas may in turn create pressures for international migration. Government leaders are keenly aware that high levels of unemployment and underemployment can lead to political instability.

In this paper, the terms "labor force" and "labor supply" are synonymous with the economically active population, defined to comprise all employed and unemployed persons, including those seeking work for the first time (International Labour Office 1986:ix). The employed population may include some people who are underemployed, especially in low-income countries. Persons who do not hold jobs and who are either unable or unwilling to work are considered to be out of the labor force. The size of any country's labor force depends on both the age-sex composition of its population in the working ages and labor force participation rates, that is, on the proportions of persons in selected age-sex categories who are in the labor force. As a result, trends in population and in labor force growth are often closely related, but usually they are not identical. Increases in labor force participation rates, for example, lead independently to a larger labor force than population growth. In addition, if population growth rates accelerate because of an increase in birth rates or a decline in infant and childhood mortality, the impact on the labor force of these larger cohorts of young people will not be felt for another ten or fifteen years.[9]

Labor force trends discussed in this section are based on International Labour Office (1986) estimates and projections of the economically active population of the Caribbean Basin. Projections of labor supply are consistent with the medium-variant projections of total population as assessed in 1984 by the United Nations (1986). The ILO also issues labor force projections based on the high and low variants of the U.N. population projections. These alternatives are not discussed here, not only for reasons of economy, but also because the differences between the figures as derived from the two variants are small in most cases and generally less than the percentage of error contained in the projection models themselves (International Labour Office 1986). Labor force participation rates, which are applied to the medium-variant U.N. population projections to yield projections of the economically active population, are produced from regression equations that take account of historical trends in rates of change in the economically active population ratios.

The resulting labor supply projections should not be confused with forecasts. That is, these projections are based on assumptions about future trends in population and in labor force participation rates, and these assumptions may be disproved by subsequent experience. Nevertheless, because the ILO labor force projections are based on a standard projection methodology that employs uniform concepts, methods, and classification schemes and that, with a few exceptions, has been applied uniformly to all countries, areas, and territories, we may consider them to be reliable for the purposes of our analysis here.

Trends in labor supply for each of the four major regions of the Caribbean Basin are shown in figure 2.[10] In 1950, when total labor supply in the Caribbean Basin numbered just 25 million persons, no region registered a labor force larger than 9 million. By 1980 the regions' combined labor force had reached 53 million—a growth of 117 percent in three decades—and Mexico's economically active population (22 million) was nearly as large as that of the entire Caribbean Basin in 1950. Labor supply throughout the four regions is projected to total 93 million by the year 2000 and to reach 140 million by 2020. At these expected levels, the Caribbean Basin's labor force will grow by 40 million persons between 1980 and 2000, and by another 47 million between 2000 and 2020. Much of this projected increase will occur in Mexico—roughly 44 percent over the entire forty-year period. As indicated in figure 2, the gap between the size of Mexico's labor force and those of the other regions steadily widens over time.[11]

Labor supply expands in all four regions of the Caribbean Basin between 1950 and 2020, but there are significant differences in rates of growth among regions. These differentials are reflected in changes in each region's labor force as a share of the total labor force (see figure 3). Mexico has the largest regional labor force and is expected to increase its share of the total from 36 percent in 1950 to 43 percent by 2020. Owing to their slower rate of population growth, the Caribbean Islands are expected to lose share relative to others, declining from 28 percent of the total in 1950, to 16 percent by 2020. Central America historically has had the Caribbean Basin's smallest labor force. In 1950, its economically active population was only half as large as the labor force in the next-smallest region (the Southern Rim). By 2020, Central America is expected to surpass the Islands' labor force and to rise to 17 percent of the total, up from 13 percent in 1950. The Southern Rim exhibits little change throughout the period; its labor supply never deviates far from one-quarter of the total.

Figure 4.2 **Labor Supply in the Caribbean Basin, 1950–2020**

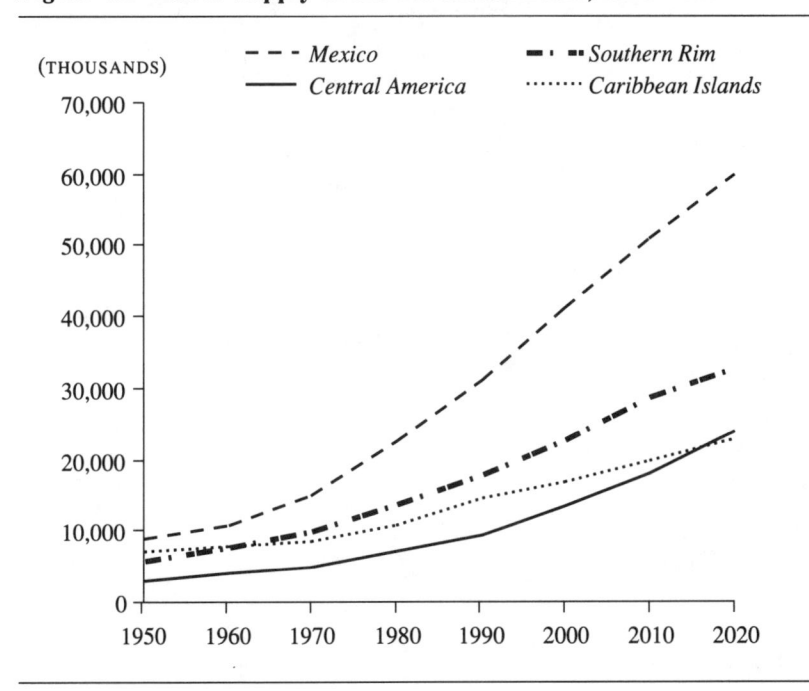

[Line graph showing labor supply in thousands from 1950 to 2020 for Mexico (dashed), Central America (solid), Southern Rim (dash-dot), and Caribbean Islands (dotted). Y-axis ranges from 0 to 70,000 thousands.]

Average annual rates of actual labor force growth for the period 1950–1980 and projected rates for 1980–2020 are shown in figure 4. The typical pattern is one of accelerating labor force growth up to the 1970s or early 1980s, followed by a leveling-off or a gradual decline in growth rates. This pattern reflects an earlier peaking in each region's overall rate of population growth combined with secular increases in labor force participation rates. In the future, the rise in participation rates is projected to slow and to be more than offset by declines in the rate of growth of population in the economically active ages. For the Caribbean Basin as a whole, the average rate of labor supply growth rose from 2.0 percent per annum in the 1950s, to a peak of 3.4 percent during the 1970s. Gradual declines are projected thereafter, with the annual rate expected to fall to 2.9 percent in the late 1980s, and eventually to 1.8 percent by 2010–2020. Even though the rate of growth is falling, however, it is being applied to an expanding base. Consequently, the projected absolute number of persons being added to the Caribbean Basin's labor supply will continue to mount until well toward the end of the projection period.

Figure 4.3 **Caribbean Basin Labor Force**

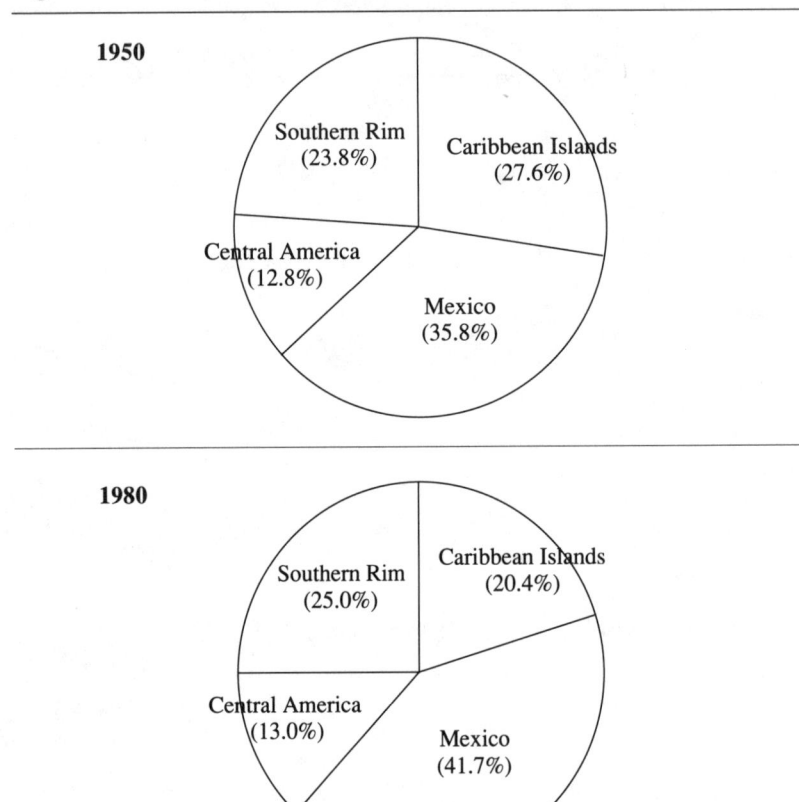

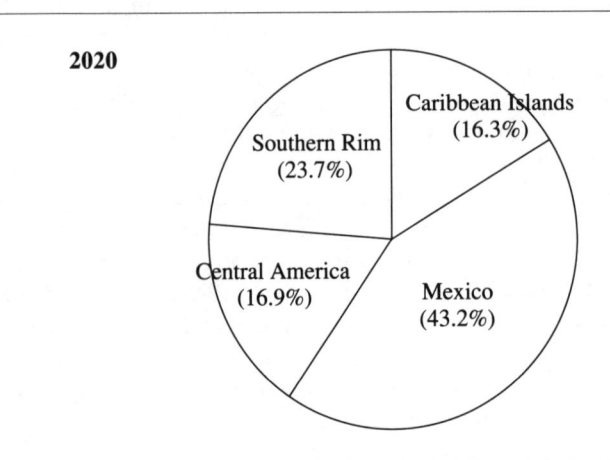

1950

- Southern Rim (23.8%)
- Caribbean Islands (27.6%)
- Central America (12.8%)
- Mexico (35.8%)

1980

- Southern Rim (25.0%)
- Caribbean Islands (20.4%)
- Central America (13.0%)
- Mexico (41.7%)

2020

- Southern Rim (23.7%)
- Caribbean Islands (16.3%)
- Central America (16.9%)
- Mexico (43.2%)

Figure 4.4 **Average Annual Growth Rates of the Economically Active Population**

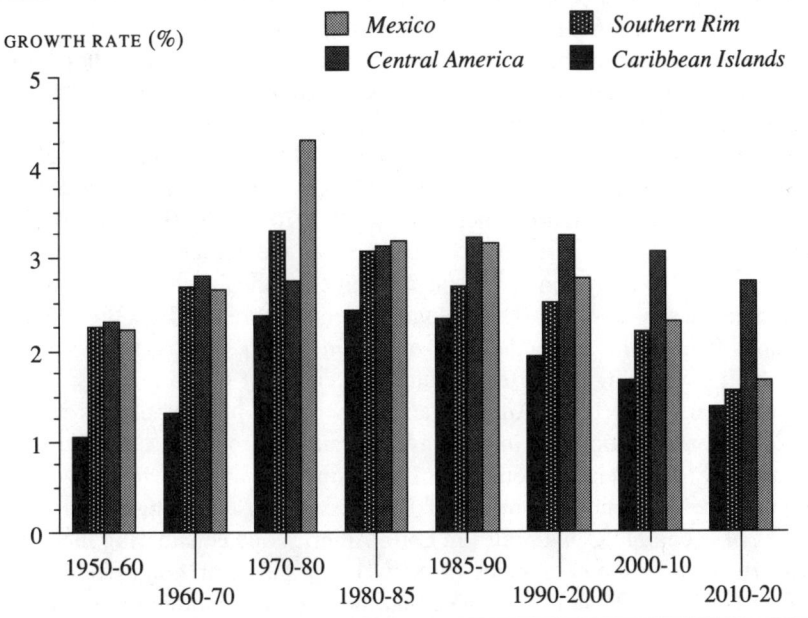

[Bar chart showing growth rates (%) for Mexico, Central America, Southern Rim, and Caribbean Islands across time periods: 1950-60, 1960-70, 1970-80, 1980-85, 1985-90, 1990-2000, 2000-10, 2010-20]

Labor Demand: 1980–2010

The previous section presented projections of labor supply. Just because people want jobs, however, does not automatically mean that jobs will be available for them. It is important, therefore, to examine projections of the future demand for workers (or job opportunities) and to compare this demand with projections of labor supply.

Published projections of labor demand are much rarer than projections of labor supply. Indeed, it has been impossible to locate projections of labor demand for the complete set of Caribbean Basin countries considered here. Part of the difficulty is that projecting labor demand is inherently more problematic than projecting labor supply. In the latter case, persons who will be entering the labor force over the next fifteen or twenty years are already alive, and one can ascertain their numbers with relative reliability. In addition, changes in the size and composition of a population—changes that drive changes in the size and composition of the labor force—occur relatively slowly, especially when compared with the speed of many economic changes. Such economic indicators as unemployment rates, interest rates, growth rates in gross national product, and rates of inflation can change quickly. A doubling or halving in the value of any of these within the space of two or three years would not be uncommon. Because the demand for labor hinges on the performance of the overall economy and because this performance is especially difficult to anticipate, researchers have typically been hesitant to make projections of labor demand.

One assessment of potential labor demand in Latin America has been provided by Gendell (1986), who compares growth rates implied by two models that contain assumptions about the region's ability to absorb its future labor supply. The first model, developed by the Programa Regional de Empleo en América Latina y el Caribe (PREALC 1976), projects the extent of labor utilization in Latin America between 1970 and 2000. Gross domestic product (GDP) is assumed to expand at an average annual rate of 6.5 percent, total employment grows at 2.7 percent annually, and open unemployment nearly doubles. The second projection, prepared by the United Nations Industrial Development Organization (1982), constructs a scenario in which developing countries produce 25 percent of world manufacturing by the year 2000 (Latin America accounts for 13 percent of this total). Given this assumption, the implied average annual growth in labor demand from 1975 to 2000 is 3.2 percent, if Latin America can achieve an average annual rate of economic growth of 8.0 percent. Based on historical estimates of economic growth rates in Latin America and considering the poor performances of the economies of many Latin American countries during the early 1980s, Gendell concludes that the rate of economic growth most likely to occur in Latin America will be even lower than the rate predicted by the PREALC model. As a result, labor demand is likely to grow by less than 2.7 percent per year.

In the absence of published data, I have prepared my own projections of labor demand for each of the Caribbean Basin regions. Three separate projections are used, partly to emphasize that these are not forecasts of the future but rather projections based on particular sets of assumptions. In each projection, assumptions about how quickly the economy will be able to generate jobs are based on the historical record. The low labor demand scenario selects the smallest decennial labor force growth rate between 1950 and 1980 in each of the four regions and assumes that total job opportunities will grow at this rate between 1980 and 2010. The medium and high growth scenarios use the intermediate and the largest decennial labor force growth rates, respectively, from 1950 to 1980 and assume that labor demand will grow exponentially at these rates through 2010. The actual growth rates used to project labor demand in each region under the high, medium, and low growth scenarios are contained in table 1. The Caribbean Islands show the slowest employment growth of any region in all three scenarios. Moreover, under the medium growth and low growth paths, the remaining three regions exhibit roughly comparable growth rates—2.7 percent per annum under medium growth and 2.3 percent under low growth.

Table 4.1 **Annual Percentage Growth Rates Used to Project Labor Demand, 1980–2010**

	Region			
Scenario	Caribbean Islands	Southern Rim	Central America	Mexico
High growth	2.36[a]	3.28[a]	2.84[b]	4.29[a]
Medium growth	1.31[b]	2.69[b]	2.77[a]	2.70[b]
Low growth	1.07[c]	2.27[c]	2.30[c]	2.27[c]

[a]Based on 1970–1980.
[b]Based on 1960–1970.
[c]Based on 1950–1960.

To generate the projections, the exponential growth rates in table 1 were applied to baseline labor demand figures for 1980. These baseline data were obtained by first estimating 1980 rates of unemployment for each of the four Caribbean Basin areas. Averages of 1980 unemployment rates for selected countries within each region provided the basis for the regional estimates (International Labour Office 1983).[12] These rates ranged from 7 percent in Mexico to 15 percent in the Caribbean Islands, with an average for the entire Caribbean Basin of 9 percent. Next, the volume of unemployment within each region in 1980 was calculated by multiplying the unemployment rates by 1980 estimates of labor supply; the resulting levels of unemployment were subtracted from total labor supply to produce estimates of regional employment levels. Finally, it was assumed that levels of employment in 1980 are a satisfactory measure of baseline labor demand. Estimated total labor demand in 1980 was 49 million in the four regions combined, compared with an estimated total labor supply of 53 million.[13]

Projections of future labor demand under the low-, medium-, and high-growth scenarios are illustrated in figures 5, 6, and 7, respectively. Under the low growth projection, job availabilities throughout the entire Caribbean Basin area are expected to increase by 86 percent between 1980 and 2010. Projected labor demand is expected to rise from 49 million to 91 million, or at an average annual rate of 2.1 percent. With the exception of the Islands, where projected growth is slowest, labor demand is expected to double in each region of the Caribbean Basin. In Mexico, for example, labor demand is expected to jump from 21 million in 1980 to 41 million by 2010.

Similar regional patterns of labor demand, albeit on a magnified scale, are evident in the medium-growth scenario. Total labor demand throughout the Caribbean Basin is expected to rise to 103 million by 2010, an increase of 111 percent over the 1980 total. Projected labor demand increases by a half in the Caribbean Islands and by approximately 125 percent in each of the three remaining regions. Job availabilities in Central America are expected to draw even with labor demand in the Caribbean Islands in 2005 and then to surpass it by 2010.

The increase in projected labor demand is especially rapid under the high growth scenario, propelled in large measure by the extraordinary increases in Mexico. For the entire Basin, job availabilities are expected to grow at an average annual rate of 3.6 percent, and labor demand is projected nearly to triple from 49 million in 1980 to 142 million by 2010. Projected labor demand in Mexico in 2010 is 3.6 times greater than in 1980 (75 versus 21 million). And, for the first time, projected labor demand doubles between 1980 and 2010 in the Caribbean Islands.

Several comments on the labor demand numbers are warranted. First, because the projections are based on labor force growth rates that were actually experienced by each of the regions between 1950 and 1980, they might be thought of as reflecting in some sense the continuation of present policies. That is, the projections in figures 5, 6, and 7 might be interpreted as the number of jobs the respective economies would produce (under the specified assumptions) if no extra efforts to create employment are undertaken, over and above those already being implemented. Second, the

Figure 4.5 **Projected Labor Demand: Low Growth**

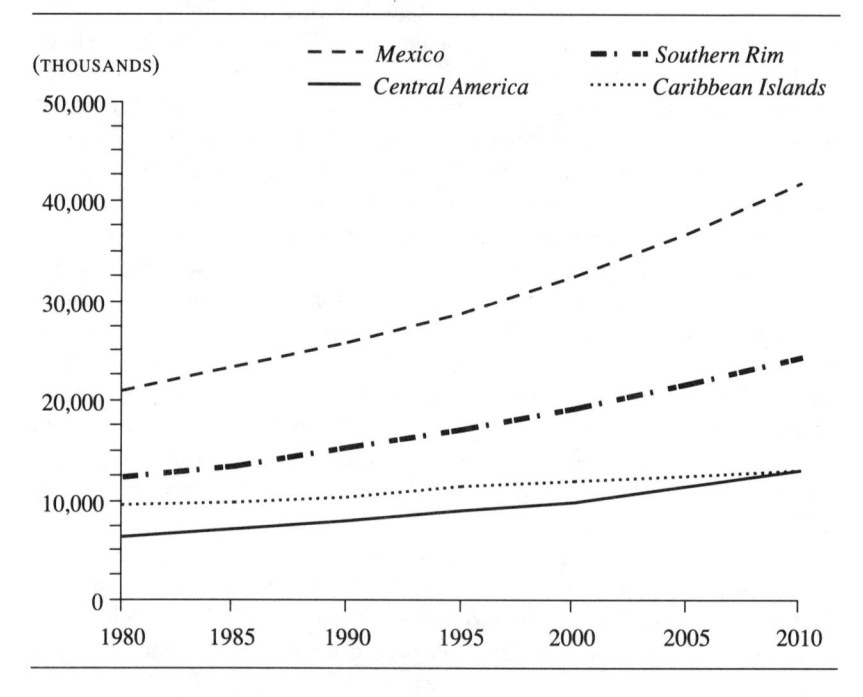

Figure 4.6 **Projected Labor Demand: Medium Growth**

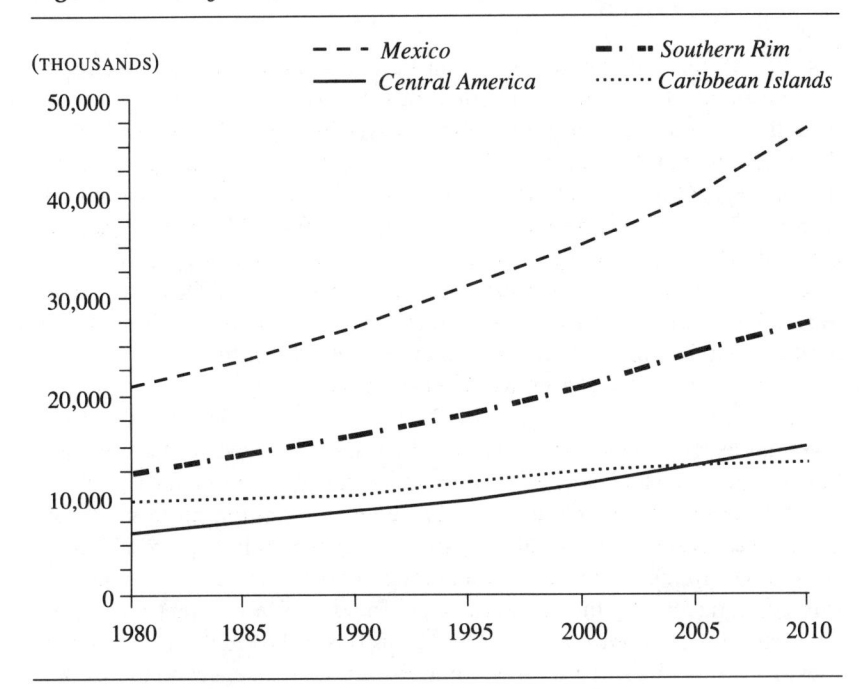

Figure 4.7 **Projected Labor Demand: High Growth**

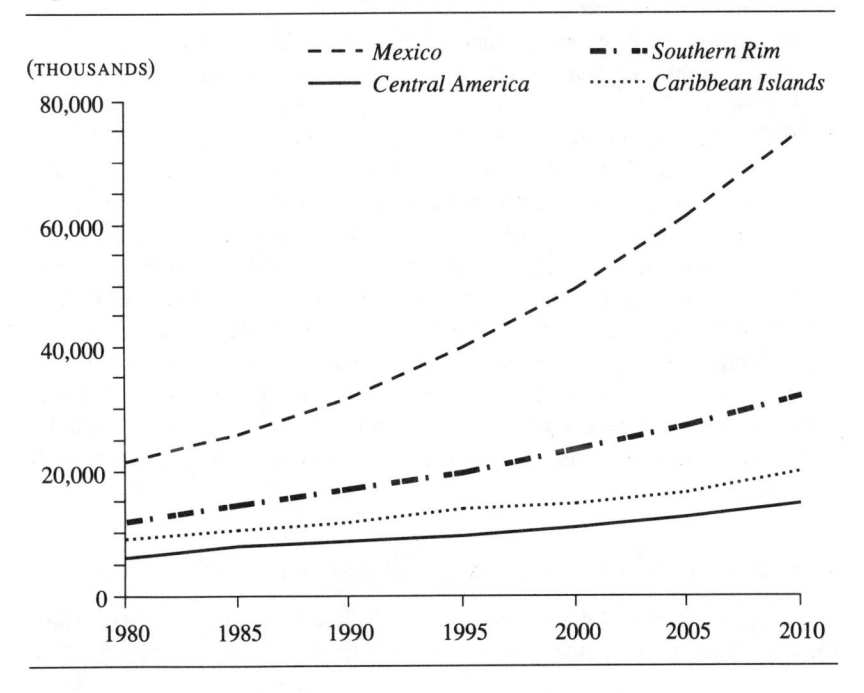

assumption that job availabilities can be expected to grow exponentially may be satisfactory in the short run, but it becomes less tenable when extended over a thirty-year period, especially when growth rates as high as those assumed in the high growth scenario are employed. Furthermore, the use of constant growth rates to project labor demand is somewhat at odds with the data in figure 4, which show projected future declines in rates of labor force growth. Building similar declines into projected growth rates of labor demand may have been preferable, although it is difficult to defend the choice of a particular path of decline against the charge of being highly arbitrary and bearing little relation to the historical record.[14]

Third, because the gap between the high growth and low growth projections exceeds 50 million jobs by 2010, it is of no little consequence to potential users of these data to know which labor demand scenario is most likely to occur. The actual economic performance of the major Caribbean Basin countries since 1980 does not leave much room for optimism. Table 2 compares average annual rates of growth since 1950 in real gross domestic product (roughly equivalent to the total annual volume of all goods and services produced by the economy when measured in constant prices) for the eight largest countries in the Caribbean Basin. For each of these countries, 1980 marks a sharp turning point. Prior to that date, economic growth was robust, often ranging between 4 and 7 percent per year. After 1980, however, economic growth slowed and actually turned negative for many countries.

This downturn in economic performance has also exerted a depressing effect on labor demand. According to the International Labour Office (1987), the world labor situation has continued to deteriorate since the early 1980s. In half of the more than forty developing countries the ILO surveyed, real wages have fallen by more than one percent annually over the past fifteen years, and in Latin America a majority of workers have suffered a drop in real income of as much as 40 percent. In Mexico, for example, real agricultural wages, which rose enormously between 1965 and 1980, are not back to their 1965 levels. In addition, regular wage employment is also stagnant or contracting, forcing an increasing number of people into self-employment or casual wage work. In light of these considerations, the labor demand projections contained in the high growth scenario appear excessively optimistic; a more realistic outcome might be expected to lie somewhere between the low growth and medium growth alternatives.

The Gap between Job Seekers and Job Opportunities

A major concern of economists, planners, and policymakers involved in the Caribbean Basin is that population growth rates have been so high that

Table 4.2 **Average Annual Percentage Growth Rates of Real Gross Domestic Product, Largest Countries in the Caribbean Basin, 1950–1986**

Country	Estimated Population Size (millions)	Growth Rate of Real GDP 1950–60	1960–70	1970–80	1980–Latest Available Year
Mexico[a]	78.5	5.9	6.8	6.4	1.6
Colombia[b]	28.2	4.5	5.3	5.4	2.6
Venezuela[c]	16.9	6.8	5.9	4.0	-1.3
Cuba[d]	10.1	—	—	—	—
Guatemala[e]	7.7	3.7	5.4	5.5	-0.9
Haiti[f]	5.2	1.5	0.9	4.6	-0.7
El Salvador[g]	5.0	2.4	5.1	3.2	-1.4
Honduras[h]	4.4	3.0	4.8	4.5	1.3

SOURCES: Population estimates are from the United Nations (1986). GDP data are contained in International Monetary Fund (1987).

NOTES:

	Date of population estimate	Latest year for GDP data
a	30 June 1985	1985
b	1 July 1984	1986
c	1 July 1984	1985
d	28 Feb. 1985	no data available
e	30 June 1984	1986
f	30 June 1984	1986
g	1 July 1982	1986
h	30 June 1985	1986

most countries seem to have very little chance of providing sufficient jobs to all those who are about to enter the labor force. Even where population growth rates have declined (as in Mexico) because of reductions in birth rates, these developments do not begin to relieve pressures on the labor market for another fifteen to twenty years. There is therefore great policy interest in comparing projections of future labor supply with labor demand to see whether future labor force growth will outstrip the capacity of these economies to generate jobs and, if so, by how much.[15] Labor surplus is conventionally measured in one of two ways, either as an unemployment rate or as the number of unemployed persons.[16] These indicators facilitate a judgment about whether labor shortages (an excess of labor demand over labor supply) or labor surpluses (an excess of supply over demand) are the more likely outcome.

Unemployment Rates. Unemployment rates are defined for a given period as the number of unemployed persons in the labor force (labor supply minus labor demand) divided by total labor supply and multiplied by 100. The resulting figure captures the percentage of persons willing and able to work who are without jobs. Projected unemployment rates for the period 1980–2010, calculated by matching the one labor supply projection to the low, medium, and high growth labor demand scenarios, are shown in figures 8, 9, and 10, respectively.

There is a rapid acceleration in unemployment rates throughout the Caribbean Basin under the low growth projections. This acceleration is concentrated during the 1980s, but unemployment rates continue to rise, in some cases to 2010. For the entire Basin area, the projected unemployment rate grows from 9 percent in 1980 to 16 percent by 1990 and again to 22 percent by 2010. Increases between 1980 and 2010 are especially pronounced for the Caribbean Islands (from 15 to 35 percent) and for Central America (from 7 to 28 percent).

Under the medium growth scenario, labor demand for the entire Caribbean Basin region is projected to grow by 2.5 percent per year (compared with 2.1 percent under low growth); this faster growth moderates the rise in unemployment rates. Continued (though smaller) increases to 2010 are still evidenced by the Caribbean Islands and Central America, but the rate peaks at 10 percent for the Southern Rim in 1990 and at 12 percent for Mexico in

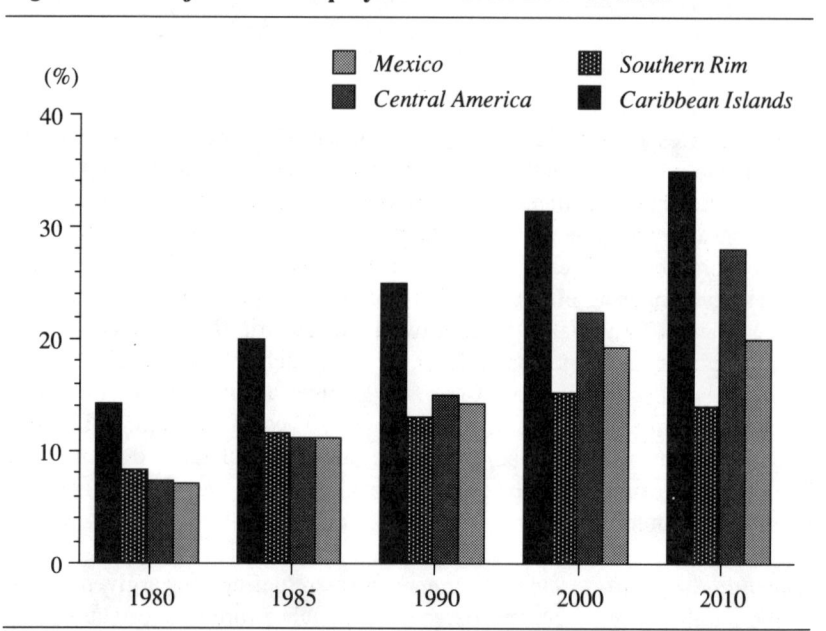

Figure 4.8 **Projected Unemployment Rates: Low Growth**

LABOR SUPPLY AND DEMAND IN THE CARIBBEAN BASIN *129*

Figure 4.9 **Projected Unemployment Rates: Medium Growth**

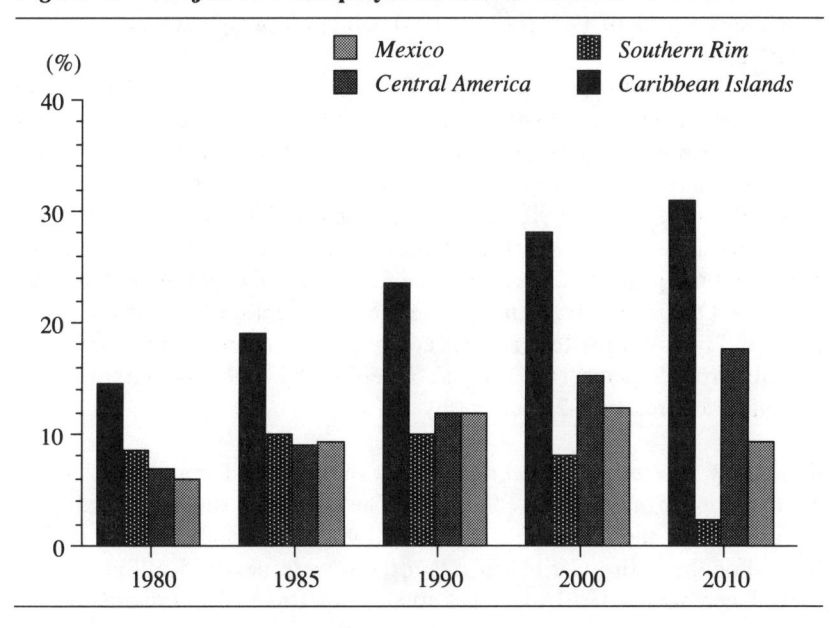

Figure 4.10 **Projected Unemployment Rates: High Growth**

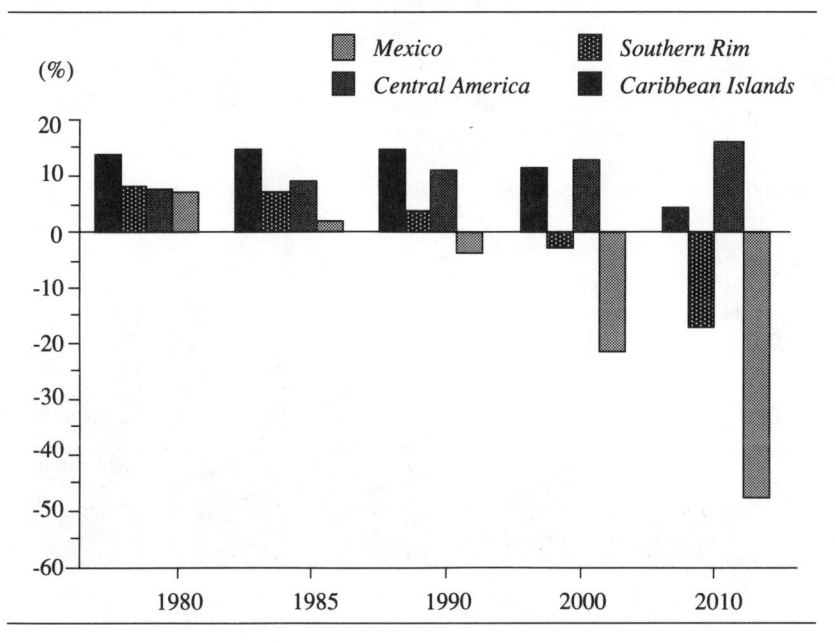

2000 before receding. For the Caribbean Basin in general, unemployment rates reach a peak of 14 percent in 2000 before dropping back to 12 percent by 2010.

If labor demand is assumed to grow at high rates (at 3.6 percent per year for the entire Basin), growth in certain regions is sufficiently fast that it overtakes labor supply before 2010 and gives rise to projected labor shortages (and therefore to negative unemployment rates). This is the case in Mexico beginning in 1990 and in the Southern Rim beginning in 2000. Unemployment rates in the Caribbean Islands remain positive throughout the period but peak at 15 percent in the 1980s before declining to 5 percent by 2010. Only in Central America do rates of employed persons continue rising to 2010. For the four regions combined, the unemployment rate falls steadily from 9 percent in 1980 to 3 percent by 1990; it turns negative thereafter and reaches -21 percent by 2010.[17]

Number of unemployed persons. Another indicator of labor surplus is simply the number of unemployed persons. These data are shown in figures 11, 12, and 13 for the low-, medium-, and high-growth labor demand projections. For the entire Caribbean Basin there were nearly 5 million unemployed persons in 1980 (out of a total labor force of approximately 53

Figure 4.11 **Number of Unemployed Persons: Low Growth**

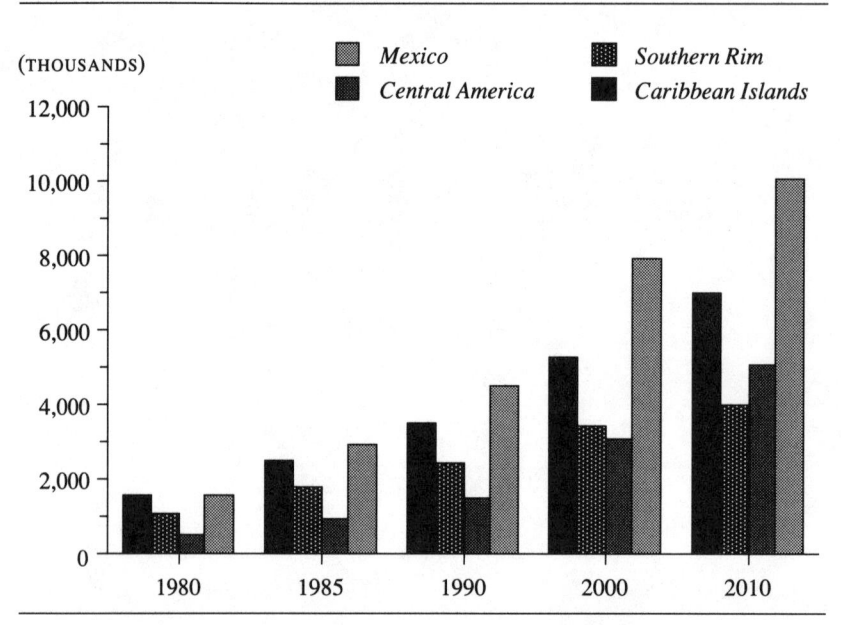

LABOR SUPPLY AND DEMAND IN THE CARIBBEAN BASIN   *131*

Figure 4.12 **Number of Unemployed Persons: Medium Growth**

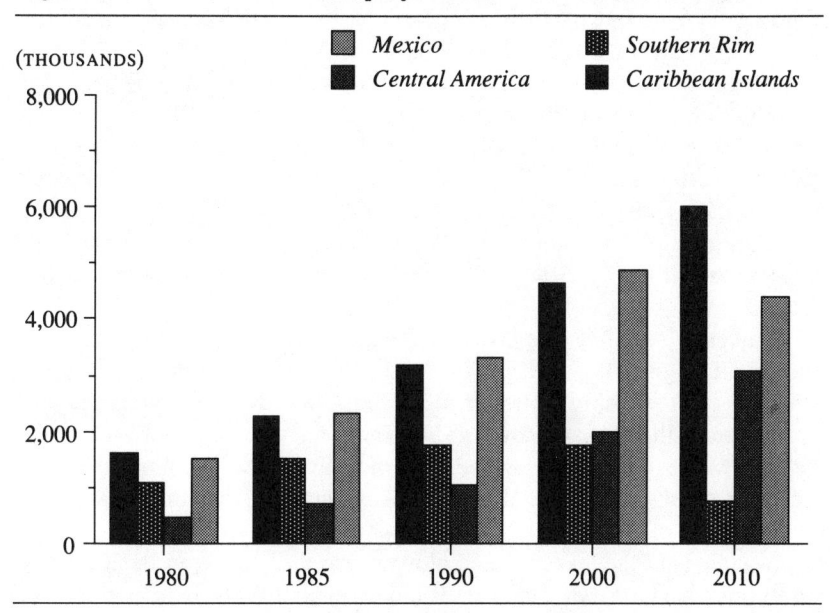

Figure 4.13 **Number of Unemployed Persons: High Growth**

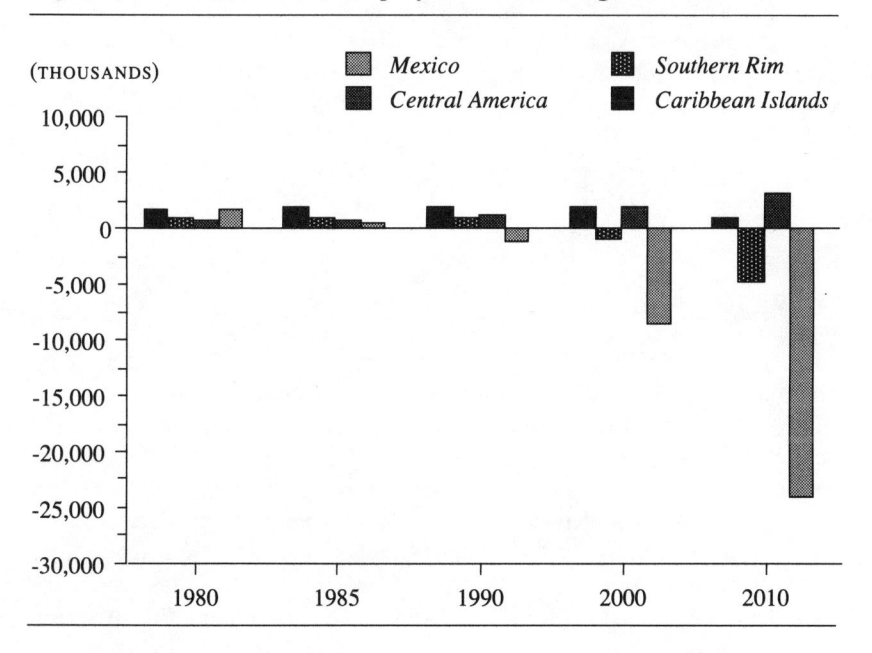

million). These persons were distributed by region as follows: roughly one-third each of the total in the Caribbean Islands and in Mexico, one million in the Southern Rim, and 500,000 in Central America.

Under the low growth scenario, the number of unemployed persons rises steadily throughout the thirty-year period and peaks in 2010 at ten million in Mexico, seven million in the Islands, five million in Central America, and four million in the Southern Rim. These figures range between four and ten times as large as their corresponding 1980 levels. For the Caribbean Basin in general, the total volume of unemployment is projected to reach twenty-six million by 2010—more than twenty-one million greater than in 1980.

Numbers of unemployed throughout the Caribbean Basin rise less under the medium growth scenario than under low growth, but they increase steadily nonetheless, to a total of fourteen million by 2010—an increase of nearly ten million persons over 1980. The total volume of unemployment by 2010 is greatest in the Caribbean Islands (six million), followed by four million in Mexico, and has already turned sharply downward in the Southern Rim.

Projections of the level of unemployment in the Caribbean Basin quickly turn into expected labor shortages if labor demand follows the high growth path. For the four regions combined, the number of unemployed persons declines from nearly five million in 1980 to two million by 1990, and then turns negative beginning in 2000. By the end of the period, labor shortages are expected in Mexico and the Southern Rim, and the projected surplus of labor in the Caribbean Islands has begun to fall. Only in Central America does the number of unemployed persons continue to rise.

Implications for U.S. Immigration

The amount of joblessness in the Caribbean Basin is already large, and it is growing. Under the medium growth scenario, for example, unemployment rates are projected to continue rising through the year 2000. If jobs are not available in their own countries, workers have a strong incentive to migrate to countries where they can find employment. Increasingly, workers from the Caribbean Basin are coming to the United States in search of a better life for themselves and their families.[18] Rates of out-migration are especially high in the Caribbean Islands. Since the 1960s, the number of people who have migrated to the United States as a proportion of the current population in their respective countries of origin has ranged from a low of 9 percent in Haiti to over 25 percent in Barbados, with a regional average of 10 percent (Pastor 1985). To some extent, this immigration is driven by economic as well as noneconomic pull factors in the

United States. But increasingly, it seems, migrants—especially undocumented migrants—are being pushed out of the Caribbean Basin by job prospects that are deteriorating rapidly and appear likely to worsen further in the next decade.

Legal immigration from the Caribbean Basin to the United States has surged in recent decades, especially since 1965, when country quotas were lifted and replaced by a preference system based on family reunification. In the 1940s legal immigrants from the Caribbean Islands, Mexico, and Central America made up just 13 percent of total U.S. legal immigration, but by the 1970s this proportion had reached 34 percent (Immigration and Naturalization Service 1986). Because the total volume of legal immigration to the United States is also rising, the number of migrants from the Caribbean Basin is growing rapidly. Between 1981 and 1985, for example, immigrants from all Caribbean Basin regions totaled 919,000—nearly as many as the 1.1 million Caribbean Basin migrants that entered in the entire decade of the 1960s (Immigration and Naturalization Service 1986). Of the 1981–1985 total legal immigrants from the Caribbean Basin, 37 percent were from Mexico, followed by 11 percent each from the Dominican Republic and Jamaica.[19]

Migrants from the Caribbean Basin have favorite destinations in the United States, depending on their place of birth. In fiscal year 1985, one-quarter of the legal migrants who were born in Mexico gave Southern California as their intended place of residence; another 20 percent said Texas; and 7 percent listed the Chicago metropolitan area. Migrants from the Dominican Republic and Jamaica tended to favor the New York metropolitan area (including northern New Jersey). More than half of the Jamaican migrants in 1985 and three-quarters of the migrants from the Dominican Republic gave the New York City region as their intended home. South Florida was the intended destination for more than one-third of Cuban migrants, followed by New York (20 percent).

Undocumented or illegal immigration to the United States has also been on the rise, prompting concerns that led to the IRCA legislation in 1986. Warren and Passel (1987) estimate that nearly 2.1 million undocumented immigrants who were residents of the United States were enumerated in the 1980 decennial census, and the Panel on Immigration Statistics (1985) of the National Academy of Sciences concludes that the total number of illegal aliens in the country was probably in the 2 to 4 million range. Warren and Passel calculate that roughly 940,000, or 46 percent, of all enumerated illegals entered the United States between 1975 and 1980, and that another 28 percent came in the five years before that. Mexico led the list of countries sending undocumented immigrants to the United States, with more than 1.1 million, or about 55 percent of the total. The Central American countries of El Salvador and Guatemala together contributed just 4 percent of the total, whereas the Caribbean Island countries of Cuba, the Dominican Republic, Haiti, Jamaica, and Trinidad and Tobago sent 7 percent.[20]

Passel and Woodrow (1984) estimated the geographic distribution of the counted undocumented immigrants in the 1980 census and concluded that half, or 1,024,000 persons, resided in California. Sizable numbers were counted in New York (234,000), Texas (186,000), Illinois (135,000), and Florida (80,000). Two out of every three Mexican undocumented immigrants live in California, with another 13 percent in Texas and 9 percent in Illinois. New York was home to about 70 percent of the illegal migrants from Haiti, Jamaica, and Trinidad and Tobago. Passel and Woodrow (1986) found that the size of the undocumented alien population continued to grow between 1980 and 1983 by about 200,000 persons per year. Mexican immigrants accounted for roughly 95 percent of this increase.

Data from the 1980 decennial census give an overall picture of the demographic impact of immigration in California, Texas, and Florida—three states in the South and Southwest that are prominent destinations for immigrants from the Caribbean Basin and that contain about 40 percent of all foreign-born persons in the United States. This immigration is large and much of it is recent. For example, three-fifths of the 1.3 million foreign-born Mexicans in California in 1980 came to the United States during the 1970s. In addition, over half of California's immigrants from other parts of Central and South America came during the same period (U.S. Bureau of the Census 1983a). In Texas, the 500,000 immigrants from Mexico made up almost 60 percent of the state's foreign-born population in 1980, and more than half of these came during the 1970s (U.S. Bureau of the Census 1983c). In Florida, Cubans—most of whom came during the 1960s—were the largest group of immigrants and made up over one-third of Florida's 1.1 million foreign-born persons in 1980. Immigrants from other parts of the Caribbean Basin are fewer in number, but there is evidence that this immigration is accelerating. For example, 5 out of every 6 of the 17,000 Haitians in Florida in 1980 came to the United States during the 1970s. Three-fifths of the 80,000 Central Americans and three-fifths of the 61,000 South Americans also came in this period (U.S. Bureau of the Census 1983b).

The Need for Additional Job Creation

The projections presented in this chapter suggest that pressures for both legal and illegal entry to the United States from the Caribbean Basin will mount for the remainder of this century. The lack of jobs and the low wages in the Caribbean Basin will be a strong incentive for migrants to leave; jobs in the United States will be a strong magnet. The United States and other industrial countries, however, cannot be a safety valve for all the unemployment in the Caribbean. Nor should they necessarily attempt to be. Although emigration generally reduces unemployment in sending countries, it also reduces the quantity of skilled labor and may represent an impediment to economic development (Pastor and Rogers 1985). Therefore, the policy question for leaders in the United States and in the Caribbean Basin is what can and should be done about the situation.

Problems surrounding the expanding imbalance between the number of potential workers and the smaller number of available jobs in the Caribbean Basin have many causes. Prominent is the rapid acceleration in population growth during the 1950s and 1960s stemming from the reduction in death rates. This suggests that part of the solution to growing joblessness lies in slower rates of population growth.[21] Many Latin American governments have in fact already taken vigorous steps to promote and support family-planning programs. But achieving substantial reductions in birth rates in low-income countries is not something that can be expected to happen immediately. And even if birth rates were to drop sharply, there would still be a delay of fifteen or twenty years before salutary effects on the labor force were felt.

Job creation in the economies of the Caribbean Basin nations has to be another element in the solution. This necessity has been recognized as part of the Reagan administration's Caribbean Basin Initiative (CBI)—a combination of trade, aid, and investment incentives designed to encourage new business while promoting political and social stability in the Caribbean area.[22] At the heart of the CBI is a twelve-year elimination of duties on Caribbean fruits and vegetables, electronic parts, meat and meat packaging, tobacco, rum, and many other products, aimed at giving Caribbean producers greater access to U.S. markets. There is evidence that the CBI has stimulated new projects in the region and succeeded in retaining some industries that were tempted to relocated (Wall Street Journal 1984; Wylie 1985).

But despite some progress, the CBI is plagued by a number of shortcomings. Critics contend that the exclusion of textiles, apparel, footwear, and other leather goods from the list of commodities receiving preferential treatment removes items that have more growth potential than anything else in the Caribbean. Moreover, they argue that the amount of aid being provided along with the CBI is small (less than $900 million in 1984) and that much of it is directed toward Honduras, Costa Rica, and El Salvador, where there is a perceived threat of Communist expansion (Wall Street Journal 1984). Finally, as Bouvier and Simcox (1986) note, "Repeated U.S. cuts in sugar imports since 1982 have cost Caribbean nations more jobs than the Caribbean Basin initiative has so far created" (p. 53).

Part of the CBI's strategy is to curtail the public sector's involvement in business expansion and to rely on the private sector for economic development and to provide new jobs. But because a well-developed industrial base, infrastructure, and pool of managerial talent are currently lacking, it is not clear that the private sector will be able to assume the additional responsibilities given to it. As a result, the short-term effects of the CBI are likely to be small, and any added development that does occur could be driven largely by U.S. investors. In some instances, this could reduce employment rather than increase it. For example, Ricketts (1985) points out that, to the extent that U.S. investors employ capital-intensive and other inappropriate technologies, deep-seated problems of structural unemployment in Caribbean Basin countries may be aggravated.[23] Also, as Pelzman and Schoepfle (1988) have concluded, a truly development-oriented program should focus on both attracting manufacturing firms away from the Pacific Basin to the Caribbean region and encouraging the development of the necessary infrastructure in the Caribbean to support the establishment of internal markets. In short, efforts stronger than the CBI will doubtless be needed if the gap between the number of job seekers and the number of available jobs is to be narrowed.

Policy initiatives conducive to fertility reduction and to job creation do not exhaust the set of possibilities. Nor are these choices mutually exclusive. Many countries make an effort to deal with these problems on several fronts simultaneously. Nonetheless, the policy questions on which the remainder of this chapter focuses relate to job creation. How many additional jobs must be created? Where must these efforts be concentrated among the four regions of the Caribbean Basin? When will the greatest efforts be needed? And how much is this additional job creation effort likely to cost?

Answers to the question of how many additional jobs have to be generated depend on the particular policy target one is trying to achieve. Here I consider three policy targets or thresholds, ordered in terms of how difficult they are to attain, how many extra jobs they require, and how much they might cost. First, and most demanding, policymakers may wish to hold the line on the number of people who were unemployed in 1980 and not let that volume increase further between 1980 and 2010. Second, 1980 unemployment rates might constitute the ceiling that policymakers do not wish to exceed. Third, and most lenient, policymakers may feel satisfied as long as unemployment rates do not exceed 150 percent of their 1980 levels at any time during the 1980–2010 period.

To assess how many extra jobs will be needed according to each of these policy thresholds, I assume that labor demand will increase according to the medium growth scenario between 1980 and 2010. As long as the number of jobs that are projected to be generated under this scenario is sufficient to meet each of the three policy targets, I assume that no additional efforts are required. My estimates in this section pertain only to those instances in which the medium growth scenario is insufficient to meet the specified policy threshold and in which extra job creation activities are then needed. Labor demand might not grow according to the medium growth scenario. If future labor demand follows a course more accurately described by the low growth scenario, then my estimates of the number of new jobs needed and the cost of creating these extra jobs will be too low. Alternatively, my calculations will lead to overestimates if labor demand follows the high growth scenario. As was suggested previously, future labor demand might be expected to grow at rates somewhere between the low and the medium growth outcomes. If this expectation materializes, then the estimates discussed here may be considered conservative estimates.

A total of 11.1 million extra jobs will be required over and above those the medium growth labor demand scenario is projected to yield (figure 14). Most of these jobs will have to be concentrated in the Caribbean Islands (40 percent) and in Mexico (30 percent). Only about 6 percent are projected to be needed in the Southern Rim. Figure 14 also shows that the most urgent efforts at job creation are needed before 1990. Almost 42 percent of the total jobs are needed in the current decade, whereas the number required between 2000 and 2010 drops to 23 percent of the total.

The job creation efforts mandated by the desire to prevent unemployment rates from rising above their 1980 levels are shown in figure 15. Under this policy threshold, 7.4 million additional jobs are needed—fewer than called for in figure 14, because constant unemployment rates permit the number of unemployed persons to increase with an expanding labor force. However, the regional and temporal patterns of job creation are similar to those in figure 14. The Caribbean Islands (43 percent) and Mexico (29 percent) again lead the list of where most of the efforts will be needed. And, as before, the evidence suggests that the greatest efforts are needed immediately.

The picture changes abruptly if one is prepared to wait until unemployment rates reach 150 percent of their 1980 levels before undertaking new employment-generating activities. In this case, as shown in figure 16, the number of additional new jobs needed between 1980 and 2010 falls to 3.6 million, and nearly 90 percent of them can be postponed until after 1990. Under this policy threshold, no additional job creation efforts will be needed at all in the Southern Rim, because projected labor demand under the medium growth scenario is adequate to hold unemployment rates in this region below 150 percent of their 1980 level. More than half of the new jobs (52 percent) will be needed in the Caribbean Islands, 30 percent in Mexico, and less than 20 percent will be needed in Central America.

The Cost of Extra Jobs

The final question this chapter addresses is how much it will cost to generate the jobs required by each of the three policy targets we have discussed. This is a difficult question and one that cannot be answered precisely. For one thing, there is uncertainty built into the projections of both labor demand and labor supply. Unlike labor supply, however, which can be forecast reasonably accurately, at least for the next twenty years or so, because practically all those individuals who will enter the labor force within that period are now alive, projections of labor demand are subject to much greater volatility because they depend on the performance of the economy, which is inherently more difficult to forecast.

Second, the cost of additional jobs depends on the types of jobs being created. Jobs requiring very little capital, such as some in agriculture, may be relatively inexpensive to generate (although the extra output one gets as a result of these jobs may be low if agriculture is already characterized by unemployment or underemployment). Jobs in the primary sector that have high capital/labor ratios may be extremely costly to create. The job mix—whether high skill or low skill and whether capital intensive or labor intensive—will therefore be important in determining the cost of new job

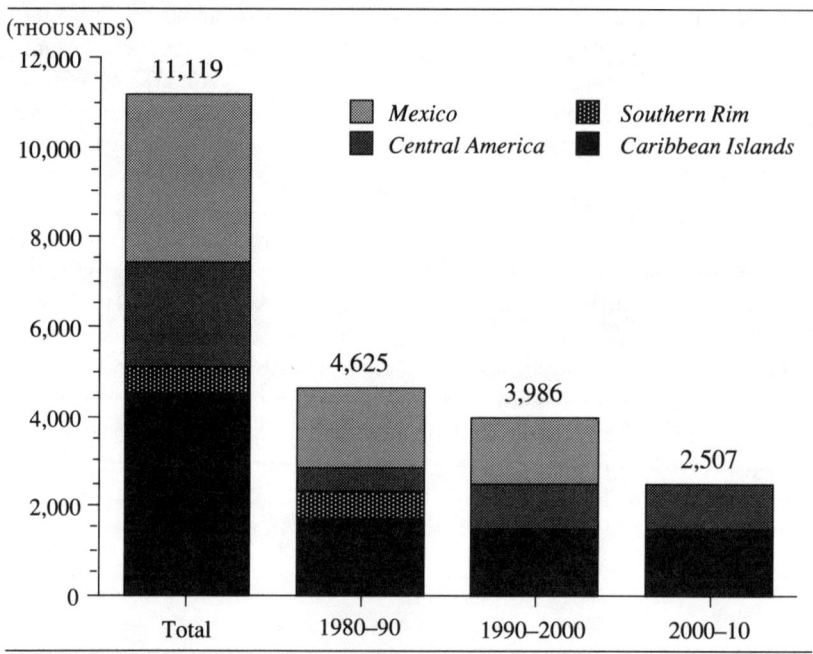

Figure 4.14 **Extra Jobs Needed: Policy Threshold, 1980 Numbers of Unemployed**

Figure 4.15 **Extra Jobs Needed: Policy Threshold, 1980 Unemployment Rates**

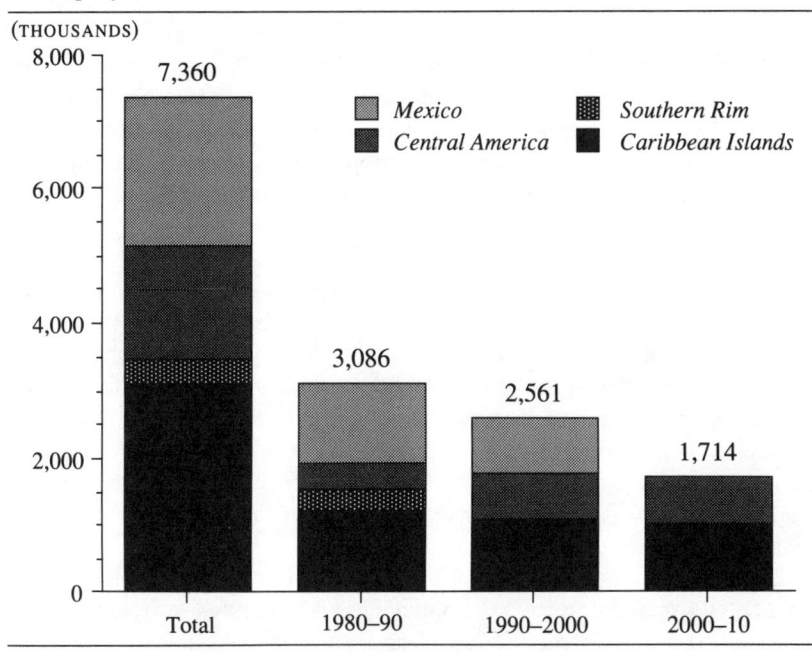

(THOUSANDS)

- Mexico
- Central America
- Southern Rim
- Caribbean Islands

Total: 7,360
1980–90: 3,086
1990–2000: 2,561
2000–10: 1,714

Figure 4.16 **Extra Jobs Needed: Policy Threshold, 150 Percent of 1980 Unemployment Rates**

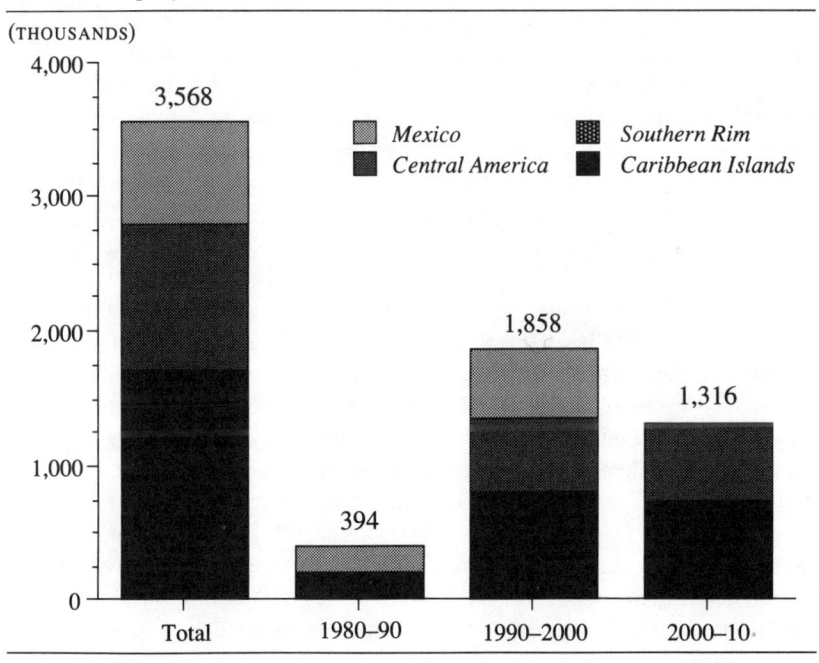

(THOUSANDS)

- Mexico
- Central America
- Southern Rim
- Caribbean Islands

Total: 3,568
1980–90: 394
1990–2000: 1,858
2000–10: 1,316

creation.[24] In addition, planners will have to decide whether new jobs should be directed to urban or rural areas, which sectors and industries are likely to benefit most from additional jobs, and whether within the Caribbean Islands, for example, it is more advantageous to concentrate new jobs in just one or two countries or to distribute them in some more uniform fashion. Each of these decisions will influence the cost of creating new jobs, but to consider the many permutations that are possible goes beyond the scope of this chapter.[25]

Finally, the cost of new job creation is likely to depend on whether one relies on the public or the private sector for the augmented activity. The ability of the indigenous private sector to generate additional jobs may already have been taken into account in the projections of labor demand. If that is the case, then new job creation may be the responsibility of the public sector. On the other hand, the role of the public sector is deliberately being scaled down under the terms of the Caribbean Basin Initiative, which suggests perhaps a greater future role for private investment from the United States and other industrial nations.

Even with these caveats, there is interest in knowing how much might have to be expended to meet the policy targets addressed in figures 14, 15, and 16. If the public sector in Caribbean Basin countries is expected to produce the extra jobs, then some estimate of the cost will be needed. Alternatively, if the industrialized nations should shoulder some of the responsibility in the form of loans, outright grants, or other forms of aid, an estimate of the size of the task again is required. The cost estimates presented here should be regarded as preliminary and only approximate; nevertheless, they serve a purpose in helping to answer a fundamental question. Even with assistance from the United States and other developed countries, can the imposing problems of job creation in the Caribbean Basin between now and the early part of the next century be surmounted?

I have approached estimating the cost of creating *one* additional job in the following way. The numbers in table 3 develop an estimate of gross domestic investment per new labor force entrant. It is an estimate based on 1982 data for most of the major countries in the Caribbean Basin area, and it shows how much investment in new plants and equipment was generated in each of these countries for each new member of the labor force. This estimate, shown in column 6, should not necessarily be interpreted as the amount these countries must invest for each new person entering the labor force. This number is, in fact, highly variable. The estimate shows instead how much each of these countries did in fact invest at one point in time. Once estimates of gross domestic investment per new labor force entrant were developed for the individual countries in table 3, an aggregate estimate was formed for each of the four major regions of the Caribbean Basin by taking a weighted average of the values of each country in the region,

Table 4.3 Gross Domestic Investment Per New Labor Force Entrant (LFE), Selected Caribbean Basin Countries, 1982

Country Group	GNP per Capita (dollars)[a] (1)	GDP (millions of dollars)[a] (2)	Investment Ratio (%) (3)	Gross Domestic Investment (billions of dollars)[a] (4)	Increase in Labor Force 1981–1982 (millions) (5)	Investment per New LFE (thousands of dollars)[a] (6)
Caribbean Islands						
Haiti	300	1,640	11	0.18	0.038	4.74
Dominican Republic	1,330	7,230	21	1.52	0.057	26.67
Jamaica	1,330	3,180	20	0.64	0.021	30.48
Trinidad & Tobago[b]	6,840	6,970	34	2.37	0.010	237.00
Southern Rim						
Colombia	1,460	34,970	26	9.09	0.322	28.23
Venezuela[b]	4,140	69,490	26	18.07	0.163	110.86
Central America						
Honduras	660	2,520	16	0.40	0.037	10.81
El Salvador	700	3,680	11	0.40	0.053	7.55
Nicaragua	920	2,940	19	0.56	0.029	19.31
Guatemala	1,130	8,730	14	1.22	0.065	18.77
Costa Rica	1,430	2,580	23	0.59	0.026	22.69
Panama	2,120	4,190	29	1.22	0.019	64.21
Mexico	2,270	171,270	21	35.97	0.739	48.67

SOURCES: International Labour Office (1977); World Bank (1984).

[a] 1982 U.S. dollars.

[b] The economies of Trinidad and Tobago and of Venezuela are dominated by oil exports, which help to explain their relatively high per capita incomes and possibly their high levels of new investment per labor market entrant.

using the estimated 1982 populations for each country as weights. These procedures produced the following estimates: $35,500 of investment for each new member of the labor force in the Caribbean Islands, $59,000 in the Southern Rim, $19,000 in Central America, and $48,700 in Mexico.

These estimates of investment expenditure for each new job added to the labor force were then multiplied by the numbers in figures 14, 15, and 16 to derive an estimate of the total cost of creating all the additional jobs required between 1980 and 2010 to meet each of the policy thresholds. Figure 17 indicates that approximately $413 billion of additional investment expenditure will be required to prevent the volume of unemployment from exceeding the number of unemployed persons in 1980. Most of this investment will have to be directed toward Mexico (40 percent) and the Caribbean Islands (38 percent). Smaller amounts will be needed in the Southern Rim and in Central America, either because fewer jobs are needed (as in the Southern Rim) or because the investment cost per job is low (as in Central America). Figure 17 also suggests the need for immediate action. Of the total investment expenditure that is projected over the thirty-year period, nearly half (47 percent) is expected to come due before 1990.

To prevent unemployment rates from exceeding their 1980 levels would take a prospective amount of investment expenditure of almost $267 billion

Figure 4.17 **Estimated Cost of Creating the Extra Jobs in Figure 14**

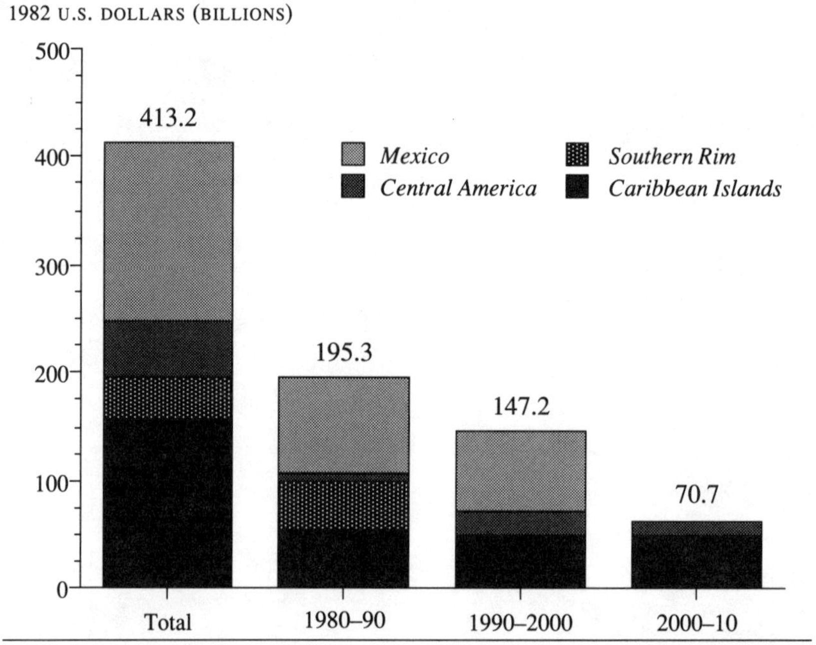

1982 U.S. DOLLARS (BILLIONS)

Figure 4.18 **Estimated Cost of Creating the Extra Jobs in Figure 15**

1982 U.S. DOLLARS (BILLIONS)

- Mexico
- Central America
- Southern Rim
- Caribbean Islands

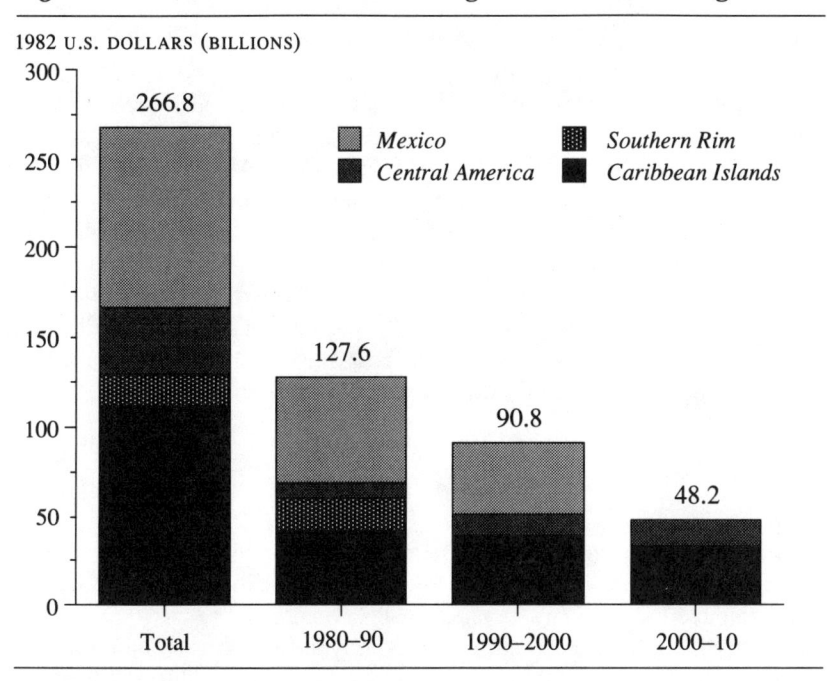

Period	Total
Total	266.8
1980–90	127.6
1990–2000	90.8
2000–10	48.2

Figure 4.19 **Estimated Cost of Creating the Extra Jobs in Figure 16**

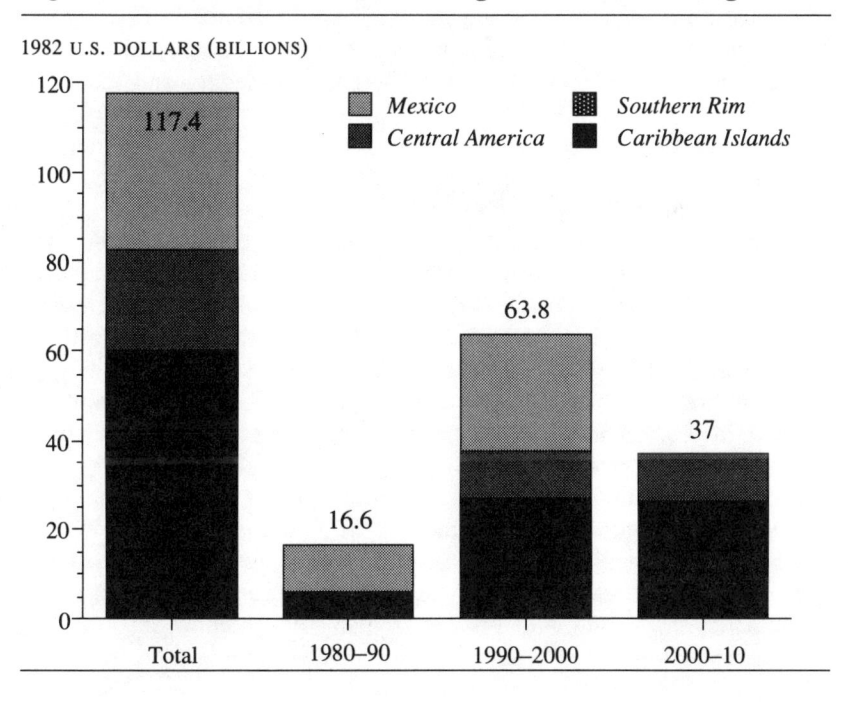

1982 U.S. DOLLARS (BILLIONS)

- Mexico
- Central America
- Southern Rim
- Caribbean Islands

Period	Total
Total	117.4
1980–90	16.6
1990–2000	63.8
2000–10	37

between 1980 and 2010 (figure 18). Most of this would have to be invested in the Caribbean Islands (42 percent) and in Mexico (39 percent), and nearly half of the total needs to be provided before 1990. The least expensive policy alternative is the one that allows unemployment rates to drift upward to 150 percent of their 1980 levels before corrective action is taken (figure 19). The total estimated cost of this policy response is $117 billion. This alternative also buys time in the sense that just 14 percent of the total cost accrues during the 1980s. More than half (54 percent) comes due during the 1990s, and almost one-third (31 percent) occurs during the first decade of the twenty-first century. The cost of delay, however, is reflected in both higher numbers and rates of unemployed persons.

Conclusions

Long-term solutions to the problem of rising joblessness in the Caribbean Basin must inevitably focus on continued fertility reduction and on accelerated efforts toward economic development. The next twenty or twenty-five years are especially critical. Beyond this time frame, rates of growth of the economically active population are projected to fall below 2 percent per annum—down considerably from their peak of 3.4 percent per annum during the 1970s. Because fertility rates in Caribbean Basin countries have been declining and are projected by the United Nations to fall further, this chapter has focused instead on the need for additional job creation to correct growing imbalances between labor supply and labor demand.

Several conclusions are worth emphasizing. First, there is an emerging awareness of the interdependence between the United States and countries below our southern border. Increasingly, what happens in Mexico, Central America, and the rest of Latin America is acknowledged to have economic, social, and political consequences for the United States. International economic relations that were once limited largely to flows of goods and services now involve significant international labor migration flows as well. As a consequence, the self-interest of the United States lies in accepting more responsibility for economic development in the Caribbean Basin. Solutions to rising joblessness in the region ought ultimately to be based on a North-South cooperative effort.

Second, according to the estimates discussed in this chapter, most of the new jobs that will be required and most of the investment expenditures that will be needed to achieve the alternative policy targets I have outlined will have to be concentrated in Mexico and in the Caribbean Islands. Regardless of the policy threshold that is invoked, roughly 70 percent of the new jobs and approximately 80 percent of the new investment expenditure will be needed in these two regions combined. Moreover, of the four major regions in the Caribbean Basin, these are the two that are closest to the United States. Thus it is perhaps not a coincidence that, as I have already noted, Mexico and the Caribbean Islands lead the Caribbean Basin nations in terms of the number of both legal and undocumented immigrants coming to the United States.

Third, there is a special urgency to the task. With the exception of the policy threshold that allows unemployment rates to increase to 150 percent of their 1980 levels, between 40 and 50 percent of both the new jobs needed and the new investment expenditure required between 1980 and 2010 must be concentrated during the decade of the 1980s.

Fourth, as noted previously, the world labor situation since 1980 has been marked by growing impoverishment of Third World populations, persistently high unemployment in many industrial democracies, and failing work incomes in most parts of the world (International Labour Office 1987). The date in table 2 that show growth rates in real GDP for selected Caribbean Basin countries suggest that the Caribbean Basin has not escaped these worldwide trends and may have fared even worse. In light of these developments, it is unlikely that a turnaround in labor demand can occur quickly enough to keep job creation efforts on track by 1990. This implies that there will be much catching up to do after 1990 and that the temporal arrangement of job-scheduling activities will need to be accelerated beyond the levels indicated by figures 14 and 15 to achieve the implied policy targets by the year 2010.

Fifth, it appears likely that the Caribbean Basin Initiative—as it is now construed—is substantially limited in its ability to meet the job requirements that lie ahead. My estimates of the thirty-year costs of the three policy targets range from $117 billion to $413 billion. On an average annual basis the range is between $4 billion and $14 billion (in 1982 U.S. dollars). In 1984 the Reagan administration spent $881 million in aid to the Caribbean, more than double the 1980 amount of $336 million (*Wall Street Journal*, 1984). But even this higher amount falls substantially short of what is required. And the fact that more than half of the 1984 total went to Central American countries, whereas the greatest need for new jobs is in Mexico (which is excluded from the CBI) and the Caribbean Islands, further suggests that the CBI by itself will prove insufficient to meet the job creation requirements of the region. The conclusion that expanded efforts are called for is valid, even if my cost estimates are off by 100 percent.

Sixth, not all of the growing labor underutilization that I project may show up as higher open unemployment. If wage rates are flexible in a downward direction, then labor surpluses should exert downward pressure on wages, thereby helping to eliminate the surplus. It may be, as Preston (1986) has reasoned, that "wages rather than unemployment statistics are where we would expect the consequences of population growth to appear [because] the poor can't afford to be unemployed" (p. 80). But lower wages for workers are equally likely to increase the stimulus for out-migration to destinations where economic opportunities appear brighter.[26]

What are the probable consequences for the Caribbean Basin and for the United States if these extra efforts toward job creation are not undertaken? The most immediate (and most likely) is that pressures resulting from unemployment and underemployment will intensify during the next five to ten years. Among other things, the failure to take fuller advantage of existing human resources will mean a drag on potential economic growth rates in the region. Second, social and political unrest is likely to accelerate as heightened aspirations for a better way of life come into conflict with the economic reality of limited avenues for productive employment. Third, push factors related to undocumented migration from the Caribbean Basin to the United States are likely to strengthen. Moreover, due to projected substantial shortfalls in the United States in the supply of unskilled entry-level workers in many industrial categories beginning in the 1990s (Wachter 1980), periods of peak pressure to emigrate in the Caribbean will coincide with the peak pressure to recruit foreign workers in the United States.

Following the enactment of IRCA, the number of border apprehensions by the U.S. Border Patrol dropped sharply. During most of 1986, monthly apprehensions averaged about 150,000, having risen in the first half of the year and then tapered off during the second half. But in November they dropped to 80,000 and they fell again to less than 60,000 during December.[27] Instead of remaining low, however, the monthly apprehension figures have followed roughly the same seasonal pattern since the beginning of 1987 that they exhibited in 1985 and 1986. Thus, the decline in apprehensions toward the end of 1986 may more accurately reflect a seasonal decline in the demand for farmworkers in California and in other major agricultural states than it does the impact of IRCA itself.[28] Unless greater efforts are made to deal with the expanding incentives originating in the Caribbean Basin for undocumented migration to the United States, one cannot be overly optimistic that reliance on employer sanctions and stepped-up enforcement activities along the U.S.–Mexico border—the main tools in IRCA for controlling the flow of undocumented workers to this country—will have their intended effect.

LABOR SUPPLY AND DEMAND IN THE CARIBBEAN BASIN   *147*

Appendix

Table 4A.1 **Labor Supply in the Caribbean Basin (thousands)**

Year	Total	Caribbean Islands	Southern Rim	Central America	Mexico
1950	24,582	6,779	5,848	3,145	8,810
1960	29,892	7,542	7,335	3,959	11,056
1970	37,947	8,597	9,602	5,259	14,489
1980	53,408	10,890	13,333	6,937	22,248
1985	61,993	12,287	15,520	8,106	26,080
1990	71,592	13,813	17,772	9,520	30,487
2000	93,134	16,732	22,771	13,189	40,442
2010	116,968	19,817	28,264	17,873	51,014
2020	139,680	22,709	33,037	23,576	60,358

Table 4A.2 **Regional Shares of Caribbean Basin Labor Force (%)**

Year	Total	Caribbean Islands	Southern Rim	Central American	Mexico
1950	100.0	27.6	23.8	12.8	35.8
1960	100.0	25.2	24.5	13.2	37.0
1970	100.0	22.7	25.3	13.9	38.2
1980	100.0	20.4	25.0	13.0	41.7
1985	100.0	19.8	25.0	13.1	42.1
1990	100.0	19.3	24.8	13.3	42.6
2000	100.0	18.0	24.4	14.2	43.4
2010	100.0	16.9	24.2	15.3	43.6
2020	100.0	16.3	23.7	16.9	43.2

NOTE: Columns may not total 100 because of rounding.

Table 4A.3 **Average Annual Growth Rates of Economically Active Population (%)**

Years	Total	Caribbean Islands	Southern Rim	Central America	Mexico
1950–1960	1.96	1.07	2.27	2.30	2.27
1960–1970	2.39	1.31	2.69	2.84	2.70
1970–1980	3.42	2.36	3.28	2.77	4.29
1980–1985	2.98	2.41	3.04	3.11	3.18
1985–1990	2.88	2.34	2.71	3.22	3.12
1990–2000	2.63	1.92	2.48	3.26	2.83
2000–2010	2.28	1.69	2.16	3.04	2.32
2010–2020	1.77	1.36	1.56	2.77	1.68

Table 4A.4 **Projected Labor Demand, Low Growth (thousands)**

Year	Total	Caribbean Islands	Southern Rim	Central America	Mexico
1980	48,714	9,311	12,266	6,424	20,713
1985	53,973	9,823	13,740	7,207	23,203
1990	59,831	10,363	15,392	8,085	25,991
1995	66,360	10,932	17,242	9,071	29,115
2000	73,638	11,533	19,314	10,176	32,615
2005	81,753	12,167	21,635	11,416	36,535
2010	90,805	12,835	24,236	12,808	40,926

Table 4A.5 **Projected Labor Demand, Medium Growth (thousands)**

Year	Total	Caribbean Islands	Southern Rim	Central America	Mexico
1980	48,714	9,311	12,266	6,424	20,713
1985	55,058	9,941	14,032	7,378	23,707
1990	62,273	10,614	16,052	8,474	27,133
1995	70,484	11,333	18,363	9,733	31,055
2000	79,829	12,100	21,006	11,179	35,544
2005	90,471	12,919	24,031	12,840	40,681
2010	102,591	13,793	27,490	14,747	46,561

Table 4A.6 **Projected Labor Demand, High Growth (thousands)**

Year	Total	Caribbean Islands	Southern Rim	Central America	Mexico
1980	48,714	9,311	12,266	6,424	20,713
1985	58,001	10,477	14,452	7,404	25,668
1990	69,160	11,789	17,028	8,534	31,809
1995	82,584	13,266	20,062	9,836	39,420
2000	98,751	14,927	23,637	11,337	48,850
2005	118,250	16,797	27,850	13,066	60,537
2010	141,795	18,901	32,813	15,060	75,021

Table 4A.7 **Projected Unemployment Rates, Low Growth (%)**

Year	Total	Caribbean Islands	Southern Rim	Central America	Mexico
1980	8.8	14.5	8.0	7.4	6.9
1985	12.9	20.1	11.5	11.1	11.0
1990	16.4	25.0	13.4	15.1	14.7
2000	20.9	31.1	15.2	22.8	19.4
2010	22.4	35.2	14.3	28.3	19.8

Table 4A.8 **Projected Unemployment Rates, Medium Growth (%)**

Year	Total	Caribbean Islands	Southern Rim	Central America	Mexico
1980	8.8	14.5	8.0	7.4	6.9
1985	11.2	19.1	9.6	9.0	9.1
1990	13.0	23.2	9.7	11.0	11.0
2000	14.3	27.7	7.7	15.2	12.1
2010	12.3	30.4	2.7	17.5	8.7

Table 4A.9 **Projected Unemployment Rates, High Growth (%)**

Year	Total	Caribbean Islands	Southern Rim	Central America	Mexico
1980	8.8	14.5	8.0	7.4	6.9
1985	6.4	14.7	6.9	8.7	1.6
1990	3.4	14.7	4.2	10.4	-4.3
2000	-6.0	10.8	-3.8	14.0	-20.8
2010	-21.2	4.6	-16.1	15.7	-47.1

Table 4A.10 **Projected Labor Surplus, Low Growth (thousands)**

Year	Total	Caribbean Islands	Southern Rim	Central America	Mexico
1980	4,694	1,579	1,067	513	1,535
1985	8,020	2,464	1,780	899	2,877
1990	11,761	3,450	2,380	1,435	4,496
2000	19,496	5,199	3,457	3,013	7,827
2010	26,163	6,982	4,028	5,065	10,088

Table 4A.11 **Projected Labor Surplus, Medium Growth (thousands)**

Year	Total	Caribbean Islands	Southern Rim	Central America	Mexico
1980	4,694	1,579	1,067	513	1,535
1985	6,935	2,346	1,488	728	2,373
1990	9,319	3,199	1,720	1,046	3,354
2000	13,305	4,632	1,765	2,010	4,898
2010	14,377	6,024	774	3,126	4,453

Table 4A.12 **Projected Labor Surplus, High Growth (thousands)**

Year	Total	Caribbean Islands	Southern Rim	Central America	Mexico
1980	4,694	1,579	1,067	513	1,535
1985	3,992	1,810	1,068	702	412
1990	2,432	2,024	744	986	-1,322
2000	-5,617	1,805	-866	1,852	-8,408
2010	-24,827	916	-4549	2813	-24,007

Table 4A.13 **Projected Number of Additional Jobs Needed to Prevent Volume of Unemployment from Rising above 1980 Levels in Any of the Four Regions, Medium Growth (thousands)**

Year	Total	Caribbean Islands	Southern Rim	Central America	Mexico
1980–1990	4,624	1,620	653	533	1,818
80–85	2,241	767	421	215	838
85–90	2,383	853	232	318	980
1990–2000	3,986	1,433	44	964	1,545
2000–2010	2,507	1,391	0	1,116	0
Total	11,117	4,444	697	2,613	3,363

Table 4A.14 **Estimated Cost of Creating Extra Jobs in Table A.13, Medium Growth (billions of 1982 U.S. dollars)**

Year	Total	Caribbean Islands	Southern Rim	Central America	Mexico
1980–1990	195.3	57.5	39.1	10.2	88.5
80–85	97.3	27.2	25.2	4.1	40.8
85–90	98.0	30.3	13.9	6.1	47.7
1990–2000	147.2	50.9	2.7	18.4	75.2
2000–2010	70.7	49.4	0.0	21.3	0.0
Total	413.2	157.8	41.8	49.9	163.7

Table 4A.15 **Projected Number of Additional Jobs Needed to Prevent Unemployment Rates from Rising above 1980 Levels in Any of the Four Regions, Medium Growth (thousands)**

Year	Total	Caribbean Islands	Southern Rim	Central America	Mexico
1980–1990	3,085	1,196	298	341	1,250
80–85	1,512	564	246	128	574
85–90	1,573	632	52	213	676
1990–2000	2,561	1,010	0	693	858
2000–2010	1,714	944	0	770	0
Total	7,360	3,150	298	1,804	2,108

Table 4A.16 **Estimated Cost of Creating Extra Jobs in Table A.15, Medium Growth (billions of 1982 U.S. dollars)**

Year	Total	Caribbean Islands	Southern Rim	Central America	Mexico
1980–1990	127.6	42.4	17.8	6.5	60.8
80–85	65.1	20.0	14.7	2.4	27.9
85–90	62.5	22.4	3.1	4.1	32.9
1990–2000	90.9	35.9	0.0	13.2	41.7
2000–2010	48.2	33.5	0.0	14.7	0.0
Total	266.7	111.8	17.8	34.4	102.5

Table 4A.17 **Projected Number of Additional Jobs Needed to Prevent Unemployment Rates from Exceeding 150 Percent of 1980 Levels in Any of the Four Regions, Medium Growth (thousands)**

Year	Total	Caribbean Islands	Southern Rim	Central America	Mexico
1980–1990	393	195	0	0	199
80–85	0	0	0	0	0
85–90	393	195	0	0	199
1990–2000	1,858	798	0	546	514
2000–2010	1,316	720	0	596	0
Total	3,567	1,713	0	1,142	713

Table 4A.18 **Estimated Cost of Creating Extra Jobs in Table A.17, Medium Growth (billions of 1982 U.S. dollars)**

Year	Total	Caribbean Islands	Southern Rim	Central America	Mexico
1980–1990	16.6	6.9	0.0	0.0	9.7
80–85	0.0	0.0	0.0	0.0	0.0
85–90	16.6	6.9	0.0	0.0	9.7
1990–2000	63.8	28.4	0.0	10.4	25.0
2000–2010	37.0	25.6	0.0	11.4	0.0
Total	117.4	60.9	0.0	21.8	34.7

Notes

1. For the purposes of this chapter, the Caribbean Basin is divided into four regions: countries in the Caribbean Islands, the northern tier of South America (Columbia, Venezuela, Guyana, and Suriname), Central America, and Mexico (see fig. 1). Patterson (1987) calls this the circum-Caribbean area.

2. The strategic implications for the United States of rapid population growth in the Caribbean and in Middle and South America have been examined in the collection edited by Saunders (1986). See Bach (1985) for a review of demographic linkages between the United States and this region. Patterson (1987) points out that these linkages have deep historical roots, dating back to well before the Spanish-American War, and involve complex flows of people and ideas.

3. The U.S.Immigration and Naturalization Service is also being provided with additional funding to augment its enforcement activities along the U.S.–Mexico border.

4. Wachter (1980) developed a labor supply forecast for the U.S. 1980s labor market, focusing on the effects of recent low fertility, and then compared that forecast with a Bureau of Labor Statistics projection of employment demand for the current decade. Wachter predicted a relative shortage of unskilled workers in the 1980s and suggested that increasing the flow of immigrants would help to relieve some of the bottlenecks.

5. Interrelations among population growth, labor supply, and economic policies for Mexico between 1940 and 1980 have been studied by Alba (1987). He also considers the prospects for generating an economic trajectory consistent with future employment needs in the country.

6. Regarding the determinants of labor force growth in Latin America, Gendell (1986) finds that population growth has been and is anticipated to continue to be much more important that changes in labor force participation rates. Indeed, he concludes that population growth is virtually the sole determinant.

7. A general discussion of trends in births and deaths in Latin America is contained in Merrick et al. (1986).

8. A discussion of the factors influencing rates of urban growth in Latin America, projections of future rates of growth in urban and rural areas, and suggested policy responses to the pressures of urban concentration is contained in Fox (1985) and Jordon (1986).

9. Mexico's experience illustrates both the independent effects of changes in labor force participation rates and the delayed impact of altered birth cohort sizes on labor force growth. Mexico's overall rate of population growth reached a post-World War II peak of 3.2 percent per annum during the 1960s. Owing in large part to the government's vigorous sponsorship of a national family-planning program in the 1970s, Mexico's total fertility rate fell from 6.7 in 1970, to 4.1 in 1980 (Alba and Potter 1986; Stycos 1986). This decline had the effect of lowering the overall rate of population growth during the 1970s to 3.05 percent per year. By 1984 the annual growth rate had dropped to 2.2 percent (Alba and Potter 1986). Nevertheless, the

rate of growth of population in the labor force ages (15–64) moved ahead—from an average annual rate of 3.0 percent during the 1960s to 3.4 percent in the 1970s—primarily because the larger youth cohorts, produced by an accelerating population growth rate during the 1950s and early 1960s, were now entering the labor force. In this connection, Alba (1987) argues that the early success of Mexico's economic policies in absorbing the labor supply was undermined once the delayed impact of the rapid population growth was more fully felt on the labor markets and some of the easy labor absorption potential of the import-substitution strategy began to be exhausted. Compounding the growth of population in the labor force ages was a sharp increase in labor force participation rates. In the age range from 25 to 49, these rates (expressed as a percentage) increased from roughly the mid-fifties in 1970 to the low to mid sixties by 1980, boosting the average annual rate of growth of Mexico's labor force from 2.7 percent during the 1960s to 4.3 percent in the 1970s (International Labour Office 1986).

10. Throughout this chapter much of the text's main story is illustrated graphically. Detailed appendix tables are included for readers interested in the specific numbers.

11. Bloom and Freeman (1986) demonstrate that, despite unprecedented rates of population growth, developing countries were generally able to "absorb" the new labor supply at increased levels of productivity and with a shift toward more productive employment in the period between 1960 and 1980. Looking to the future, they stress that "the economies of the less developed countries are about to face perhaps the greatest challenge in their histories: generating a sufficient number of jobs at reasonable wages to 'absorb' their rapidly growing populations into productive employment" (p. 381).

12. By ILO criteria, persons who are underemployed are more likely to be included with the employed than with the unemployed (International Labour Office 1983, chaps. 2 and 3). Underemployment in Latin America is widespread and frequently concentrated in the informal sectors of low-income economies (Merrick et al. 1986). As a result, rates of labor underutilization are not fully captured by rates of open unemployment. Gendell (1986), in fact, argues that for Latin America "*under*employment is a more important form of labor underutilization than *open* unemployment" (p. 61). He reports that 42 percent of the labor force was in sectors of low labor utilization in 1980. My subsequent projections of unemployment rates exclude a measure of underemployment or "equivalent unemployment." Gregory (1986) presents a discussion of the difficulties of developing a meaningful measure of underemployment that is not subject to factors unrelated to labor market conditions. Furthermore, regarding Mexico, Gregory notes that "the large measure of underemployment will not represent an accurate measure of the idle labor resources available for immediate employment in newly created vacancies" (p. 275). To the extent that low wages rather than joblessness per se constitute the driving force behind undocumented immigration to the United States, focusing on the potential for rising unemployment in the Caribbean Basin can possibly result in understating the power of push factors motivating migration out of the region.

13. Baseline total labor demand in each region in 1980 was as follows: 98.3 million in the Caribbean Islands, 12.3 million in the Southern Rim, 6.4 million in Central

America, and 20.7 million in Mexico. Additional detail is included in the appendix.

14. It simplifies the analysis to assume that trends in labor demand are independent of changes in labor supply. A more complicated model would recognize that population growth and economic growth are dynamically related.

15. In related work, Bradshaw and Frisbie (1983) estimate the potential demand for and supply of Mexican male labor by using the labor force replacement ratio—the ratio between the number of men who would reach working age during a decade and the projected number of deaths and retirements during a decade among men in the working ages at the beginning of the decade. Numbers above replacement indicate the approximate number of men for whom jobs must be created. Based on historical trends of economic growth in Mexico, the authors doubt whether new employment can be expanded by the 200 percent necessary to accommodate the influx to the labor market by 2000.

16. As noted earlier, labor underutilization in the form of disguised unemployment or underemployment can still be a problem, even if rates of open unemployment are low. As Gendell (1986) has noted, Latin American adult men who are heads of households cannot afford to be without any income for more than a brief period.

17. The negative unemployment rates in the high growth scenario do not appear reasonable, and not just for the reason that the assumptions underlying the high growth case seem unduly optimistic in general, as I have already noted. The growth rates in table 1 that are used to project labor demand in the high growth scenario for the Southern Rim (3.28 percent) and for Mexico (4.29 percent) are the highest in the table and the only two that exceed 2.9 percent. Moreover, these unusually high growth rates were caused primarily by large gains during the 1970s in female labor force participation rates—gains that are not likely to be repeated. For example, between 1970 and 1980 the female labor force in Mexico grew at an average annual rate of 8.8 percent. The comparable figure for Venezuela was 7.2 percent (International Labour Organization 1986). The declines in unemployment rates observed for the Southern Rim and Mexico in the medium growth scenario occur because by the year 2010 rates of labor force growth will have slowed sufficiently to be below projected rates of labor demand. In Mexico, for example, the labor force is projected to grow at an annual rate of 2.35 percent between 2000 and 2010, whereas labor demand is assumed to grow by 2.70 percent annually (International Labour Office 1986).

18. Massey and García España (1987) show that much of the migration from Mexico during the 1970s was facilitated by the social process of network growth, that is, by the expanding web of social ties that link potential migrants in sending countries to people in receiving societies.

19. Cooper (1985) found that for Jamaica the immigration policies of receiving countries are more influential in shaping the volume and composition of the migrant population than is the policy orientation of the domestic administration.

20. It is important to add that, unlike the majority of undocumented workers from Mexico and Central America, many of the illegal migrants from the Caribbean Islands arrive in the United States legally and subsequently overstay their visas (Pastor 1985).

21. Despite the plausibility of this proposal, however, a National Academy of Sciences study of the relationships between population growth and economic development concludes that "a reduced rate of urban labor force growth in developing countries . . . is not likely to be systematically accompanied by corresponding reductions in joblessness" (National Research Council 1986:87). And Preston (1986) has observed that "rates of labor force growth across countries and over time are not found to be statistically related to unemployment levels. The low-wage informal sector in developing countries evidently has substantial capacity to 'absorb' labor" (p. 80). Bloom and Freeman (1986) conclude that "population and labor force growth are not necessarily strongly related to labor absorption" (p. 382). If anything, the empirical evidence supports what they call "population neutralism."

22. The Caribbean Basin Initiative does not extend to Mexico, but Mexico has substantially benefited from the Generalized System of Preferences (GSP)—a tariff program antedating the CBI but not focused on a particular region. The GSP includes about 120 countries—primarily non-Communist developing countries.

23. This argument is substantiated by Massey et al. (1987). In a personal communication, Douglas Massey notes that this argument is important because many people, including a congressman he has spoken with, believe that simply sending tractors down to "improve" Mexican agriculture will stop migration, when precisely the opposite will most likely happen, because mechanization will disrupt the traditional social organization of agricultural production and displace many workers.

24. On a related point, Murray Gendell has suggested to me that if it is reasonable to assume that productivity and the investment cost per job are positively related, then raising productivity also raises the cost of job creation. As he notes elsewhere (Gendell 1986), this indicates that the goals of increasing employment and raising levels of living (via wage-enhancing productivity gains) are difficult to reconcile.

25. Other considerations can help to narrow the range of alternatives. The available skills possessed by the indigenous labor force, for example, will influence the types of jobs one aims to create. As a consequence, economic policy and educational policy ought to be closely coordinated in planning for the economic futures of Caribbean Basin nations. Such coordination appears to be badly needed. According to a new study, *Employment and Youth in Latin America*, carried out by PREALC, young people in Latin America are finding that their education is not in line with the real needs of the labor market. The economic crisis together with structural changes in production have limited many young job seekers to the informal and agricultural sectors. Jobs in the formal sector have diminished, and the percentage of young people who have found their way into it has tended to be lower than that of the older work force (International Labour Office 1987). With government efforts to spread literacy in the region, particularly in urban areas, and with the school system encompassing every-growing numbers of young people, the percentage entering the work force before the age of twenty is much lower than it was in 1950 (International Labour Office 1987). The rise in secondary education enrollments is reflected in declining labor force participation rates for persons under age twenty. In Mexico, for example, participation rates for persons ten to fourteen years old fell

from 16.20 in 1950, to 6.55 in 1980. In the ILO labor force projections, these rates are expected to fall further, to 0.10 by 2025. In the fifteen to nineteen age range, participation rates declined from 48.10 in 1950 to 41.60 in 1980, and are projected to reach 30.70 by 2025 (International Labour Office 1986). Similar trends are evident for the other regions in the Caribbean Basin. Because those persons aged fifteen to twenty-four represent a third of the economically active population throughout all of Latin America, the opening of educational doors has been a major factor in reducing the rate of labor force growth. It is doubtful, however, that expanding enrollments will eventually tie people to their domestic labor market if the kind of education they are receiving fails to match the needs of the domestic economy.

26. Both higher unemployment and lower wages in the Caribbean Basin are likely to lead to greater migration to the United States. But as David Bloom, in a personal communication, points out, "the migratory response may differ considerably depending on whether the price or the quantity side of the market takes the brunt of the shock. Thus, labor market institutions will be an important element conditioning future developments."

27. These data were supplied in a personal communication by Michael Hoefer, Statistical Analysis Branch, U.S. Immigration and Naturalization Service.

28. Seasonal fluctuations in the number of undocumented farmworkers in California agriculture are discussed in Espenshade and Taylor (1988) and Taylor and Espenshade (forthcoming).

References

Alba, Francisco. 1987. "Forty Years of Population Growth and Labor Absorption in Mexico: 1940–1980." Paper presented at the Annual Meetings of the Population Association of America, Chicago.

Alba, Francisco, and Joseph E. Potter. 1986. "Population and Development in Mexico since 1940: An Interpretation." *Population and Development Review* 12, no. 1 (March):47–75.

Bach, Robert L. 1985. *Western Hemispheric Immigration to the United States: A Review of Selected Research Trends. Occasional Paper Series,* Hemispheric Migration Project, Center for Immigration Policy and Refugee Assistance, Georgetown University, Washington, D.C.

Bloom, David E., and Richard B. Freeman. 1986. "The Effects of Rapid Population Growth on Labor Supply and Employment in Developing Countries." *Population and Development Review* 12, no. 3 (September):381-414.

Bouvier, Leon F., and David Simcox. 1986. *Many Hands, Few Jobs: Population, Unemployment and Emigration in Mexico and the Caribbean.* CIS Paper 2, Washington, D.C.: Center for Immigration Studies.

Bradshaw, Benjamin. S., and W. Parker Frisbie. 1983. "Potential Labor Force Supply and Replacement in Mexico and the States of the Mexico Cession and Texas:

1980-2000." *International Migration Review* 17, no. 3 (Fall):394-409.

Cooper, Dereck W. 1985. "Migration from Jamaica in the 1970s: Political Protest or Economic Pull?" *International Migration Review* 19, no. 4 (Winter):728-745.

Espenshade, Thomas J., and J. Edward Taylor. 1988. "Undocumented and Seasonal Workers in the California Farm Workforce." In Barbara D. Dennis, ed., *Industrial Relations Research Association Series*, Proceedings of the 40th Annual Meeting (December 28-30, 1987), pp. 182-191.

Fox, Robert. 1985. Urban Growth in Latin America." *Populi* 12, no. 3:4-13.

Gendell, Murray. 1986. "Population Growth and Labor Absorption in Latin America, 1970-2000." In John Saunders, ed., *Population Growth in Latin America and U. S. National Security*. Boston: Allen & Unwin, pp. 49-78.

Gregory, Peter. 1986. *The Myth of Market Failure: Employment and the Labor Market in Mexico*. Baltimore, Md.: The Johns Hopkins University Press.

Immigration and Naturalization Service. 1986. *1985 Statistical Yearbook of the Immigration and Naturalization Service*. Washington, D.C.: U.S. Department of Justice.

International Labour Office. 1977. *Labour Force Estimates and Projections: 1950-2000*. 2d ed. Geneva.

———. 1983. *1983 Yearbook of Labour Statistics*. 43d ed. Geneva.

———. 1986. *Economically Active Population, 1950-2025. Estimates: 1950-1980, Projections: 1985-2025*. Latin America, vol. III. 3d ed. Geneva.

———. 1987. *ILO Information* 15, no. 4 (October).

International Monetary Fund. 1987. *International Financial Statistics Yearbook*, vol. 40. Washington, D.C.

Jordan, Ricardo S. 1986. "Urban Concentration in Latin America." *Populi* 13, no. 1:26-31.

The Kissinger Commission on Population and Development in Central America. 1984. *Population and Development Review* 10, no. 2 (June):381-389.

Massey, Douglas S., et al. 1987. *Return to Aztlan: The Social Process of International Migration*. Berkeley & Los Angeles: University of California Press.

Massey, Douglas S., and Felipe García España. 1987. "The Social Process of International Migration." *Science* 237 (August 14):733-738.

Merrick, Thomas W., et al. 1986. "Population Pressures in Latin America." *Population Bulletin* 41, no. 3.

National Research Council. 1986. *Population Growth and Economic Development: Policy Questions*. Washington, D.C.: National Academy Press.

Panel on Immigration Statistics. 1985. *Immigration Statistics: A Story of Neglect*. Washington, D.C.: National Academy Press.

Passel, Jeffrey S., and Karen A. Woodrow. 1984. "Geographic Distribution of Undocumented Immigrants: Estimates of Undocumented Aliens Counted in the 1980 Census by State." *International Migration Review* 18, no. 3 (Fall):642-671.

———. 1986. "Change in the Undocumented Alien Population in the United States, 1979–1983." Revision of a paper presented at the Annual Meetings of the Population Association of America, Boston.

Pastor, Robert A. 1985. "The Policy Challenge." In Robert A. Pastor, ed., *Migration and Development in the Caribbean: The Unexplored Connection*. Boulder, Colo.: Westview Press, pp. 1–39.

Pastor, Robert A., and Rosemarie Rogers. 1985. "Using Migration to Enhance Economic Development in the Caribbean: Three Sets of Proposals." In Robert A. Pastor, ed., *Migration and Development in the Caribbean: The Unexplored Connection*. Boulder, Colo.: Westview Press, pp. 321–347.

Patterson, Orlando. 1987. "The Emerging West Atlantic System: Migration, Culture, and Underdevelopment in the United States and the Circum-Caribbean Region." In William Alonso, ed., *Population in an Interacting World*. Cambridge: Harvard University Press, pp. 227–260.

Pelzman, Joseph, and Gregory K. Schoepfle. 1988. "The Impact of the Caribbean Basin Economic Recovery Act on Caribbean Nations' Exports and Development." *Economic Development and Cultural Change* 36, no. 4:753–796.

Portes, Alejandro. 1982. "International Labor Migration and National Development." In Mary M. Kritz, ed., *U.S. Immigration and Refugee Policy: Global and Domestic Issues*. Lexington, Mass.: Lexington Books, pp. 71–91.

Preston, Samuel H. 1986. "Are the Economic Consequences of Population Growth a Sound Basis for Population Policy?" In Jane Menken, ed., World *Population and U.S. Policy: The Choices Ahead*. New York: W.W. Norton, pp. 67–95.

Programa Regional de Empleo en América Latina y el Caribe (PREALC). 1976. *The Employment Problem in Latin America: Facts, Outlook and Policies*. Santiago: International Labour Office, Regional Employment Program for Latin America and the Caribbean.

Ricketts, Erol. 1985. "The Relationship between U.S. Investment and Immigration from the Caribbean: Prospects for the Reagan Administration's Caribbean Basin Initiative." City University of New York Graduate School and University Center.

Saunders, John, ed. 1986. *Population Growth in Latin America and U.S. National Security*. Boston: Allen and Unwin.

Stycos, J. Mayone. 1986. "Medium-Range Prospects for Fertility Reduction in Latin America."In John Saunders, ed., *Population Growth in Latin America and U.S. National Security*. Boston: Allen and Unwin, pp. 31–47.

Taylor, J. Edward, and Thomas J. Espenshade. Forthcoming. "Seasonality and the Changing Role of Undocumented Immigrants in the California Farm Labor Market." In Wayne A. Cornelius, ed., *The Changing Roles of Mexican Immigrants in the U.S. Economy: Sectoral Perspectives*.

United Nations. 1982. *World Population Trends and Policies: 1981 Monitoring Report*. Vol. 1, *Population Trends*. New York.

———. 1986. *World Population Prospects: Estimates and Projections as Assessed in 1984*. Department of International and Economic and Social Affairs, Population Studies, no. 98, New York.

U.S. Bureau of the Census. 1983a. *1980 Census of Population*, Vol. 1, Characteristics of the Population, Chap. D, Detailed Population Characteristics, P. 6, California. Washington, D.C.: U.S. Government Printing Office.

———. 1983b. *1980 Census of Population*, Vol. 1, Characteristics of the Population, Chap. D, Detailed Population Characteristics, P. 11, Florida. Washington, D.C.: U.S. Government Printing Office.

———. 1983c. *1980 Census of Population*, Vol. 1, Characteristics of the Population, Chap. d, Detailed Population Characteristics, P. 45, Texas. Washington, D.C.: U.S. Government Printing Office.

———. 1984. *Projections of the Population of the United States, by Age, Sex, and Race: 1983 to 2080*. Current Population Reports, Series P-25, No. 952. Washington, D.C.: U.S. Government Printing Office.

Wachter, Michael L. 1980. "The Labor Market and Illegal Immigration: The Outlook for the 1980s." *Industrial and Labor Relations Review* 33, no. 3 (April):342–354.

Wall Street Journal. 1984. "Reagan's Caribbean Basin Initiative Yields Mixed Results After 11 Months." December 3.

Warren, Robert, and Jeffrey S. Passel. 1987. "A Count of the Uncountable: Estimates of Undocumented Aliens Counted in the 1980 United States Census." *Demography* 24, no. 3 (August): 375-393.

World Bank. 1984. *World Development Report*, 1984. Oxford: Oxford University Press.

Wylie, Scott. 1985. "CBI: One Year Later." *Business America* (January 7):2–4.

5.

Population and Immigration Policy: State and Federal Roles

Charles B. Keely

The Immigration Reform and Control Act of 1986 (IRCA) is not only a major piece of immigration legislation, but probably the most far-reaching employment and Civil Rights legislation since the heyday of the Great Society. The bill will have profound effects on the demographic, economic, social, and political life of America, especially the Southwest. This chapter will focus on the major components of the act and the steps taken or planned for its implementation. Based on that descriptive foundation, four issues will be addressed to stimulate thinking about the implications of the recent immigration legislation for states in the Southwest: immigration and population dynamics; immigration and the economy; states and international migration policy; and states and internal migration policy. There will also be a short excursus about how to establish what "causes" migration in order to discuss sensible ways to change or manage migration flows.

The Immigration Reform and Control Act of 1986 (IRCA)

The immigration bill passed by Congress and signed by the president on November 6, 1986, was described as a corpse that would not die. In 1984, a prior version was overwhelmingly passed by the Senate, only to die because of inaction in the House. In 1985, both houses passed a bill, but it never made it out of the conference committee. In 1986, it was only at the last minute, as a result of major compromises, that the bill finally was approved by both houses and sent to the president. The story of the bill's passage is a fascinating lesson in how competing interests can come to agreement. That history, however, is beyond the boundaries set out here.

IRCA contains five major programs: legalization; prohibition of employment of undocumented aliens (employer sanctions), including extensive discrimination protections and a program of enforcement for immigration-related discrimination; a program to reimburse states for added costs due to legalization of up to $1 billion a year for four years (or a total of $4 billion); a program of welfare applicant screening to determine migration status and eligibility (the Systematic Alien Verification for Entitlement [SAVE] program); and a variety of agricultural worker provisions. The Act contains a number of other narrower provisions, some of which will have minimal impact and some, major implications. The ceiling on immigrant admissions from colonies in any one year, for example, is raised from six hundred to five thousand. More important for the impact on the United States, warrantless searches of open fields are prohibited.

IRCA, indeed, has great potential for affecting American society. How it will all turn out cannot be confidently forecast, however. Too many variables are unknown, like how many aliens are eligible for legalization or how much voluntary compliance will be forthcoming from employers regarding screening of job applicants and not hiring ineligible aliens. The outlines of what the law says and how it is being implemented are clear. These define the boundaries within which (or around which) immigration practice will take place.

Legalization

IRCA permits anyone resident in an illegal status in the United States since January 1, 1982, to apply to regularize his or her status. To qualify, a person must be eligible for immigrant status (not excludable because of criminal behavior or contagious disease, for example) and not likely to become a public charge. Applicants have to have been residents continuously since January 1982 (brief absences from the United States are permitted) and must prove that residence and show—by establishing a work history, for example—that they are not likely to become public charges. If approved, applicants may stay as temporary residents, but must apply within eighteen months for permanent resident (immigrant) status. The applicants must at that time also show knowledge of English and U.S. political history and government or at least enrollment in a bona fide training program. If approved, a new immigrant can sponsor a spouse and children for immigrant status. Five years after becoming an immigrant, a person can apply for citizenship.

The law also contains a legalization program with special eligibility criteria for agricultural workers (described below).

The INS set up 109 offices to process applications and signed agreements with hundreds of voluntary agencies (unions, church organizations, refugee resettlement groups, ethnic organizations, and so on) to help recruit applicants, to prepare their applications, and to gather supportive documents for submission to the INS for decision. These agencies, referred to by the unwieldy "qualified designated entities," or QDEs, are presumed to be a key link in the legalization process, based on other countries' experiences. The agencies are trusted by their constituents and provide both a psychological and actual buffer between the immigrant and the INS—the government agency charged with catching and deporting immigration law violators while at the same time the decision maker on legalization. The law also explicitly forbids any use of the application materials for purposes other than to make a decision on legalization. The materials may not be used by the INS as a basis for apprehending applicants who have been denied legalization.

The INS estimates that 2.9 million people are eligible for legalization, but has programmed for 1.9 million applicants. Fees are charged for application ($145 per adult and $50 per minor, or, $420 per nuclear family), and the program is meant to pay for itself. Experience in the first two months showed a rate of application below expectations. In July 1987, the number of applicants picked up appreciably; by October 9 almost 800,000 applications for legalization had been received. If that rate were to continue up to the May 1988 deadline (a date beyond the writing of this paper), the 1.9 million target would be reached. Rates of preliminary approval also ran high (well over 90 percent). Applications through QDEs, however, were slower than expected and there is disagreement between the INS and QDEs as to why this is the case. Neither have applications been uniformly high in all states. Some states, particularly those in the northeast, received applications at a rate below expectations. The INS considered reducing hours of operation in some legalization offices or even closing some and forecast cash flow problems in what was supposed to be a self-liquidating program unless a monthly rate of 160,000 was maintained.

Early reports are not always a good guide to program progress. The five-month experience of the legalization program provides a basis for modest optimism that the U.S. program will be the most successful amnesty program of any country to date in its size and the proportion of estimated eligible population who actually become legalized.

The final outcome will probably see between one and a half and two million people being legalized. These will not be new entrants; by definition they have been residents of the United States for five years. But their status will be changed to "permanent resident alien" or bona fide immigrant. As immigrants, they may also petition for family members to obtain immigrant status.

Immigrant visas are distributed by a visa preference system. Visas for spouses and children of permanent resident aliens are the second preference, which already is much oversubscribed, meaning there is a long waiting list, with a delay of over fifteen months currently. The families of some newly legalized aliens will already be in the United States, but not eligible for legalization (if, e.g., they entered after January 1, 1982). The INS plans no special effort to deport members of such "mixed" families, however the ineligibles will still be in a legal limbo, ineligible to work and still deportable if discovered. They (and the families who may return to a foreign country) will have to wait probably for at least two years for an immigrant visa. Congress may decide to let these family members also get an immigrant visa. In that case, the Congress will also likely act to clear up the second preference backlog, a move that will add another one-time bulge of immigrants, most likely young adults and children.

Making people legal residents may well have the paradoxical effect of developing a geographically more mobile population of aliens who have firm anchors in their home country and use the "green card" as, in effect, an entry permit for work during part of the year in the United States. This already is the case for some "immigrants" from Mexico and the Caribbean. The ineligibles, on the other hand, may become less mobile, if jobs become harder to find for illegal aliens and illegal reentry becomes more problematic due to stepped-up and more effective border enforcement. There are many "ifs" in this proposition about less-mobile ineligibles. It is distinctly possible that, after an initial slowdown in illegal border crossings and employer hesitation about hiring, the situation will revert to something like the status quo ante.

In sum, legalization will probably result in 1.5 to 2 million residents qualifying to become immigrants. They should generate additional applications for family reunification, although some of those families who are to be "reunified" may already be resident in the United States, but ineligible for legalization. How many actual new entrants will result from sponsorship by the newly legalized remains to be seen, but the number could affect service provision like schools and hospitals. The possession of a green card, on the other hand, could spur some return migration, as the breadwinner(s) use the card as an entry and work document within the prescriptions of the law. Those ineligible for legalization may become less mobile than currently, although that depends on the effectiveness of border and employer sanctions enforcement.

Employer Sanctions

The cornerstone of IRCA makes the hiring of an alien unauthorized to work an illegal act. The reasoning behind this policy is that work is the biggest magnet drawing illegal aliens to the United States. If an effective employer sanctions program demagnetizes the workplace, illegal migration should dwindle to marginal levels.

The law mandates a phasing in of its provisions. Hiring an undocumented person became illegal as of November 6, 1986, the date of the law's signing by President Reagan. On June 1, 1987, employers were to begin inspecting identification of *all* new hires regarding the right to work and completing a form (the I-9) for each new hire attesting to review of identification as specified in law or regulation about work eligibility. To avoid discrimination, every new hire without exception, whether citizen or not, must show eligibility to work. I-9's were to be completed retroactively for all hires after November 6, 1986, as soon as the forms became available (scheduled for June). (Hires before November 6 are not subject to the law.)

The first six months after enactment (from December 1, 1986, until May 31, 1987) were strictly a public education period. There were no citations, proceedings, or court orders to cease and desist hiring people not authorized to work. The next twelve months (June 1, 1987, to May 31, 1988) were designated in the law as a first citation period. For the first instance of alleged violation, a citation was to be issued without further proceedings and with no penalty. In effect the citation was a warning. Second instances of alleged violations in this citation period could incur civil charges and fines.

After eighteen months of education and warning, that is, by June 1, 1988, employer sanctions are now fully effective. The first offense of knowingly hiring unauthorized aliens has a civil penalty of $250 to $2,000 per unauthorized alien; the second offense, $2,000 to $5,000 per alien; the third offense, $3,000 to $10,000 per alien. If a pattern and practice of hiring unauthorized aliens is proven, criminal penalties may be imposed of a $3,000 fine and/or six months imprisonment per violation.

The distribution of I-9 forms and employer handbooks to every U.S. employer by June 1, 1987, was such a formidable task, it was not completed, and the June 1 deadline was pushed back a month. Congress in an appropriations bill acted on in late June permitted a further delay to September 1, 1987, in employer sanctions enforcement (i.e., the citation stage). The INS did not delay the citation stage to September, but began that phase of enforcement during the summer months. Great effort is being given to employer education. The timetable for full enforcement still began on June 1, 1988.

The unanswered question about sanctions is how effective they will be. Will there be a great deal of voluntary compliance that will last (like, for example, the minimum wage, which is an institutional guideline) or will the analogy be more like the fifty-five-mile-an-hour speed limit, which waned in its effectiveness after an initial period of acceptance and compliance? It will be some time until the answer is clear. It should not be concluded that effective employer sanctions will reduce the number of aliens entering the United States for temporary work. As will be detailed below, IRCA provisions on agricultural workers and on asylum open up new avenues for worker entry. Even if employer sanctions are as fully effective as authorities expect, the number of persons entering the United States for work may remain the same, but their status will be legal. The law may redirect these migrant workers to the agricultural sector in greater proportion than has been the case in recent years with illegal migrants.

An adjunct of employer sanctions was the creation of the Office of Special Counsel in the Justice Department to deal with immigration-related discrimination claims. The law added citizenship to the roster of criteria that cannot be used to discriminate in hiring practices. Many feared that employer sanctions would lead to avoidance in hiring persons who either "looked or sounded" foreign or all aliens as a way for employers to make sure they were in compliance with the law. IRCA makes such a practice illegal, and the Office of Special Counsel is meant to reinforce for both employers and government agencies implementing IRCA (especially as they design and implement public education about the law) that IRCA is not a license to discriminate on ethnic, racial, or citizenship bases.

An acting special counsel was appointed in late spring and the president nominated a permanent candidate on June 17, 1987, Lawrence Siskind.

Final regulations regarding the discrimination provisions of IRCA were quite delayed. Civil rights groups are watching the discrimination provisions and preparing to file complaints as they occur. Few complaints have been filed or received by the special counsel. However, a few employers had settled or lost lawsuits under both IRCA and the employment discrimination provisions of Title VII of the Civil Rights Act by late June of 1987.

IRCA may trigger a large number of suits regarding employment discrimination, but there are no strong signs of that happening in the first year of implementation. A whole new group of employers (those with between three and fourteen employees) are now under Title VII of the Civil Rights Act because of IRCA. The citizen/alien criterion is now added to other criteria (like race and religion) that cannot be used to discriminate in hiring. A period of negotiating the "rules of the game" through regulation, suits, pressure on the executive for enforcement, and perhaps even subsequent legislation, is in its initial stages. How deeply employment practices and costs are affected and how effective the new law is in discouraging and prohibiting employment of unauthorized aliens remain to be seen.

Finally, a note should be made of the potential impact of one of the regulations promulgated by the Department of Justice in connection with the implementation of IRCA. All nonfrivolous applicants for asylum are automatically to receive authorization to work while their cases are being decided. Prior to IRCA regulations, employment authorization for asylum applicants was at the discretion of the Immigration and Naturalization Service district directors. This authorization was routinely denied as a deterrent to the mushrooming of asylum claims, as occurred in Europe. A new channel of at least temporary migration may now open up, especially from

Central America, because asylum claims from that region, even if ultimately denied, will probably not be treated as frivolous on the face of it.

State Reimbursement

A constant theme of states and local governments in the immigration debate is that they bear many costs, especially of locally financed educational, health, and social services, caused by the failure of federal immigration policy. A compromise introduced with the legislation provided for reimbursing states for additional costs incurred due to legalization. The Department of Health and Human Services (HHS) is to distribute a pool of about $4 billion to states and to federal departments over four years beginning in fiscal 1988 to cover extra costs due to legalization.

As of October 1987, HHS had not issued final regulations so that states would know what would qualify for reimbursement. The newly legalized are not eligible for most federally funded income transfer or other programs that would make them a "public charge." HHS has articulated no specific goals or objectives for this program. It seems to see its role as merely a conduit for funds. States were at one point being advised to submit their proposals, absent guidelines, and await decisions when HHS saw what states proposed as the ways to spend the money. Most states have adopted a strategy of awaiting final federal regulations before submitting state plans.

Each state is required to appoint an official contact person for the program. Many states have turned to their refugee coordinators, who devise state refugee resettlement plans and deal with the HHS Office of Refugee Resettlement, to coordinate their reimbursement applications. Although convenient for state governments to turn to refugee coordinators' offices, refugees and legalized permanent residents are not necessarily people with similar needs or similar impacts on state and local services and certainly are quite different in terms of entitlements.

Whether a refugee coordinator is the contact person or not, states are faced with reconciling conflicting messages and delivering general services to persons with differing specific needs and legal entitlements. States must provide emergency medical care, for example, but would not want to jeopardize a legalized alien's status by providing a service that makes him or her a "public charge." Information and communication between federal and state governments in this entire area of benefits to noncitizens is woefully lacking. Much confusion exists, primarily because the federal government's goals are uncoordinated. It is left to states, as service providers, to figure out what to do— and often, how to pay.

Four billion dollars is to be set aside for this program. The law also provides for excess federal costs due to legalization for programs the Federal

Government funds to come out of this pot. Up to half the money, it is estimated, will be retained at the federal level.

Systematic Alien Verification for Entitlement Program

The INS has run a series of pilot programs to verify eligibility of aliens applying under certain federally financed programs. The law requires all states to participate in the new Systematic Alien Verification for Entitlement (SAVE) program or to have an equivalent program in place. Costs of participation will be reimbursed by the federal government. Programs can be exempted from participation in SAVE if the verification program is not cost-effective. Applicants will be entitled to a hearing regarding unresolved immigration status.

The program clearly introduces a new procedure in welfare determinations. Its impact on the operation of resource transfer programs (and on the INS), especially in electronic record cross-checks, is an issue of importance to many audiences. The bureaucratic (and, some would say, the personal) convenience of an alien identity card for employment, other federal programs, and so on, could provide the initial step for an ID card system for aliens, and then perhaps for all residents. Even short of such a result, the cross-checking among agencies has as yet unidentified and unevaluated implications for agency operation, delivery of services, and individual rights.

Agricultural Worker Programs

IRCA provides for expedited review of requests for temporary agricultural workers (the H-2A program, named after the section of immigration law in which visas for temporary workers is discussed). The intent is to admit workers unless the government can clearly demonstrate the current availability of U.S. workers in the locality with requisite skills.

The law also allows migrants who worked for ninety days in agriculture related to perishable crops during 1984, 1985, and 1986 to apply for immigrant status. Eligible persons will be given temporary status for one year and then be given permanent status. Up to 350,000 qualified applicants can be approved. Other agricultural workers who worked for ninety days in 1986 will also qualify, but will have temporary status for two years. There is no limit to the size of this group, to which may be added those workers over and above the 350,000 who qualified for the one-year temporary status. The workers eligible under these provisions are collectively referred to as SAWs, special agricultural workers.

IRCA also establishes an agricultural worker replenishment program. If the secretaries of agriculture and labor certify that shortages exist, workers will be admitted under the replenishment program to replace those who were legalized under IRCA's agricultural provisions. The replenishment process will take place during 1990–1993. If replenishment workers perform ninety days of seasonal agricultural labor in each of three years, they become eligible for permanent residence. They must work ninety days in agriculture for another two years (or a total of five years) before being eligible for naturalization.

The H-2A and replenishment provisions are compromises made with the agricultural sector to make sure labor supply is not interrupted while adjustments are made regarding the presumed unavailability of illegal migrant workers who either have become legal or who no longer enter the United States because of better border enforcement and employer sanctions. The program to give immigrant status to agricultural workers also assumes that many of them will be available for at least one more season of agricultural work as they take advantage of the law. Many of them are presumed to be ineligible for the normal legalization program, since they did not establish continuous residency while holding seasonal jobs in an undocumented status.

The variety and complexity of these provisions are recognized by Congress. How many SAWs become eligible, how large H-2A gets, the size of the replenishment worker group, and how many of them qualify for permanent resident status, the different effects of these provisions on sectors of agriculture dealing with perishable versus nonperishable crops are all unknown. (The Department of Agriculture regulation process defining and justifying what is perishable or not, what constitutes "planting, cultural practices, cultivating, growing and harvesting," and what is a "fruit or vegetable of every kind" or an "other perishable commodity" is a fascinating exercise in legal reasoning. Christmas trees are perishable and sugarcane is not under the regulations.

The Commission on Agricultural Workers was established to study the effects of these provisions on farmworkers and the structure of agricultural employment in affected sectors. The commission is to report by 1991, although the full effects will not have been felt by then. Some sectors of agriculture may have to adjust rapidly to fewer temporary workers, and others may or may not have a greater supply of labor or no great incentive to restructure the production process to rely less on labor.

These, in sum, are the major programs mandated by IRCA. Exactly how they will "play out" in terms of numbers, characteristics of immigrants, effects on regional distribution of U.S. population, impacts on employment and various sectors of the U.S. economy, and so on cannot yet be discerned in detail. We do know that a large group will be legalized, concentrated in a few states—mostly southwestern states plus New York, Florida, and Illinois—and heavily Hispanic, particularly Mexican. What these people will do in terms of employment or geographical mobility after legalization is not clear. Whether and how their integration into U.S. society will differ from that of other immigrants we do not know. Whether sanctions will work and whether legalization is a one-time event—even with congressional insistence that it is and must be so—is still to be seen. The United States has chosen a path by adopting legislation, but we cannot see very far beyond the bend.

Immigration and U.S. Population Dynamics

In 1972, the Commission on Population Growth and the American Future made its report. That commission was formed because of a concern that the United States would have 300 million people by the year 2000. It examined the implications of a three- versus a two-child family and developed its report just as the "baby boom" was changing to a "baby bust." It is the "birth dearth" in developed countries that is exercising some commentators these days, not population explosions.

Fear of population decline is not a new phenomenon in developed countries. It was a frequent theme in nineteenth-century French political and social commentary, revived and spread by the fertility declines in the Depression years of the 1930s. A number of countries have pronatalist policies to try to convince their populations that an extra child or two is desirable. Republican presidential candidate Pat Robertson suggested in the fall of 1987 that Americans increase their fertility. If anything, however, pronatalist policies have an unbroken record of failure.

What is the role of immigration in current U.S. population dynamics? The United States is characterized by low fertility, or an average of about 1.85 children born per woman in her reproductive years (the total fertility rate). This rate will lead to a decline in population in about two generations as couples do not replace themselves. At a total fertility rate of 2.1—the extra .1 accounts for mortality—births and deaths would approximately equal one another, the total population size would stabilize at a fixed number, and the age structure would not change. How rapidly this steady state—a stationary population—would emerge depends on how high the original fertility level is and how long it takes to decline to the 2.1 level.

Of course, it is far-fetched to expect that fertility will decline to 2.1 and then stay there. Exactly the opposite has happened in capitalist and socialist industrial societies: fertility has declined and continued to go below replacement levels. There is no theoretical or experiential reason to presume that the population of nation-states will somehow automatically return to a 2.1 level once it has gone below it.

Without immigration, then, the United States is on a path to population decline. However, due to the age structure (the large number of baby boomers who themselves are now in their own reproductive years), the population is still growing, but at slower rates. Net immigration now accounts for 30 to 40 percent of the annual population increase. (The range is due to how many illegal migrants one thinks settle permanently each year in the United States.) The word "net" is important because people still emigrate from the United States. Estimates since 1900 are consistently in a range of 30 percent of all immigrants subsequently emigrating, so for each ten immigrants, about three leave in any year. Some native-born Americans also emigrate. Illegal migrants may also settle for a number of years and then return home. At what rate that happens, we do not know. Different nationality groups emigrate at different levels. Refugee groups, of course, have low emigration rates. So do most Asian groups. European and legal Latin American immigrants are more likely to return before or at retirement.

Net migration has been at a level of about 350,000 to 500,000 legal migrants. The trend has been slightly downward as refugee admissions have declined from the high levels of Indochinese boat people and the Mariel boatlift.

If we tie all of these various strands together, we can conclude that America is not about to decline in population soon. The age-structure effect of the baby boomers who are now having families, even at low fertility rates, is more births than deaths. Immigrants add to population growth. The United States is growing at about 0.9 percent a year. But that growth rate is getting smaller. We will not get to 300 million by 2000; in fact, we will be twenty-five or more million below that mark if current conditions prevail. The three hundred million mark hardly seems credible for any reasonable assumptions, nor is population decline on the immediate horizon.

If population size is not going to be subject to radical swings under any conditions barring an event like nuclear war (in which case all reasonable planning exercises will be futile), what about composition? Are we about to be, if not overrun, unable to absorb so many foreigners? This nation of immigrants has fewer foreign-born than Argentina, Venezuela, France, Germany, England, or Switzerland. Canada, Australia, and New Zealand—other traditional immigrant countries—have two to three times the proportion of foreigners that we do. (These results are all from the 1980 round of national censuses.) The United States had about 6.2 percent foreign-born in 1980. Given our history of immigrant absorption and comparison with the other countries mentioned, which do not seem about to fall apart culturally or socially due to migration, an objection to too many foreigners seems to be primarily an expression of taste rather than of demonstrated economic or social problems.

What of the future, however? Will immigrants "outbreed" the native-born and also continue to enter so that the nature and character of society will change? Some sets of projections have been published trying to assess the ethnic composition a century from now. The real interest, if we are honest, is what proportion would be Hispanic and, secondarily, Asian.

I will not go into detail on any particular set of such projections, because such projection exercises require a suspension of judgement. Is it reasonable to assume constant fertility for one hundred years, fixed ethnic composition among immigrants, no intermarriage across ethnic lines, and a society so unchanging that "Hispanic" or "Asian" as a social category will mean the same in 2080 as in 1980?

It is not sufficient, in my judgment, to justify such exercises as relevant policy by saying that they are not predictions of forecasts but projections to tell us what would happen under certain conditions or assumptions. Relevance in that case depends on the reasonableness of assumptions. How reasonable, how probable are the assumptions? If they are improbable, then why present such scenarios as opposed to any other unlikely futures?

Put yourself back in 1900 for a minute. Migration has been rising for twenty years or so and seems poised for larger changes. Native fertility has been falling, as noted by the census director of 1870 and MIT president, Francis A. Walker, in an influential 1891 article. The composition of immigrants has changed to larger number and proportions of Southern and Eastern Europeans.

There are a number of similarities to today's trends. Suppose someone had a computer and projection software in 1900 and set to work producing a set of population projections. Most telling, I think, is what would have been made of the projections in 1900 of the number of Italians and Jews (and other "new immigrants" since 1880 coming from non-Nordic Europe) under the presumption that the social image of them, their achievements, and their contributions to society would be no different in 1980 than in 1900.

This scenario shows how ludicrous, and ultimately how misleading and policy irrelevant, such exercises can be. The 1900 projection would have missed tremendous fertility variation, wide swings in immigration, and the very changes in the ethnic composition since 1965 that seem to exercise some people today. It would have scared people, however, with visions of unmeltable ethnics in the lower East Sides, East Harlems, and other Jewish, Italian, and Slavic immigrant ghettos of turn-of-the-century American cities.

The bottom line seems to be whether the United States is receiving "unmeltable ethnics." Are the concentration, the connections with homelands, the contemporary respect for pluralism, barriers to integration? Some wish to return to previous social policy to "Americanize," to discourage the "hyphenated American," and to think of schools as the "forcing houses of Americanism" and of English as the national language to be acquired without the transfer of other mother tongues.

To ask what holds America together is a serious question. To raise it is not in and of itself bigoted. The problem, as I see it, is that the question is not being raised in a nonbigoted way. Those who question the size and composition of today's immigration seem to be raising a red flag. No historical context is given, no experience of other countries is referred to.

Immigration and U.S. population dynamics, therefore, seem to be an issue not of size or growth but of ethnic composition. The ethnic composition issue seems to revolve around whether immigrants are "too different" and whether "they" will make us become like them. When social discourse is full of words like "invasion," "hordes," "inundated," and "floods," the implication is that destruction is just around the corner. Perhaps more time should be spent in framing the issues when immigration and population relations are discussed rather than stating armageddonlike conclusions. We might miss the important question: What does hold a society like America together, and is immigration a threat to that cohesion or a necessary ingredient continually revitalizing the cohesive force of a pluralistic society?

Immigration and the Economy

Immigrants get blamed for many things, and understandably so, An outgroup is often an easy target. To blame immigrants for the high unemployment of the 1970s and early 1980s or for youth and minority unemployment rates (or even for female and disabled unemployment) is to oversimplify. Perhaps we should recall the European experience. Europeans hoped to have temporary labor or "guest workers" to fill their passing labor shortages. If an economic slowdown came, the guests were to go home and the locally unemployed fill their vacated spots. The slowdown came. Not only did the guests not all go home, the Europeans found that they were integrated into the economy. They were needed—not perhaps to the extent that they stayed—but they were not all expendable, either.

The United States has yet seriously to ask itself how dependent it is on illegal migrant labor—or more generally on a foreign labor supply that is a combination of temporary and permanent settlers, whether legal or illegal. There is no simple all-or-nothing answer to this question. The answer will be phrased in terms of costs (monetary, social, political) of an adjustment of the economy to a more or less purely domestic labor supply. The answer is that the costs are too high. IRCA does nothing about high-level labor coming as exchange visitors or multinational corporation executives or scientists transferred to the United States under a special visa category. In the agricultural sector, it bends over backward not to reduce the foreign labor supply at least until 1993 (and even beyond, with the H-2A program). It wants the labor to be present legally—but to be present. The newly legalized (the SAWs and others) may also go into other sectors like the garment industry, electronics, services, and construction (along with applicants for asylum for whom the regulators, not the legislators, will allow work authorization).

The answer to the question of how dependent America is on foreign labor may well be answered not by a study but by experience with employer sanctions. Will employers voluntarily comply, especially over the long haul? It would seem that growers were not convinced nor were the arguments against their position powerful enough to catalyze counterforces to their influence. "Special interests" are not all-powerful. Merely to throw up one's hands and bemoan their power is sour grapes. The American system is built so that in political life we do not have to rely on goodwill, altruism, or the unselfish pursuit of a "common good." Although no social or political life exists if there is a war of all against all, neither is the common good a Platonic idea apparent to all persons of goodwill. The common good, if pursued at all, usually required a pursuit of self-interest, a test of strength and commitment. Although hardly a perfect process, it is not the same as despotism (benevolent or not), nor is it a thinly veiled "common good," which is an expression of a dominant group's interest.

Immigration reform has set up a regime of employer sanctions, agricultural worker programs, and legalization that is a contemporary "playing field" to test how committed various interests are in continuing to use foreign labor or to curtail its use. IRCA is not simply a commitment to open jobs to Americans (assuming legislation can do that). It is that, but it is also a commitment to bring in labor, especially agricultural labor, and then to let a large proportion have permanent-resident status. Both views, both commitments are expressed. If immigration policy is likened to a boxing match, the IRCA legislation is round one and it is a draw. Implementation is the successive rounds, and they are just under way.

Excursus on Causality

When discussing demographic and labor force aspects of immigration, many focus on the supply side. Rapid population growth in general and expansion of the labor force age group beyond any apparent absorptive capacity in particular are focused on. The conclusion is usually some variant of an irresistible push force.

The problem with variations on this sort of demographic determinism is that it does not explain size or direction of flows. Not all rapidly growing populations (or labor force groups) go to the United States or to industrial countries. Some move hardly at all (e.g., in China). And the direction is not always to the nearest place (e.g., many Caribbean migrants preferred England to the United States until England's restrictive legislation, and Koreans favor America over Japan, Algerians favor France, and Turks favor Germany over France). The examples show two things: population pressure does not mean automatic exit; what happens in receiving countries ("pull") is also important. Colonial, economic, military, linguistic and cultural ties, and contiguity act in many ways, as do exit and entry rules.

The economic development of the Southwest is as important as Mexican demography to understanding immigration to the United States in the last twenty years. Causation is not simple. To focus on Mexican demography and job creation and to conclude that migration north is inevitable can be misleading. The Depression saw net movement back to Mexico. Since 1960 we've seen a demand for labor in the Southwest, a growth in jobs, a disciplining of American labor, and attempts to weaken organized labor. Immigrants were one of the tools, but by no means the only tool, used. The economic growth in the Southwest and the Sunbelt until recently was not exclusively due to immigrants. In other words, developments took place in the United States that immigrant labor (often illegal) complemented. The supply of labor in Mexico and in the Caribbean Basin (and, for much of the highly skilled legal migration under the 1965 Immigration Act, in Asia) was clearly present, but there were also historical ties of economic connections, prior labor migration, colonial ties (e.g., in the Philippines), and military ties (e.g., in Korea). There was supply, demand, and the ties that facilitated movement between the countries involved. Mexicans had a supply of labor but were not European guest workers in the 1960s. Nor are Caribbean migrants found in large numbers among migrant workers in Saudi Arabia or the Persian Gulf countries. Labor supply is a necessary but not sufficient explanation of specific flows.

This excursus is not meant to map all the factors that contribute to ("cause") a movement of a certain number of people with specific characteristics (e.g., skill levels) between points A and B. What is intended is to point out that focusing only on what is happening at the place of origin and then to conclude that movement to B is inevitable is less than helpful and perhaps misleading. Even further, demographic determinism focusing on population growth is usually quite fuzzy about the size and characteristics of the impending flows except to imply that they will be big and unskilled.

States and International Migration

The U S. Constitution, as interpreted by judicial decisions, vests control over immigration in the Congress. In 1876 the Supreme Court concluded that states have no right to regulate immigration; Congress has virtually unlimited rights. It argued that Congress could mandate the most bigoted, arbitrary criteria to decide who could immigrate and who could not. An argument can be made that Congress did just that when Asians were barred and visas were distributed on nationality quotas that made place of birth the paramount criterion. At one point a person born in the Asian part of Turkey or in the Soviet Union was barred but his brother born in the European regions of those countries was not.

States at one time controlled or regulated immigration by imposing head taxes and regulating conditions on ships. The Supreme Court prohibited that in the 1876 ruling. States also tried to circumscribe the rights of aliens concerning ownership of property and practice of professions or occupations. Legislation and court decisions have constantly chipped away at these mechanisms to discourage entry or settlement. IRCA added to this trend by adding citizenship status to the list of prohibited criteria for employment. (IRCA, however, says that if two job candidates are equally qualified, then preference may be given a citizen over a noncitizen.)

States then are limited in their powers to regulate international migration. Indirectly, they may cooperate with foreign counterparts with which they share a border. Such cooperation on a variety of issues like environment, economic development, or cultural activities is possible. Of these, economic development seems to have the most direct bearing on immigration (as would environmental cooperation if it allowed or promoted otherwise difficult or impossible development). What usually comes to mind is working within national agreements to promote certain kinds of complementary activities that would, it is hoped, have the effect of reducing migration by employment creation.

The record is not encouraging. Most cross-border programs do not create jobs that are filled by the unemployed already in the area. Frequently, new people—young women, for example—are drawn into the labor market; some even migrate to the area. In a broader vein, economic development, especially of a modern sector that is export oriented, in the short and medium term is more often associated with increased mobility. In short, state economic efforts undertaken to reduce migration are probably misplaced. Cooperative development, environmental projects, or other efforts ought to be evaluated and undertaken on the basis of other objectives.

States can take little direct action, since by the Constitution and its interpretation, immigration is solidly reserved to the federal government. Attempts to reduce migration by economic cooperation are probably doomed, since the forces at work are probably beyond the scale of economic initiatives available to states, and such initiatives would probably stimulate migration rather than reduce it. Economic cooperation ought to be justified on other grounds than indirect immigration control.

States and Internal Migration

Can states control their populations by controlling internal migration, by prohibiting settlement by U.S. citizens or legal (or illegal) resident aliens? The answer apparently is no. The Commission on Population Growth and the American Future addressed this question. Current legal doctrine is that states cannot prohibit movement and settlement. International migrants likewise can resettle. Some states feel the impact of immigration not only when immigrants enter but also because of secondary migration. Indochinese emigration to California is an excellent example of this second-order effect. If states could control internal migration, a focus on U.S. citizens, not on immigrants, would have the biggest impact. The point, however, seems to be moot. Direct state action is not lawful. Immigrants admitted can go to any state they wish on entry. Immigrants can resettle, just as any citizen can move from state to state. Like interstate and foreign commerce, immigration is reserved to the federal government. There is really nothing more to be said.

Conclusions

This chapter has focused on the provisions of the 1986 immigration law. That law creates a framework for radical changes in social and economic policy that go beyond immigration in their impact. Because of the nature of recent and current immigration patterns, legalization, sanctions, SAVE and agricultural labor programs will have particular salience in the Southwest. Although what the law provides and programs to implement the Act can be outlined, the results are not yet discernible or predictable. Immigration has and will play a role in U.S. population dynamics. The role is not dominant in terms of population growth or composition at this time, however. As for the future, we seem incapable yet (still) of addressing the important issue of what holds this society together (and therefore needs attention and nurturing) in a way that allows for detached analysis. When raised, the question usually seems to have a bigoted tone. Those who want to disassociate themselves from such a tone often drift off into a nostalgia-invoking image of ethnic neighborhoods, strong families, struggle, hard work, the value of education, and the eventual realization of the American dream of upward mobility measured by income, education, family size, and occupational prestige (for example, an Italian-American professor of English becomes commissioner of baseball's National League after being president of Yale University). Can the center still hold in this pluralistic society? How? Is immigration a threat to stability or a requirement if the "American experiment" is to have any credible chance of continued success?

In like manner, this society has not addressed the issue of how seriously the United States is willing to reduce reliance on foreign labor. IRCA is not an affirmation of commitment to do that, but a statement of conflicting opinions and framework within which those conflicting views will contest the issue—in the agricultural sector, certainly, but probably in other sectors of the economy as well. The Southwest and some other large immigrant-receiving states (New York, Florida, and Illinois) are the playing fields or battlefields.

When discussing immigration, I caution that we look not only or even primarily at sending countries. Rapid population growth may be handled in ways other than immigration. The consequences for the United States of rapid population growth may be more in the realm of lost markets and supply sources due to instability and unfriendly governments than of migration per se. We should perhaps look more to ourselves and our policies than to the population policies and dynamics of our neighbors (and others) to discern how many and what kinds of people will come here.

Finally, I suspect that states can have little direct impact on immigration and population distribution. The exception to this is, of course, if state governments (and local governments and their organizations) are successful in influencing the Congress, the Executive, and perhaps even the federal courts on immigration policy. Such efforts, and even the interest in immigration and foreign policy as a concern of state and local government, are a recent development. For the near term, states will probably have to react to rather than shape events.

6.

Implications of Mexican Demographic Developments for the United States

Sidney Weintraub

The Hispanic population of the United States is growing faster than any other ethnic or racial group. In the Southwest, this represents largely growth of the Mexican-origin population. The growth of the Hispanic population as a whole or of its Mexican segment is the result of a combination of immigration and natural increase, roughly half and half for the Mexican-origin population between 1970 and 1980 (Bean et al., this volume).

This demographic development has profound cultural implications for both the country as a whole and the Southwest.[1] A Hispanization of the Southwest is occurring, which affects language usage, education, music, food habits, and the direction of attention of residents of the region. Hispanics tend to look south to Mexico and Latin America more than east or west, as was (and is) the case for other waves of immigrants from Europe and Asia. The Hispanic population of the Southwest already exerts considerable political influence, particularly in the region itself, and this power will undoubtedly grow. The Hispanic presence is altering the economies of the regions in which it is located, although the changes are not uniform throughout the country: the Cuban-origin presence in Miami, the Puerto Rican in New York City, the Central American on the two coasts and in the Southwest, and the Mexican-origin in the cities and rural areas of the Southwest are producing different outcomes.

The growth of the Hispanic population is in part the result of natural tendencies, such as the proximity of Mexico and the U.S. Southwest. History has played a role in the process. The Southwest was once Mexico; the Puerto Rican relationship with the United States grew out of the Spanish-American War; turmoil in Central America is stimulating emigration; and the growth of the Cuban-origin population in Miami and elsewhere received its impulse from the nature of the Castro regime.

In addition, policy, both of the United States and the sending countries, has affected migration. The use of Mexican workers for certain occupations in the U.S. Southwest has had a lasting effect on the ethnic composition of the region. The inability of the Mexican development model to create sufficient jobs at wages comparable to those in the United States created the economic push-pull that encourages migration. The United States is now engaged in a policy designed to discourage the pull factor in immigration, at least for low-skilled nonagricultural workers (Keely, this volume).

This chapter has three main parts. The first examines population and employment projections, primarily for Mexico. These data for Mexico, Central America, and the United States are presented in detail in other chapters in this volume; they will be set forth here only as necessary to make this presentation self-contained. The second part examines the impact on the United States of demographic-employment developments in Mexico. The third part analyzes U.S. policy options that can affect immigration from Mexico. The emphasis is on the implications of developments for the U.S. Southwest.

Population and Employment Projections

Mexico has experienced a significant shift in population trends since the 1970s. This can be illustrated by a few figures. The average annual rate of population growth exceeded 3 percent from 1950 until 1980. It now appears to be closer to 2.2 percent and is projected to decline still further. The crude birth rate fell from 46 per thousand in 1970 to 33 per thousand in 1981; the fertility rate fell over this period from 6.7 births to 4.3 and is now estimated to be 4.0 (Alba, this volume). The changes are the result both of economic-social trends leading to declining birth rates as Mexican income and education levels have risen, and of a deliberate policy of providing family-planning services since the administration of President Luis Echeverría (1970–1976).

Past population increases can be attributed largely to sharp declines in mortality rates coupled with an increase in life expectancy at birth. Mortality rates dropped from more than 23 per thousand in the latter 1930s to 8.6 in the early 1970s. Life expectancy at birth, which was about 40 years in 1940 (40.4 years for men and 42.5 years for women) was 66 years in 1980. Mexico's population has increased from 17 million in 1930 to more than 80 million today.

The result of this rapid increase is a young population, about 40 percent under age fifteen and more than 95 percent under age sixty-five. The implication of this youth is that the momentum of past births will be felt in the labor market for the rest of this century and beyond even as the population growth trend exhibits further declines. Projections by the Mexican authorities indicate that the crude birth rate is likely to stabilize between now and 2010 at between 5.1 and 5.6 percent, but that the crude death rate should decline from its current 26 percent to 18.5 percent. By 2010, under these projections, the proportion of the population under age fifteen will have declined to 25 percent.

These data can be used as the basis for projecting Mexican population and employment trends to the year 2010. Table 1 projects total Mexican population. The first column accepts the Mexican calculation of the current rate of population increase of 2.2 percent a year and the time path of decline to 1.2 percent a year after 2000. The second column accepts the first calculation regarding the current rate of population increase, but then looks at the population results if the decline after the year 2000 is to only 1.6 percent a year. This modest difference, stretched out over some twenty years, results in an end population in 2010 of 123 million rather than 111 million, a difference of 8 percent.[2]

The significance of small differences in assumptions is worth emphasizing, since they affect all the projections made in this and the other chapters. The workings of compound interest, operating over thirty years (the projections in this chapter run from 1980 to 2010), magnify what are modest differences in assumptions at the start of the period. It would be unwise, therefore, to consider the projections as precise predictions. They do serve, however, to provide general trends from which analytical and policy conclusions can be drawn.

Table 2, using the projection in column 1 of table 1, examines Mexico's labor supply (the economically active population) to the year 2010. Its main assumptions are made explicit in the notes to the table. However, some additional explanatory points should be given. The figure of twenty-two million for the economically active population (EAP) for 1980 is not universally accepted. Alba uses it in his chapter, as does the Mexican government in many of its analyses. Gregory uses a figure of twenty million; he is inclined to accept as more accurate an estimate of the labor force made in 1979, which is consistent with the twenty million figure and not that of twenty-two million (Gregory 1986:20, 57). Espenshade, using data elaborated in 1977 by the International Labour Office, also shows the EAP at roughly twenty million in 1980 (Espenshade, this volume).

The starting point of the EAP in 1980 does make a big difference in projecting its size in subsequent years, as well as in calculating actual participation in the labor force. It makes a difference as well, although a more modest one, in projecting the balance between labor supply and demand, as long as the same starting figures are used in both projections. Column 3, the labor-force participation rate, shows steady increases between 1980 and 2010, flowing from the assumptions made in calculating columns 1 and 2.

Table 6.1 **Alternative Mexican Population Projections, 1980–2010 (millions)**

	Average Annual Growth Rate Declining Gradually from 2.2% in 1980s to 1.2% after 2000	Average Annual Growth Rate Declining Gradually from 2.2% in 1980s to 1.6% after 2000
1980	70	70
1990	86	86
2000	100	104
2010	111	123

SOURCE: Alba, this volume, tables 7 and 8.

Table 6.2 **Projections of Mexico's Total Population Aged 15–64 and of Economically Active Population, 1980–2010 (millions)**

	Population Aged 15–64[a] (1)	Economically Active Population[b] (2)	Column 2 as Percent of Column 1 (3)
1980	52.4	22.0	42
1990	60.6	28.7	47
2000	66.5	38.6	58
2010	68.5	49.4	72

SOURCE: Alba, this volume, tables 9 and 11.

[a]Based on annual population growth declining gradually from 2.2 percent during 1980s to 1.2 percent from 2000 to 2010.

[b]Growth of EAP projected at 2.7 percent a year in the 1980s, 3 percent a year in the 1990s, and 2.5 percent a year between 2000 and 2010. The bulge in labor force entry is thus during the twenty years 1980–2000, after which the declining birth rate should slow down increases in the labor force.

The overall participation figure, by itself, is not startling; male participation in the labor force in the United States exceeded 75 percent in 1980, although female participation was only 50 percent. Gregory (1986:52–53) shows the labor force participation rate for Mexico in 1979 as 45.5 percent, made up of 71.3 percent for males and 21.5 for females. What is implicit in the projections of table 2 is a steady increase in female participation in the labor force in Mexico.

Table 3 projects labor demand in Mexico from 1980 to 2010 under various assumptions about the level of annual increase. The projection showing an annual increase in demand at 2.5 percent a year, the figure used in table 4 to compare labor demand and supply projections, implies a consistent

Table 6.3 **Projections of Growth in Labor Demand in Mexico, 1980–2010 (millions)**

	At 3% Annually	At 2.5% Annually	At 2.3% Annually	At 2.0% Annually
1980	21.2[a]	21.2[a]	21.2[a]	21.1[a]
1990	28.5	27.1	26.6	25.8
2000	38.3	34.7	33.4	31.5
2010	51.5	44.5	41.9	38.4

SOURCE: My calculations.

[a]Based on open unemployment of 4 percent of twenty-two million economically active population.

Table 6.4 **Projections of Mexican Labor Supply and Demand, 1980–2010 (millions)**

	1980	1990	2000	2010
Labor supply	22.0	28.7	38.6	49.4
Labor demand[a]	21.2	27.1	34.7	44.6
Excess supply	0.8	1.6	3.9	0.9

SOURCE: Tables 2 and 3.

[a]Based on 2.5 percent annual increase in labor demand. Based on historical experience, this would require sustained real growth of GDP of 5 percent a year.

growth of GDP of about 5 percent for thirty years, based on the past relationship between GDP growth and labor absorption. The Mexican industrial development model in the past tended to be more capital-intensive than in other countries, South Korea, for example, so that the past relationship may not be valid under current conditions (Watanabe 1974).

Table 4 brings together the labor-supply projections of table 2 and the labor-demand projections of table 3. Too much should not be made of the absolute figures for the excess supply of labor over the period projected, since they flow from a number of assumptions, all of which may not prove to be accurate. However, two points merit emphasis. One is that even when projecting a steady increase in GDP over thirty years (part of which already is inaccurate for the 1980s), Mexico's labor surplus shows consistent growth. This has implications for migration pressures.

However, an opposite point also emerges. Assuming that there is steady growth in GDP in Mexico once the current economic crisis is surmounted, the possibility of accommodating all those seeking employment in Mexico exists by the year 2010 (or, more likely, 2020, in light of the economic stagnation of the 1980s). This would require a steady increase in GDP of at least 6 percent a year, or combining a slightly lower overall growth rate with greater use of labor in Mexico's capital-labor factor mix.

This more optimistic outcome is feasible because of the demographic changes that have occurred, and are continuing, in Mexico. The conventional wisdom is that population pressure in Mexico leaves no alternative to the safety valve of emigration. This may be true for the short term; it may also turn out to be accurate for the longer term. However, there are feasible scenarios that demonstrate that this outcome is not inevitable. Mexican economic and education policy, combined with the continuation of demographic programs instituted during the 1970s, does have the possibility of altering Mexico from a labor surplus nation to one able to handle its own employment problems by the second or third decade of the next century without resort to emigration.

A few words of caution are necessary. Emigration is not merely, probably not even mainly, an outgrowth of the lack of job opportunities at home. Most Mexicans who come to the United States seeking jobs do have jobs at home in the period immediately prior to departure. The earning differential between staying at home in a job and a sojourn in the United States is a potent explanatory factor of why Mexicans emigrate. This difference in the earning power of jobs is not captured in simple job supply-demand projections. Having said this, there is a big difference between having to emigrate due to lack of job opportunities at home, which is the main premise of the safety-valve theory, and wanting to emigrate to increase one's income.

Before turning to the implications for the United States of demographic and employment developments in Mexico, a word should be said about emigration from Central America. The economic-demographic features of the five countries of the region (Costa Rica, El Salvador, Guatemala, Honduras, Nicaragua) and of Panama are provided in the chapter prepared by Sergio Díaz-Briquets (in this volume). The emigration drive from these countries comes not merely from population pressures, which have long been intense in El Salvador, but also from the political situation and its consequences on the national economies. The natural entry point for undocumented immigration from these countries, as with Mexico, is the Southwest. Of all deportable aliens located by the Immigration and Naturalization Service in U.S. fiscal year 1985, those from El Salvador and Guatemala ranked second and third behind those from Mexico.[3] This is a function of where the INS concentrates its apprehension personnel, but also of real entries from Central America.

Implications for the United States

There are important implicit assumptions built into an analysis that examines Mexican population and employment trends as the starting point of an explanation of migration to the United States. The main one is acceptance of the proposition that inadequate job creation in Mexico, both in numbers and in quality, is the main factor pushing emigration from Mexico. The logical corollary to this is that as more and better jobs are created or, put differently, as Mexican incomes increase, a dampening effect on migration will occur. Over some unspecified long term, improved economic prospects at home undoubtedly will remove or reduce the economic incentive to leave one's country; this has been evident in Asia, when incomes increased substantially, and for a short period in Ireland after it joined the European Economic Community, when there was even some short-term migration back.

However, there is also much evidence that as incomes increase marginally in a low-income country such as Mexico, emigration increases in the short term. The higher income makes the emigration more affordable. Emigration pressure from Mexico did not cease during the years of economic growth prior to the 1980s, when GDP increased almost monotonically by 6 percent (between 2.5 and 3 percent per capita) a year. For the majority of Mexicans, the increase in income still left them below what would be considered the poverty level in the United States.

What seems to occur in Mexico in the face of the income pull of the United States is that emigration increases in the short term as incomes rise moderately and increases even more when incomes decline, as they have since 1982. The point of turnaround, when increased income leads to reduced emigration, cannot be specified. This turnaround is unlikely to take place before 2010.

The impact on the United States of emigration from Mexico or from Central America is felt in many spheres: the U.S. labor market; budgets, both federal and state; national and regional politics; and the ethnic makeup of the United States. The United States has experienced these effects over and over again from previous waves of immigration. In each case, the wave was accompanied by dire predictions of the economic, political, and social consequences on the United States, only to be contradicted in practice.

Before examining potential effects on the United States, it may be useful to focus briefly on the quantitative importance of the Southwest in immigration from Mexico. Detailed data are provided in the paper by Frank D. Bean and others in this volume. Table 5 summarizes some of these data. Table 6 converts the absolute numbers of table 5 into percentages to show the dominance in the Southwest of persons of Mexican origin.

Table 6.5 **Mexican-Origin Population in the United States, 1980 Census (thousands)**

Total Mexican origin	8,740
U.S. born[a]	6,209
Mexican born	2,531
Legally resident[b]	1,208
Undocumented[b]	1,131
Resident in Southwest[c]	7,020
U.S. born[a]	5,042
Legally resident Mexican born	1,038
Undocumented Mexican born	940

SOURCE: Bean et al., this volume; Passel and Woodrow, 1984; and Warren and Passel, 1987.
[a] All non-Mexican born are counted as U.S. born.
[b] These figures do not add up to 2,531. Figures given are those shown in sources, which may include both adjusted and nonadjusted estimates.
[c] The Southwest is defined to include Arizona, California, New Mexico, and Texas.

Table 6.6 **Mexican-Origin Population in the Southwest, 1980 Census (%)**

Total Mexican-origin population	80
U.S. born of Mexican origin	81
Mexican born	85
Legally resident Mexican born	86
Undocumented Mexican born	83

SOURCE: Table 5.

The data speak for themselves in showing the concentration of persons of Mexican origin, both those born in the United States and those in Mexico, in the four states of the Southwest: Arizona, California, New Mexico, and Texas. Of these, by far the most important in absolute numbers are California and Texas. Whatever impact past, present and undoubtedly future immigration from Mexico has had or will have on the United States as a whole is magnified in the Southwest, where upwards of 80 percent of the Mexican-origin population is located.

This magnification is particularly notable at the border itself. Of twelve border counties stretching from Texas to California, the 1980 census showed the Hispanic population as 35 percent of the total, going about 90 percent in two Texas border countries, Webb and Maverick. San Diego had the lowest concentration of Hispanics, less than 15 percent in 1980.

This is a statistic of some interest. San Diego is the leading point of entry for Mexican aliens, particularly undocumented aliens, but most keep going north toward Los Angeles. Table 7 of the Bean et al. chapter shows the

Hispanic proportion in U.S. standard metropolitan statistical areas with 100,000 or more Hispanics in 1980. The San Diego proportion of 15 percent can be compared with the 62 percent of El Paso, the roughly 80 percent of SMSAs in the Rio Grande Valley of Texas, the 28 percent of Los Angeles, and the 45 percent of San Antonio.

San Diego County is atypical of U.S. border counties in other respects as well. The median family income there in 1979, $20,000, exceeded the national average; in most other border counties, the median family income was well below the national average. Hispanic family income was lower in every border county than for families as a whole. More than a third of the population was below the poverty level in some Texas counties. The proportion of high school graduates in San Diego, 78 percent, exceeded that of any other border county.[4]

Labor-Market Impact

The effect of immigration on the U.S. economy as a whole is generally conceded to be unambiguously favorable. As phrased in the *Economic Report of the President, 1986* (p. 222), "the net effect of an increase in labor supply due to immigration is to increase the aggregate income of the native-born population." The reasoning behind this assertion is that immigration of labor increases the returns to other factors of production. The precise effect on the economy will undoubtedly depend on the economic cycle, whether there is full employment or high unemployment; it presumably depends also, in the short term, on the skills brought by the immigrants, although this feature may have less significance in the long term as subsequent generations acquire skills. This point will be developed further.

There are, however, distributional effects of immigration. The statement in the *Economic Report of the President* refers to one such effect, the increased returns to other factors, such as capital. The question most thoroughly examined, without definite conclusion, is the distributional impact within the labor force itself. Most Mexican immigration, legal and undocumented, is of relatively unskilled persons. The mean years of schooling of Mexican immigrants is 7.5, compared with 11.1 for other Hispanics and 11.6 for non-Hispanic whites (Chiswick 1986:97). These persons do not compete with skilled workers, at least not at the time of entry, but with other unskilled persons. The labor-market issue, therefore, is the effect of Mexican immigration on the wages and employment of persons in comparable situations. The evidence does not permit reaching a definite conclusion.

There are difficult conceptual and procedural problems in making an examination of the wage impact of Mexican immigrants. Greenwood and

McDowell (1986:1767) point out that a rigorous examination requires limiting assumptions concerning competitive markets, constant returns to scale, and mobile labor within the United States coupled with immobile capital. It is evident that labor is not homogeneous, since there are many levels of skills; what is not often taken into account is that unskilled labor is not homogeneous, either. The formation of Mexican immigrants is different from that of unskilled U.S. workers, and the initiative of an immigrant, who exerted an effort to come to the United States, is apt to be different from that of a native-born American.

The labor-market impact of immigration is often examined through statistical techniques at a national level. That is, the implicit assumption is made that unskilled labor is mobile nationally. A conclusion about the national impact of immigrants may have no relevance for particular areas where immigrants tend to congregate or specific industries to which they are likely to be drawn.

There is no agreement on the short-term effect of Mexican immigration at the broad aggregation of the national level. Borjas and Tienda (1987:646–647), looking at all legal immigration, not just Mexican, conclude that the effect on the native wage rate is small, reducing it by at most two-tenths of one percent, but that the adverse effect is more substantial for resident foreign workers with whom the immigrants are more likely to compete, reducing their wage rate by 2 to 9 percent. Bean, Lowell, and Taylor (1988), looking only at undocumented Mexican immigrants, conclude that the impact of their entry into the work force is small but positive, adding two-tenths of one percent to earnings of resident females. Given the number of assumptions that are built into exercises of this type, a figure as low as two-tenths of one percent either way is not meaningful; the significance of the Borjas and Tienda study of native-born workers and the Bean, Lowell, and Taylor work on resident female workers is that the effect they found was nil.

Studies that are more disaggregated, that examine specific regions and industries, are more interesting because they are able to use more precise data and because they are based on a relevant outcome more than on an abstract exercise with limiting and often unreal assumptions. Several of these regional/sectorial studies dealing with the Southwest merit discussion.

McCarthy and Valdez (1986) made wage comparisons for the United States, California, and Los Angeles for the manufacturing sector as a whole and for fifteen selected industries. What they discovered was that while earnings levels in California in 1980 generally exceeded the national average, the growth in earnings from 1970 to 1980 was lower than for the nation as a whole. The earnings growth was uniformly lower in Los Angeles, where there is a large concentration of Mexican immigrants, than in California as a whole.

These findings can be interpreted many ways. One possible conclusion is that in a nation as mobile as the United States, a leveling process was taking place having little to do with immigration. McCarthy and Valdez conclude that Mexican immigration is what led to the slower growth in earnings. They base this evaluation on two related findings: first, already mentioned, that earnings growth was lower in Los Angeles than in California as a whole; and second, that wage differentials were most noticeable in the low-wage manufacturing sector, such as leather goods, textiles and apparel, and furniture, which are relatively heavy users of Mexican labor.

The face that the two authors put on their finding is that Mexican immigration "may actually have stimulated manufacturing employment in California by keeping wage levels competitive" (p. 40). Their evidence for this conclusion is that the level of employment in these low-wage industries grew by over 50 percent in Los Angeles while declining 5 percent nationally.

One can accept the reasoning put forth by McCarthy and Valdez, that a lag in wages in what are in any event low-wage industries is useful to keep these activities competitive, without endorsing their value judgment that keeping these wages low is useful to the economy. Perhaps it is in times of high unemployment, but the conclusion is more doubtful in times of fuller employment. The reasoning also requires a steady influx of new, low-skill immigrants to keep these activities in existence and makes a mockery of any rational international division of labor, since the United States is unable to compete with developing countries in most of these industries on the basis of low wages. Import protection is also required. The complete analysis of the effects of survival in noncompetitive industries on the basis of low wages requires a wider scope, including the effect on exports of what are truly competitive industries in both California and the United States.

Muller et al. (1985:112), who also studied immigration into California, also found evidence of wage depression from Mexican immigration. Philip Martin (1986), in an examination of the Southern California lemon industry, found that growers resisted unionization, which implied wage increases, by encouraging labor contractors who used much undocumented labor. In 1979, the unionized cooperatives harvested 80 percent of the area's lemons; in 1986, the contractors had an 80 percent share. "Contractors dependent on illegal aliens displaced American workers and depressed wages" (p. 28). Martin also found a concentration of undocumented immigrants in shaky businesses, such as furniture, shoe, and garment production in Los Angeles, and in restaurant and other low-skill service activities.

Pearce and Gunther (1985) examined a set of sixteen occupations in which many non-English-speaking immigrants work in Texas. Wages tended to be on the low side, although above the minimum wage. The authors note that the picture they found in these occupations was consistent with the stylized facts, that undocumented immigrants compete with people who have little education and who do manual work.[5] This examination required a number of limiting assumptions, the main one being that the supply of labor, both domestic and immigrant, was mobile among these sixteen occupations but not into other occupations. The implication of this assumption is that a shortage of labor in any one of the sixteen occupations would put upward pressure on all sixteen, because of the total shortage and the mobility among them.

The authors' conclusions vary by occupation. They include the probability Íthat the loss of access to undocumented immigrants from Mexico would raise prices for fruits and vegetables, probably for residential construction as well, and might reduce the returns to other factors of production and even make Texas less attractive to manufacturers of durable goods.

Campbell and Weintraub (1986) examined income in particular regions and industries in Texas and found that it was systematically lower for Hispanics than for Anglos, even after accounting for differences in education and work experience. The SMSAs examined were Beaumont, Dallas/Fort Worth, Houston, Austin, San Antonio, and El Paso. There was a definite pattern that the higher the proportion of Hispanic population, the lower the male income. The same pattern was not found for female income, which in every case was substantially lower than for males. Male income was consistently lower in those industries located in SMSAs with higher proportions of Hispanics.[6] Based on this examination, we cannot conclude that the presence of Mexican immigrants is an important contributor to lower male incomes in industries and locations in which Hispanics concentrate. However, if one accepts that Mexican immigrants tend to settle where there are concentrations of Hispanics, their contribution to lower Hispanic wages cannot be dismissed.

The evidence is quite strong, when one examines the impact of Mexican immigration at the regional and industry levels, that there is wage depression. This is felt most strongly for Mexican immigration in the U.S. Southwest. However, this is at best a partial conclusion. The wage depression may be short term unless reinforced by steady immigration. Even in this case, the overall impact on the region may be positive because of returns to other factors of production, including skilled labor, and because of complementarities between industries kept in existence by wage depression and other regional activities. Wage depression does not raise the equality of income distribution, since those adversely affected are themselves low-income persons.

A related issue, one in which the evidence is far from settled, is that of job displacement from Mexican immigration. The U.S. General Accounting

Office (1986) examined the research from fifty-one studies on possible and actual displacement effects. The studies, as the GAO put it, were "overrepresented by Mexicans" in the Southwest, particularly Southern California and Texas (p. 2). Only three of twelve studies (unspecified in the report) were found relevant to the issue of actual displacement, and each of these indicated that there was displacement.

The GAO report was inconclusive in one other respect. It stated that the studies examined were inadequate on the issue of whether native workers do or do not fill jobs left vacant by undocumented workers (p. 19). This is an important theme. The argument of many persons who favor the use of temporary foreign workers, whether undocumented or under authorized recruitment programs, is that they fill jobs native workers will not take. This is the central theme of Piore's well-known *Birds of Passage* (1979). It is the implicit argument of the position taken by Bean, Lowell, and Taylor (1988), that "after all, everyone benefits when the 'dirty-work' gets done." The special provisions for importing agricultural workers in the Immigration Reform and Control Act of 1986 are predicated on the thesis that native workers cannot be found for harvesting perishable crops.

Yet, as the GAO asserted, this proposition has not been fully tested, especially outside agriculture. Restaurants get their work done in areas where undocumented workers are available, as in the Southwest, and where they are not, in the majority of localities in the country. The "dirty work," such as cleaning streets and collecting garbage, gets done using native and foreign workers. The unpleasant work gets done in countries that do not import large numbers of foreign workers, in a populous country like Japan and a less populous one like Norway.

This is not the place to develop this argument fully, since it would require a full-fledged study, but one element missing from the undesirable-jobs argument is the price attracting native labor. Hill (1985), in studying the labor-market effect of more effective border control, concludes that this would probably raise costs somewhat; it would involve, he argues, a trade-off of some economic efficiency for more equal U.S. income distribution. There would also be other effects, such as the loss of some industries to foreign competition, increased efficiency in others, a shift in factor use from labor to capital in still others, and various combinations of all of these.

The Cost of Social Services

Keely (this volume) points out that the 1986 Immigration Reform and Control Act authorizes up to $1 billion a year for four years to reimburse the states for the potential added costs of legalization. Some municipalities and localities doubt whether this will be sufficient. The issue of sufficiency will now be tested under the act.

There have been a number of studies, particularly in California and Texas, of the net cost to states and municipalities of providing services to undocumented aliens. Muller et al. (1985:157) conclude that the cost to California and to Los Angeles County to provide public services to Mexican immigrants exceeds the revenue received from them. McCarthy and Valdez (1986:53) conclude that the tax contribution of Mexican immigrants exceeds the cost of the public services they use, with the notable exception of public education. They point out that areas with substantial concentrations of immigrants bear a disproportionate share of the public-service costs. Weintraub and Cardenas (1984) find that taxes paid to Texas by undocumented Mexican immigrants exceed the cost to the state to provide public services. They also find that cities and counties, particularly those with concentrations of undocumented immigrants, have to spend more to provide public services than they receive in taxes, because the public-service costs are greatest for education and hospital and health services, for which state reimbursement is incomplete.

Each of these studies was completed before amnesty, which was instituted to compensate the states for the increased public-service costs of legalization. The concern is that the use of welfare by legalized immigrants will be greater than for undocumented immigrants. Both McCarthy-Valdez and Weintraub-Cardenas studies find that undocumented immigrants are not large users of welfare programs, such as AFDC and food stamps.

The issue of cost to the states from legalization, although important, is a transitional one. The greatest cost is for education, and it is evident that the social cost of not educating young people who will live their lives in the United States would be even greater. This was the reasoning in the Supreme Court decision of Plyler v. Doe, in which it was decided that Texas had an obligation to provide education to undocumented alien children. The more central issue for the Southwest and the nation as a whole is whether immigrants to the United States contribute more over a lifetime to the national and state economies than they take. Put differently, the question relates to the very nature of the citizens' contribution to their locality and country.

The expectation, based on the repeated experience of U.S. history, is that educated citizens do make a net contribution to society. The only reason to raise this issue again is that the argument has been made that Mexican immigrants are different because they come less educated and then continue to be less educated than other groups even into subsequent generations. Only 21 percent of Mexican immigrants have completed high school; this is a lower percentage than for any other immigrant group (Bouvier and

Gardner 1986:22). About 38 percent of Mexican Americans have completed high school, a lower percentage than for blacks or Americans as a whole (Bean et al., this volume).

The full contribution of the Mexican immigrant to U.S. society will be evident in time. Progress may be slow, but the data do show increasing levels of education in subsequent generations of Mexican Americans. The income of first-generation Mexican immigrants tends to be lower than for other immigrant groups. Incomes rise for the second generation, although they are still lower than for non-Hispanic whites (Poston, Rogers, and Cullen 1986:112, 114). However, there is generational progress. This was the pattern as well with earlier immigrant groups. It is worth keeping in mind that the argument that uneducated immigrants become a drain on the public purse has been made repeatedly, for previous waves as well as for what Muller and Espenshade have called the fourth wave. The cries of alarm have proved false, and there is no reason not to expect them to be false once again as they pertain to Mexican Americans.

Political Implications

The history of the United States is replete with examples of racial ethnic groups concentrating in particular localities and then, over time, taking a commanding position in the politics of the area. Italians in New York City, Irish in Boston, Scandinavians in the upper Midwest, and blacks in Newark are but a few examples of this. Local political dominance has then served as a base for expanding the power of the group on a national level. Each ethnic or racial group does not necessarily have an agenda that transcends differences among the members, but many do, particularly of an economic nature. Political power is an objective in its own right, but even more as the means to achieve other goals.

Mexican Americans have been slow in organizing their political potential, but the organizing effort is becoming increasingly well developed. The first arena for this group will be the Southwest. Table 5 shows the Mexican-origin population in the United States as measured in the 1980 census at 8.7 million. What is remarkable is that the growth from 1970, when this population was 4.5 million, was 93 percent, or more than eight times the growth of the national population. Although the states of the Southwest have the largest Mexican-origin population, the rate of growth of other states from 1970 to 1980 was 150 percent. In the four states defined in this chapter as constituting the Southwest, the rate of growth of the Mexican-origin population between 1970 and 1980 was close to 100 percent in California and New Mexico, 70 percent in Texas, and 65 percent in Arizona (Browning and Cullen 1986).

Each of the states of the Southwest now has a large base of Mexican-origin population. Many of their metropolitan areas have large concentrations of Mexican-origin population, in some cases (El Paso and many smaller cities near the Mexico border), a majority. At current relative rates of growth, the Mexican-origin population will constitute a majority in many more metropolitan areas and probably in many of the states themselves. This regional concentration is increasingly being complemented by the growth of Mexican-origin population elsewhere in the United States. One should assume that the political power of this population will grow, first in the Southwest and then nationally.[7]

There are several reasons why the political potential of the Mexican-origin population has not been realized in the past: the political, social, and economic discrimination to which the members of this population have been subjected (McLemore and Romo 1985); the presence of undocumented persons, who are unable to vote (13 percent of the Mexican-origin population of the United States in 1980); and the slow pace of naturalization of Mexican-born persons resident in the United States. In 1980, less than 10 percent of these persons had been naturalized (Warren and Passel 1987:table 1.1). However, the tendency for naturalization has been greater the longer the residence in the United States. Data from Warren and Passel show that only one-tenth of one percent of the Mexican born who entered the United States between 1975 and 1980 were naturalized. The figures for naturalization rise to 1.4 percent for entrants between 1970–1974, 6.9 percent for entrants from 1960 to 1969, and 51.6 percent for entrants before 1960.

As time passes, the proportion of Mexican-origin population born in the United States will increase steadily and the issue of naturalization will be less significant. Beyond this, Mexican American groups are carrying out active drives to convince the Mexican-born to naturalize so that they can vote. The Mexican-origin population of the Southwest is moving along a well-trodden path taken by other immigrant ethnic groups, of regional concentration coupled with dispersion throughout the country, of gradually greater involvement in civic matters, from political disenfranchisement to positions of power, and slowly but surely, the ability to achieve political-economic-social objectives.

Policy Options

Three sets of policies are relevant. The first and most important is Mexican economic and social policy. Economic policies pursued in the past resulted in high rates of economic growth for roughly forty years, until the repeated crises of the 1980s. The accompanying high rate of population growth made it difficult to find suitable employment for all potential entrants into the labor force. Mexico's demographic picture has changed during the last decade, however. It is now technically feasible for Mexico to create enough jobs to meet the labor supply that will exist in thirty to forty years. Whether this is achieved depends primarily on future Mexican economic and demographic programs. Even if there are jobs in Mexico in the year 2020 for all who seek them, it is unlikely that the quality of the jobs will be high enough to eliminate the urge to emigrate to the United States.

This chapter looks to U.S. policy. The rules of the game until the passage of the immigration act of 1986 were to keep the door half open to unskilled immigrants from Mexico. This took the form of inviting them under the bracero program, official refusal to make it illegal to hire an undocumented immigrant, and underfunding of the INS so that enough persons without documents would make it to jobs in the United States. These rules were known to all the players—the employers, the immigrants themselves, and the U.S. Congress and Executive branch. An average of more than sixty thousand immigrants a year from Mexico were also permitted to enter legally during the 1970s.

The ostensible policy is now to punish employers who knowingly hire undocumented aliens, although still leaving the door mostly open for agricultural workers. The United States presumably will continue to permit legal entry of roughly the same number of Mexicans as it has in recent years. The unknown in U.S. immigration policy is the vigor with which the current law will be applied with respect to undocumented Mexicans. If applied stringently, this could place pressure on the Mexican authorities as the pull of higher wages in the United States is frustrated for ambitious would-be emigrants.

The other set of relevant U.S. policies is economic, dealing with the extent to which the United States will permit, foster, or frustrate Mexico's own economic program. The current Mexican economic development program is predicated on an increase in nonoil exports, especially of manufactured goods. The main market for these goods is now the United States—some 90 percent of Mexico's manufactured exports go to the United States. U.S. protectionism could frustrate Mexico's economic-development program.

In order to achieve its objective of expanding exports of manufactures, Mexico must also go through an industrial modernization. This effort is now being made. It will be abetted to the extent that U.S. private investment provides some of the necessary technology and savings not available from domestic Mexican sources.

Mexico is not a recipient of significant amounts of concessional aid from the United States, either bilaterally or through the multilateral development banks. However, the United States is the most important source of foreign capital for Mexico from private investment and especially from private and official lenders. The U.S. government controls the credit provided by its agencies, such as the Export-Import Bank and the Commodity Credit Corporation. It does not control the lending policies of private commercial banks, but does have an influence on these. Because of the need to service its large external indebtedness, Mexico requires some combination of increasing exports and continued capital inflows.

One additional point should be made. The Mexican economy is highly vulnerable to domestic U.S. economic policy. An expanding U.S. economy provides a growing market for Mexican goods and services. To the extent that U.S. monetary and fiscal policies keep interest rates reasonably low, this eases Mexico's debt-service burden. Mexican needs are not taken into account when U.S. macroeconomic policy measures are taken, but Mexico is clearly an interested party.

It is evident that U.S. economic policy, both that which is explicitly labeled "foreign" and that which is considered "domestic," will have a large impact on Mexico's own economy. U.S. economic policy, even if favorable to Mexico in every respect, is unlikely to have a major effect on Mexican emigration in the short term, that is, until 2010, because marginally higher Mexican incomes are unlikely to lead to reduced emigration over that time frame (Weintraub 1983). However, U.S. policies are important to the success of Mexico's own economic program; and this, in turn, will be the major determinant of emigration pressures over the long term.

Conclusions

The conclusions of this chapter can be summarized quite briefly.

1. Mexico is apt to continue to have a labor surplus through the projection period, to the year 2010, but a labor surplus is not inevitable in subsequent decades. Whether the surplus emerges or not depends primarily on Mexico's own economic and social policies, including its family-planning program, but U.S. economic policy can play either a supporting or an opposing role to what Mexico itself does.

2. The pressure to emigrate from Mexico will exist even if there is no labor surplus in the years after 2010, because of the play of economic push-pull factors.

3. By far the most important destination for Mexican emigrants, legal and undocumented, is the U.S. Southwest. However, the number of Mexican-origin persons is growing more rapidly than the U.S. population as a whole in many sections of the United States, from both immigration and natural increase.

4. The presence of Mexican immigrants does affect the U.S. labor mar-

ket. In the short term, in all but times of high unemployment, Mexican immigration increases total income in the United States; increases the income of other factors of production, including labor more skilled than the Mexican immigrant; but may depress the income of competing labor when these measurements are made for specific industries and locations where Mexican immigrants congregate.

5. Mexican immigrants have lower educational levels than other immigrants, including other Hispanic immigrants. Their earnings also tend to be lower than those of other immigrants. In the long term, that is, for generations subsequent to the immigrant, incomes of Mexican Americans do rise. They have not in the past risen as much for the Mexican Americans as they have for other immigrant groups, but this is likely to be corrected with the passage of time.

6. The political power of Mexican Americans is certain to increase, primarily in the Southwest, but elsewhere as well, from the sheer weight of numbers if nothing else, coupled with the drives of leadership groups to convince Mexican Americans to naturalize and register to vote.

Notes

1. The Southwest is usually defined as comprising four states: California, Arizona, New Mexico, and Texas. In their chapter for this volume, Bean et al. add Colorado to this listing.

2. The age breakdown of the population in 2010 noted earlier is based on the government projection of a decline in the annual rate of population increase to 1.2 percent a year from 2000 to 2010.

3. Department of Justice, 1985. *Statistical Yearbook of the Immigration and Naturalization Service*, p. 177.

4. U.S. Census.

5. The sixteen occupations studied were farmworkers, construction, other nonconstruction labor, carpenters excluding apprentices, janitors, welders and cutters, painters and construction maintenance, machine operators, groundskeepers, assemblers, textile sewing machine operators, maids, hand packers, private household servants, cooks other than short-order, and miscellaneous food preparation.

6. The industries examined were furniture, apparel, chemicals, fabricated metals, construction, nonelectrical machinery, computers, electrical machinery, primary metals, and petroleum.

7. The Mexican-origin population, according to the 1980 census, was 68 percent of the Hispanic population of 14.6 million in the United States.

References

Bean, F. D.; B. L. Lowell; and L. J. Taylor. 1986. "Undocumented Mexican Immigrants and the Earnings of Other Workers in the United States." Revision of paper presented at annual meetings of the Population Association of America, San Francisco, April 1986.

———. 1988. "Undocumented Mexican Immigrants and the Earnings of Other Workers in the United States." *Demography* 25:35–52.

Borjas, G. J., and M. Tienda. 1987. "The Economic Consequences of Immigration." *Science* 235:645–651.

Browning, H. L., and R. M. Cullen. 1986. "The Complex Demographic Formation of the U.S. Mexican Origin Population." In H. L. Browning and R. O. de la Garza, eds., *Mexican Immigrants and Mexican Americans: An evolving Relation*. Austin: University of Texas, Center for Mexican American Studies.

Bouvier, L. F., and R. W. Gardner. 1986. "Immigration to the U.S.: The Unfinished Story." *Population Bulletin* 41.

Campbell, J. P., and S. Weintraub. 1986. "The Impact of Undocumented Immigrants on Wages in Texas." Unpublished.

Chiswick, B. R. 1986. "Mexican Immigrants: The Economic Dimension." *The Annals* (of the American Academy of Political and Social Science) 487:92–101.

Economic Report of the President, 1986. Washington, D.C.: U.S. Government Printing Office.

Greenwood, M. J., and J. M. McDowell. 1986. "The Factor Market Consequence of U.S. Immigration." *Journal of Economic Literature* 24:1738–1772.

Gregory, P. 1986. *The Myth of Market Failure: Employment and the Labor Market in Mexico*. Baltimore, Md.: The Johns Hopkins University Press.

Hill, J. K. 1985. "The Economic Impact of Tighter U.S. Border Security." *Economic Review* (Federal Reserve Bank of Dallas) (July):12–20.

Martin, P. 1986. *Illegal Immigration and the Colonization of the American Labor Market*. Washington, D.C.: Center for Immigration Studies.

McCarthy, K. F., and R. B. Valdez. 1986. *Current and Future Effects of Mexican Immigration in California*. Santa Monica, Cal.: Rand Corporation.

McLemore, S. Dale, and Ricardo Romo. 1985. "The Origins and Development of the Mexican American People." In R. de la Garza et al., eds., *The Mexican American Experience: An Interdisciplinary Anthology*. Austin: University of Texas Press, pp. 9–32.

Muller, T., et al. 1985. *The Fourth Wave: California's Newest Immigrants*. Washington, D.C.: Urban Institute Press.

Passel, J. S., and K. A. Woodrow. 1984. "Geographic Distribution of Undocumented Immigrants: Estimates of Undocumented Aliens Counted in the 1980 Census by State." *International Migration Review* 18:642–671.

Pearce, J. E., and J. W. Gunther. 1985. "Illegal Immigration from Mexico: Effects on the Texas Economy." *Economic Review* (Federal Reserve Bank of Dallas) (September):1–14.

Piore, M. 1979. *Birds of Passage: Migrant Labor and Industrial Societies.* New York: Cambridge University Press.

Poston, D. L., Jr.; R. G. Rogers; and R. M. Cullen. 1986. "Income and Occupational Attainment Patterns of Mexican Immigrants and Nonimmigrants." In H. L. Browning and R. O. de la Garza, eds., *Mexican Immigrants and Mexican Americans: An Evolving Relation.* Austin: University of Texas, Center for Mexican American Studies, pp. 100–119.

U.S. General Accounting Office. 1986. *Illegal Aliens: Limited Research Suggests Illegal Aliens May Displace Native Workers.* Washington, D.C.

Warren, R., and J. S. Passel. 1987. *A Count of the Uncountable: Estimates of Undocumented Aliens Counted in the 1980 United States Census.* Appendix 1 of processed paper.

Watanabe, S. 1974. "Constraints on Labour-Intensive Export Industries in Mexico." *International Labour Review* 109:23–45.

Weintraub, S. 1983. "Treating the Causes: Illegal Immigration and U.S. Foreign Economic Policy." In D. G. Papademetriou and M. J. Miller, eds., *The Unavoidable Issue: U.S. Immigration Policy in the 1980s.* Philadelphia, Pa.: Institute for the Study of Human Issues.

Weintraub, S., and G. Cardenas. 1984. *The Use of Public Services by Undocumented Aliens in Texas.* Austin: Lyndon B. Johnson School of Public Affairs, University of Texas.

7.

Final Report of the Regional Assembly for the Southwestern Region

At the close of their discussion, the participants in the Regional Assembly for the Southwest, held at the Houston Area Research Center's Center for Growth Studies, October 22–24, 1987, reviewed as a group the following statement. This statement represents a general agreement; however, no one was asked to sign it. Furthermore, it should be understood that not everyone agreed with all of it.

Introduction and Background

Since 1963, the total population of Mexico, Belize, Costa Rica, El Salvador, Guatemala, Honduras, Nicaragua, and Panama has more than doubled, to nearly 110 million people. The population of Mexico alone is approximately 83 million. The annual growth rates of these populations average about 2.7, a rate that means the current population would double in 26 years. The current annual rate of growth in Mexico alone is estimated to be between 2.0 percent and 2.6 percent. Substantial declines in fertility (in Mexico, Costa Rica, and Panama) have slowed the momentum of population growth, but the effects of these declines have been partly offset by decreases in mortality. High rates of population growth are likely to continue for 10 to 20 years, because of the low age levels of the population, continuing relatively high fertility rates, and the potential in most of the countries for further mortality reductions.

The limits imposed by rapid population growth on social and economic development were recognized by the Twenty-third American Assembly in 1963. That Assembly published *The Population Dilemma*, which created greater awareness of global population issues in the United States and other countries. Subsequent U.S. population policies have been consistent with the policy recommendations of the 1963 Assembly. U.S. policies have encouraged developing countries to create and implement voluntary family planning programs and policies designed to achieve reduced fertility.

This view appeared to enjoy broad consensus in the United States, as well as foreign support. For example, in the 1970s Mexico adopted its own strong family-planning program. Although the Mexican government has not received direct financial assistance from the United States for those programs, its policies for well over a decade have been consistent with the premise that rapid population growth might have negative effects on some economic and social objectives.

At the 1984 International Conference on Population sponsored by the United Nations in Mexico City, the United States articulated a new policy that shifted in two important ways. First, the premise that rapid population growth curtails economic development was called into question; the alternative view was advanced that the effect of population increases on economic growth depends on other factors, many of which may be specific to a given country. The United States also argued that free-market policies act as the great spur to economic development; this, in turn, would help bring about voluntary fertility reduction. Second, the U.S. emphasized its opposition to the use of government funds to pay for abortions performed for family-planning purposes. In implementing these policy changes, it terminated funding for the International Planned Parenthood Federation (IPPF) and the United Nations Fund for Population Activities (UNFPA). It was against the backdrop of these changes in U.S. population policy that the Seventy-first American Assembly was held in April of 1986.

Elements of U.S. Population Policy

Population Growth

The focus of the Seventy-first American Assembly was on U.S. policies aimed at reducing high fertility. The major rationale for such policies is that, over the long term, high fertility exerts negative effects on social and economic conditions—such as those relating to education, health, and income—and on natural resources and environment. Reduced fertility and population growth also are likely to facilitate the development of policies aimed at avoiding the depletion of renewable resources and the degradation of the environment.

U.S. approaches designed to promote these ends through the reduction of high fertility have included the support of family-planning programs; the funding of contraceptive research; the encouragement of special programs to increase the education, status, and opportunities of women; and the promotion of primary health-care programs in developing countries.

The participants of the 1987 Regional Assembly agree that the consequences of rapid population growth are often negative and that policies designed to reduce high fertility are desirable. The group also emphasizes that policies promoting fertility reduction are not substitutes for policies that more directly improve social and economic conditions, yet fertility reduction can have beneficial economic effects, especially in the case of countries with the highest fertility levels.

In the case of Mexico, high population growth rates have resulted in large numbers of young persons who are potential members of the labor force. With a population less than one-third the size of that of the United States, Mexico must annually absorb 60 to 80 percent as many job seekers as the United States. During times of high economic growth, Mexico was in a position to absorb a large proportion of these new workers; however, in recent years, as economic growth has declined, Mexico has been less able to provide employment.

Population growth has also contributed to excess population in the agricultural sector, which, in combination with inappropriate economic policies, has resulted in deforestation of rural land and topsoil retention problems. In turn, this has contributed to urban congestion as rural populations move to urban centers. Urbanization has brought in its wake water shortages and pollution. Although the relationship between population growth and environmental problems is mediated by many factors, governments in the region have often given insufficient attention to environmental hazards as they pursue economic development efforts.

Immigration Policy

Since the early 1960s, both the volume and composition of immigration to the United States have changed considerably, largely as the result of three developments. The first was the passage of the 1965 Amendments to the Immigration and Nationality Act. The amendments eliminated the discriminatory national origins quota system in favor of the equal number immigrant visas for each nation; brought the Western Hemisphere within this system of equal numbers; and substantially redirected overall immigration preferences toward spouses, minor children, and parents of U.S. citizens by allowing them to immigrate with no numerical limitations. The second was the admission of large numbers of political refugees, particularly from Cuba and Indochina. The third was an increase in undocumented immigration to the United States. In the years since 1970, immigration to the United States has averaged over 500,000 persons a year, compared with less than 250,000 per year during the 1950s. The ethnic composition of legal immigrants has changed from a preponderance of Europeans to mostly Asians and Latin Americans.

These changes have generated considerable policy debate in the United States over the past 20 years, especially with respect to undocumented immigration. In 1978, a National Select Commission on Immigration and Refugee Policy was created and charged with the twin responsibilities of making a thorough assessment of immigration and refugee laws and of developing recommendations concerning future law. In its final report the Commission noted: "One issue has emerged as most pressing—the problem of undocumented/illegal migration." In 1986, Congress passed the Immigration Reform and Control Act (IRCA), the main provisions of which were designed to curtail undocumented immigration—through employer sanctions—and to legalize many undocumented aliens in residence in the United States.

The participants in this Regional Assembly addressed the question of the impact on the United States of legal and undocumented immigration, as well as questions pertaining to the passage and likely effects of IRCA. The U.S. Census Bureau counted 14 million foreign-born residents in the United States in the 1980 census. Of those, 12 million were legal residents, with Mexico contributing the largest number—1.2 million. On the basis of indirect methods, about 2 million have been estimated to be undocumented immigrants, of whom 1.1 million were from Mexico. In addition, an unknown number of both permanent and temporary undocumented immigrants in the United States were not included in the census.

In the view of the participants, the research evidence is inconclusive about whether the presence of undocumented alien workers displaces U.S. workers or depresses wage rates. In general, it is thought that the impact on labor markets is locality- and industry-specific.

The participants agree that the process of legalization under IRCA is running relatively smoothly. Because the legalization program has been in effect only a short time and because the implementation of employer sanctions was delayed, little data are available on these aspects of IRCA. Final regulations have not yet been published on the implementation of State Legalization Impact Assistance Grants. States will not submit applications for grant funds until final guidelines are available. Although $1 billion per year over four years will be appropriated for services to newly legalized aliens, the federal government's costs will be covered first, leaving only the remainder for state and local governments.

The participants also agree that the services available to certain categories of immigrants are uneven and often inadequate, particularly for education and health services. While government revenues from and expenditures on undocumented workers roughly balance out at the federal level and possibly at the state level, they may not at the municipal level. It is this lowest level of government that generally shoulders a disproportionate share of the most expensive burdens—that is, education and health services.

Economic Development Policy

The Mexican economy has been passing through a critical transition since 1982 and has been unable to absorb into productive employment the 800,000 to 1,000,000 persons entering the labor force each year. The government has taken courageous steps during the last five years to restructure the economy to promote exports, increase industrial efficiency, and act more flexibly in accepting foreign investment. These measures should bear fruit in years to come. The success of Mexican policies, however, also depends on cooperative measures by the United States.

The United States is Mexico's major trading partner; it is the market for 60 percent of its exports and the source of 60 percent of its imports. Three-quarters of foreign direct investment in Mexico is by the U.S. firms. The *maquiladora* assembly plants in Mexico bring $1.5 billion in foreign exchange each year, and employ about 250,000 Mexicans. Mexico earns more than $1 billion in foreign exchange from tourists, most of whom come from the United States, and perhaps $2 billion from remittances by Mexicans working in the United States.

Consequently, Mexico's ability to carry out its development program depends partly on access to the U.S. market for its exports and on foreign exchange generated from its increasing economic integration with the United States. Mexican job creation would be prejudiced by U.S. protectionism. Any increase in U.S. import restrictions would create pressures for Mexicans to migrate north of the border. If U.S. immigration legislation effectively curtails undocumented immigration, this would reduce the flow of worker remittances.

The economic progress made in Central America until the 1970s has since been halted by political turmoil in the region. At the same time, new social and regional inequalities have emerged. In some of the countries, these inequalities provided the material base for political strife that, in turn, worsened the economic performance of the region. It will be difficult for the Central American countries to regain their earlier development momentum until the armed conflict ends and social and economic reforms are undertaken.

Continuation of U.S. economic assistance is crucial to restore economic growth. The Central American countries also benefit from the Caribbean Basin Initiative (CBI), which exempts many of their exports from U.S. import duties. The CBI however, is limited by the exclusion of a number of products important to the Central American countries from duty-free import treatment.

U.S. economic policy has the potential to encourage development and job creation, but it also has the ability to frustrate economic progress in the region.

Recommendations

Population issues must be addressed in the context of economic development, environmental, immigration, educational, health, and related policies. The foregoing assessment of trends in population growth, fertility, job creation, and migration leads participants in the Regional Assembly to the following recommendations. The recommendations presume the need for a recognition of and sensitivity to the different histories and conditions in the countries of the region. U.S. bilateral relations with each country have their own characteristics.

The participants in the Regional Assembly

1. Strongly recommend that U.S. assistance for population programs be maintained at least at its current share of overall U.S. development assistance. The participants fully endorse the voluntary basis of U.S. family-planning assistance and the principle of informed consent.

2. Recommend that the U.S. government reinstate full financial support for the United Nations Fund for Population Activities and for the programs of the International Planned Parenthood Federation.

3. Recommend that the governments of the United States, Mexico, and the Central American countries engage in consultation on issues concerning immigration and its consequences.

4. Agree that public education and basic health services should be made available to all residents of the United States regardless of immigration status.

5. Recommend federal assistance to lower levels of government for providing services to immigrants. The financial burden of providing education and health services falls primarily on local and state governments. Because of the federal government's role in setting immigration policy, it has an obligation to provide support for meeting these costs.

6. Agree that the relationship between Mexico and the United States should be reflected in preferential treatment of Mexico by increasing the current immigration ceiling.

7. Agree that better information and more research are needed about immigration and its consequences for the United States. Important issues include estimating the size and geographic distribution of the undocumented population, the economic impact of both legal and undocumented immigrants, and labor market effects. The estimates of the size and distribution of the undocumented population, using 1980 census data, were based on annual registration of the legal alien population. The annual registration has been discontinued. In order to improve estimates about the undocumented population, this or preferably some better system of providing reliable data needs to be developed.

8. Recommend that business leaders and governments from the United States, Mexico, and Central America sponsor discussions to better inform interested parties of available investment and trade opportunities, as well as ways to reduce barriers to cooperation.

9. Agree that protectionist measures, if adopted, will impair economic development in the region, particularly in Mexico. Such protectionist tendencies, therefore, must be resisted. In like manner, the success of the Caribbean Basin Initiative for job creation in Central America and the Caribbean nations requires granting of duty-free entry of those imports that at present are subject to tariffs.

APPENDIX

Participants, Regional Assembly for the Southwestern Region

FRANCISCO ALBA
Department of Demography
El Colegio de México

AL ALVENOSO
Department of Natural Science
University of Houston

SUSAN GONZÁLEZ BAKER
Population Research Center
University of Texas at Austin

FRANK D. BEAN
Population Research Center
University of Texas at Austin
and The Urban Institute
Washington, D.C.

CABELL BRAND
Recovery Systems, Inc.
Salem, Va.

HARLEY BROWNING
Department of Sociology
University of Texas at Austin

JORGE CASTAÑEDA
Department of Political Science
National University of Mexico

M. RUPERT CUTLER
Population-Environment Balance, Inc.
Washington, D.C.

RAFAEL DEL CID
Department of Sociology
University of Honduras

SERGIO DÍAZ-BRIQUETS
Commission on International
  Migration and Cooperative
  Economic Development
Washington, D.C.

THOMAS ESPENSHADE
Office of Population Research
Princeton University

BENITO FLORES
College of Business
  Administration
Texas A&M University

KRISTEN FOSKETT
Washington Office
State of Florida
Washington, D.C.

TOMAS FREJKA
The Population Council
New York, N.Y.

JOSEPH GALLIPEAU
U.S. Immigration and
  Naturalization Service
Houston, Tex.

LOUISA GERKING
International Advocates Council
Planned Parenthood of Central
  and Northern Arizona
Tempe, Ariz.

VIRGINIA GUEDEA
Secretaría Académica
Institutos de Investigaciones
  Históricas
Mexico City

JACQUELINE HAGAN
Department of Sociology
University of Houston

ROBERTO HAM CHANDE
Department of Demography
El Colegio de la Frontera Norte

ALDYS HOOD
Action Committee for the Americas
  on Population Issues
Washington, D.C.

JOSEPH HOOD
Action Committee for the Americas
  on Population Issues
Washington, D.C.

BEVERLY HUNTER-CURTIS
(representing Sen. Art Torres)
Joint Committee on Refugee
  Resettlement, International
  Migration, and Cooperative
  Development
Sacramento, Calif.

SIOMA KAGAN
Department of International
  Business
University of Missouri–St. Louis

CHARLES B. KEELY
Department of Demography
Georgetown University

JAY S. KITTLE
Palo Seco Corporation
Tucson, Ariz.

JERRY LADMAN
Center for Latin American Studies
Arizona State University

PHIL LANE
Border Business Institute
Laredo, Tex.

BRIAN LATELL
U.S. National Intelligence Council
  and Department of Latin American
  Studies
Georgetown University

LINDSAY LOWELL
Population Research Center
University of Texas at Austin

REYNALDO MACÍAS
Department of Education
University of Southern California

M. GUILLERMINA MAGALLÓN
Watt, White, Gill & Craig,
  Attorneys at Law
Houston, Tex.

LEO G. MAHONEY
Department of Economics
Laredo State University

DAVID H. MORTIMER
The American Assembly
Columbia University

STEVE MURDOCK
Department of Rural Sociology
Texas A&M University

ANDREW W. NICHOLS
Rural Health Office
University of Arizona College of
  Medicine
Arizona Health Science Center

NORMA OJEDA
Department of Demography
El Colegio de México

SUSAN ORR
ESL Programs, Continuing
  Education
North Harris County Community
  College

DEMETRIOS G. PAPADEMETRIOU
Population Associated
  International
Fairfax, Va.

JEFFREY PASSEL
Department of Commerce
U.S. Census Bureau
Washington, D.C.

JAMES T. PEACH
Department of Economics
New Mexico State University

FERNANDO POZOS
Population Research Center
University of Texas at Austin

JAMES RODRÍGUEZ
Department of History
University of California

W. THAD ROWLAND
Action Committee for the Americas
  on Population Issues
Henderson, N.C.

R. RICHARD RUBOTTOM
The Owens Foundation
Dallas, Tex.

JURGEN SCHMANDT
Houston Area Research Center
and LBJ School of Public Affairs
University of Texas at Austin

PATRICIA SEED
Department of History
Rice University

SUSAN SHULTZ
SS&A Executive Search
Paradise Valley, Ariz.

DAVID E. SIMCOX
Center for Immigration Studies
Washington, D.C.

DIANNE STEWART
Commissioner's Office
Texas Department of Human
  Services
Austin, Tex.

SHOSHANA TANCER
Tancer Law Offices, Ltd.
Phoenix, Ariz.

EDUARDO TELLES
Department of Sociology
University of Texas at Austin

JESSE TREVIÑO
State Comptroller's Office
Economic Analysis Center
Austin, Tex.

JOHN WEEKS
International Population Center
San Diego State University

SIDNEY WEINTRAUB
LBJ School of Public Affairs
University of Texas at Austin

NANCY WITTENBERG
Department of Health &
 Rehabilitation Services
State of Florida

MARTHA S. WILLIAMS
School of Social Work
University of Texas at Austin

ESTHER LEE YAO
Department of Education
University of Houston at Clear
 Lake

EMILY YAUNG
National Governor's Association
Washington, D.C.

Observers

CHANDLER THOMPSON
El Paso Times

JOE KUTCHIN
Mitchell Energy & Development
 Corp.
The Woodlands, Tex.